Thomas Moore

Life of Lord Byron

Volume I

© 2025, Thomas Moore (domaine public)
Publisher : BoD · Books on Demand, 31 avenue Saint-Rémy,
57600 Forbach, bod@bod.fr
Print : Libri Plureos GmbH, Friedensallee 273,
22763 Hamburg (Allemagne)
ISBN : 978-2-3225-9582-2
Dépôt légal : Avril 2025

Life of Lord Byron Volume I

Thomas Moore

NOTICES

OF THE

LIFE OF LORD BYRON.

It has been said of Lord Byron, "that he was prouder of being a descendant of those Byrons of Normandy, who accompanied William the Conqueror into England, than of having been the author of Childe Harold and Manfred." This remark is not altogether unfounded in truth. In the character of the noble poet, the pride of ancestry was undoubtedly one of the most decided features; and, as far as antiquity alone gives lustre to descent, he had every reason to boast of the claims of his race. In Doomsday-book, the name of Ralph de Burun ranks high among the tenants of land in Nottinghamshire; and in the succeeding reigns, under the title of Lords of Horestan Castle, we find his descendants holding considerable possessions in Derbyshire; to which, afterwards, in the time of Edward I., were added the lands of Rochdale in Lancashire. So extensive, indeed, in those early times, was the landed wealth of the family, that the partition of their property, in Nottinghamshire alone, has been sufficient to establish some of the first families of the county.

Its antiquity, however, was not the only distinction by which the name of Byron came recommended to its inheritor; those personal merits and accomplishments, which form the best ornament of a genealogy, seem to have been displayed in no ordinary degree by some of his ancestors. In one of his own early poems, alluding to the achievements of his race, he commemorates, with much satisfaction, those "mail-covered barons" among them,

who proudly to battleLed their vassals from Europe to Palestine's plain.

Adding,

Near Askalon's towers John of Horiston slumbers,

Unnerved is the hand of his minstrel by death.

As there is no record, however, as far as I can discover, of any of his ancestors having been engaged in the Holy Wars, it is possible that he may have had no other authority for this notion than the tradition which he found connected with certain strange groups of heads, which are represented on the old panel-work, in some of the chambers at Newstead. In one of these groups, consisting of three heads, strongly carved and projecting from the panel, the centre figure evidently represents a Saracen or Moor, with an European female on one side of him, and a Christian soldier on the other. In a second group, which is in one of the bed-rooms, the female occupies the centre, while on each side is the head of a Saracen, with the eyes fixed earnestly upon her. Of the exact meaning of these figures there is nothing certain known; but the tradition is, I understand, that they refer to some love-adventure, in which one of those crusaders, of whom the young poet speaks, was engaged.

Of the more certain, or, at least, better known exploits of the family, it is sufficient, perhaps, to say, that, at the siege of Calais under Edward III., and on the fields, memorable in their respective eras, of Cressy, Bosworth, and Marston Moor, the name of the Byrons reaped honours both of rank and fame, of which their young descendant has, in the verses just cited, shown himself proudly conscious.

It was in the reign of Henry VIII., on the dissolution of the monasteries, that, by a royal grant, the church and priory of Newstead, with the lands adjoining, were added to the other possessions of the Byron family. The favourite upon whom these spoils of the ancient religion were conferred, was the grand-nephew of the gallant soldier who fought by the side of Richmond at Bosworth, and is distinguished from the other knights of the same Christian name in the family, by the title of "Sir John Byron the Little, with the great beard." A portrait of this personage was one of the few family pictures with which the walls of the abbey, while in the possession of the noble poet, were decorated.

At the coronation of James I. we find another representative of the family selected as an object of royal favour,—the grandson of Sir John Byron the Little, being, on this occasion, made a knight of the Bath. There is a letter to this personage, preserved in Lodge's Illustrations, from which it appears, that notwithstanding all these apparent indications of prosperity, the inroads of pecuniary embarrassment had already begun to be experienced by this ancient house. After counselling the new heir as to the best mode of getting free of his debts, "I do therefore advise you," continues the writer, "that so soon as you have, in such sort as shall be fit, finished your father's funerals, to dispose and disperse that great household, reducing them to the number of forty or fifty, at the most, of all sorts; and, in my opinion, it will be far better for you to live for a time in Lancashire rather than in Notts, for many good reasons that I can tell you when we meet, fitter for words than writing."

From the following reign (Charles I.) the nobility of the family date its origin. In the year 1643, Sir John Byron, great grandson of him who succeeded to the rich domains of Newstead, was created Baron Byron of Rochdale in the county of Lancaster; and seldom has a title been bestowed for such high and honourable services as those by which this nobleman deserved the gratitude of his royal master. Through almost every page of the History of the Civil Wars, we trace his name in connection with the varying fortunes of the king, and find him faithful, persevering, and disinterested to the last. "Sir John Biron," says the writer of Colonel Hutchinson's Memoirs, "afterwards Lord Biron, and all his brothers, bred up in arms, and valiant men in their own persons, were all passionately the king's." There is also, in the answer which Colonel Hutchinson, when governor of Nottingham, returned, on one occasion, to his cousin-german, Sir Richard Biron, a noble tribute to the valour and fidelity of the family. Sir Richard having sent to prevail on his relative to surrender the castle, received for answer, that "except he found his own heart prone to such treachery, he might consider there was, if nothing else, so much of a Biron's blood in him, that he should very much scorn to betray or quit a trust he had undertaken."

Such are a few of the gallant and distinguished personages, through whom the name and honours of this noble house have been transmitted. By the maternal side also Lord Byron had to pride himself on a line of ancestry as illustrious as any that Scotland can boast,—his mother, who was one of the Gordons of Gight, having been a descendant of that Sir William Gordon who was the third son of the Earl of Huntley, by the daughter of James I.

After the eventful period of the Civil Wars, when so many individuals of the house of Byron distinguished themselves,—there having been no less than seven brothers of that family on the field at Edgehill,—the celebrity of the name appears to have died away for near a century. It was about the year 1750, that the shipwreck and sufferings of Mr. Byron (the grandfather of the illustrious subject of these pages) awakened, in no small degree, the attention and sympathy of the public. Not long after, a less innocent sort of notoriety attached itself to two other members of the family,—one, the grand-uncle of the poet, and the other, his father. The former in the year 1765, stood his trial before the House of Peers for killing, in a duel, or rather scuffle, his relation and neighbour Mr. Chaworth; and the latter, having carried off to the Continent the wife of Lord Carmarthen, on the noble marquis obtaining a divorce from the lady, married her. Of this short union one daughter only was the issue, the Honourable Augusta Byron, now the wife of Colonel Leigh.

In reviewing thus cursorily the ancestors, both near and remote, of Lord Byron, it cannot fail to be remarked how strikingly he combined in his own nature some of the best and, perhaps, worst qualities that lie scattered through the various characters of his predecessors,—the generosity, the love of enterprise, the high-mindedness of some of the better spirits of his race, with the irregular passions, the eccentricity, and daring recklessness of the world's opinion, that so much characterised others.

The first wife of the father of the poet having died in 1784, he, in the following year, married Miss Catherine Gordon, only child and heiress of George Gordon, Esq. of Gight. In addition to the estate of Gight, which had, however, in former times, been much more extensive, this lady possessed, in ready money, bank shares, &c. no inconsiderable property; and it was known to be solely with a view of relieving himself from his debts, that Mr. Byron paid his addresses to her. A circumstance related, as having taken place before the marriage of this lady, not only shows the extreme quickness and vehemence of her feelings, but, if it be true that she had never at the time seen Captain Byron, is not a little striking. Being at the Edinburgh theatre one night when the character of Isabella was performed by Mrs. Siddons, so affected was she by the powers of this great actress, that, towards the conclusion of the play, she fell into violent fits, and was carried out of the theatre, screaming loudly, "Oh, my Biron, my Biron!"

On the occasion of her marriage there appeared a ballad by some Scotch rhymer, which has been lately reprinted in a collection of the "Ancient Ballads and Songs of the North of Scotland;" and as it bears testimony both to the reputation of the lady for wealth, and that of her husband for rakery and extravagance, it may be worth extracting:—

MISS GORDON OF GIGHT.

O whare are ye gaen, bonny Miss Gordon?

O whare are ye gaen, sae bonny an' braw?

Ye've married, ye've married wi' Johnny Byron,

To squander the lands o' Gight awa'.

This youth is a rake, frae England he's come;

The Scots dinna ken his extraction ava;

He keeps up his misses, his landlord he duns,

That's fast drawen' the lands o' Gight awa'.

O whare are ye gaen, &c.

The shooten' o' guns, an' rattlin' o' drums,

The bugle in woods, the pipes i' the ha',

The beagles a howlin', the hounds a growlin';

These soundings will soon gar Gight gang awa'.

O whare are ye gaen, &c.

Soon after the marriage, which took place, I believe, at Bath, Mr. Byron and his lady removed to their estate in Scotland; and it was not long before the prognostics of this ballad-maker began to be realised. The extent of that chasm of debt, in which her fortune was to be swallowed up, now opened upon the eyes of the ill-fated heiress. The creditors of Mr. Byron lost no time in pressing their demands; and not only was the whole of her ready money, bank shares, fisheries, &c., sacrificed to satisfy them, but a large sum raised by mortgage on the estate for the same purpose. In the summer of 1786, she and her husband left Scotland, to proceed to France; and in the following year the estate of Gight itself was sold, and the whole of the purchase money applied to the further payment of debts,—with the exception of a small sum vested in trustees for the use of Mrs. Byron, who thus found herself, within the short space of two years, reduced from competence to a pittance of 150 *l.* per annum.

From France Mrs. Byron returned to England at the close of the year 1787; and on the 22d of January, 1788, gave birth, in Holles Street, London, to her first and only child, George Gordon Byron. The name of Gordon was added in compliance with a condition imposed by will on whoever should become husband of the heiress of Gight; and at the baptism of the child, the Duke of Gordon, and Colonel Duff of Fetteresso, stood godfathers.

In reference to the circumstance of his being an only child, Lord Byron, in one of his journals, mentions some curious coincidences in his family, which, to a mind disposed as his was to regard every thing connected with himself as out of the ordinary course of events, would naturally appear even more strange and singular than they are. "I have been thinking," he says, "of an odd circumstance. My daughter (1), my wife (2), my half-sister (3), my mother (4), my sister's mother (5), my natural daughter (6), and myself (7), are, or were, all *only* children. My sister's mother (Lady Conyers) had only my half-sister by that second marriage, (herself, too, an only child,) and my father had only me, an only child, by his second marriage with my mother, an only child too. Such a complication of *only* children, all tending to *one*family, is singular enough, and looks like fatality almost." He then adds, characteristically, "But the fiercest animals have the fewest numbers in their litters, as lions, tigers, and even elephants, which are mild in comparison."

From London, Mrs. Byron proceeded with her infant to Scotland; and, in the year 1790, took up her residence in Aberdeen, where she was soon after joined by Captain Byron. Here for a short time they lived together in lodgings at the house of a person named Anderson, in Queen Street. But their union being by no means happy, a separation took place between them, and Mrs. Byron removed to lodgings at the other end of the street. Notwithstanding this schism, they for some time continued to visit, and even to drink tea with each other; but the elements of discord were strong on both sides, and their separation was, at last, complete and final. He would frequently, however, accost the nurse and his son in their walks, and expressed a strong wish to have the child for a day or two, on a visit with him. To this request Mrs. Byron was, at first, not very willing to accede, but, on the representation of the nurse, that "if he kept the boy one night, he would not do so another," she consented. The event proved as the nurse had predicted; on enquiring next morning after the child, she was told by Captain Byron that he had had quite enough of his young visitor, and she might take him home again.

It should be observed, however, that Mrs. Byron, at this period, was unable to keep more than one servant, and that, sent as the boy was on this occasion to encounter the trial of a visit, without the accustomed superintendence of his nurse, it is not so wonderful that he should have been found, under such circumstances, rather an unmanageable guest. That as a child, his temper was violent, or rather sullenly passionate, is certain. Even when in petticoats, he showed the same uncontrollable spirit with his nurse, which he afterwards exhibited when an author, with his critics. Being angrily reprimanded by her, one day, for having soiled or torn a new frock in which he had been just dressed, he got into one of his "silent rages" (as he himself has described them), seized the frock with both his hands, rent it from top to bottom, and stood in sullen stillness, setting his censurer and her wrath at defiance.

But, notwithstanding this, and other such unruly outbreaks,—in which he was but too much encouraged by the example of his mother, who frequently, it is said, proceeded to the same extremities with her caps, gowns, &c.,—there was in his disposition, as appears from the concurrent testimony of nurses, tutors, and all who were employed about him, a mixture of affectionate sweetness and playfulness, by which it was impossible not to be attached; and which rendered him then, as in his riper years, easily manageable by those who loved and understood him sufficiently to be at once gentle and firm enough for the task. The female attendant of whom we have spoken, as well as her sister, Mary Gray, who succeeded her, gained an influence over his mind against which he very rarely rebelled; while his mother, whose capricious excesses, both of anger and of fondness, left her little hold on either his respect or affection, was indebted solely to his sense of filial duty for any small portion of authority she was ever able to acquire over him.

By an accident which, it is said, occurred at the time of his birth, one of his feet was twisted out of its natural position, and this defect (chiefly from the contrivances employed to remedy it) was a source of much pain and inconvenience to him during his early years. The expedients used at this period to restore the limb to shape, were adopted by the advice, and under the direction, of the celebrated John Hunter, with whom Dr. Livingstone of Aberdeen corresponded on the subject; and his nurse, to whom fell the task of putting on these machines or bandages, at bedtime, would often, as she herself told my informant, sing him to sleep, or tell him stories and legends, in which, like most other children, he took great delight. She also taught him, while yet an infant, to repeat a great number of the Psalms; and the first and twenty-third Psalms were among the earliest that he committed to memory. It is a remarkable fact, indeed, that through the care of this respectable woman, who was herself of a very religious disposition, he attained a far earlier and more intimate acquaintance with the Sacred Writings than falls to the lot of most young people. In a letter which he wrote to Mr. Murray, from Italy, in 1821 after requesting of that gentleman to send him, by the first opportunity, a Bible, he adds—"Don't forget this, for I am a great reader and admirer of those books, and had read them through and through before I was eight years old,— that is to say, the Old Testament, for the New struck me as a task, but the other as a pleasure. I speak as a boy, from the recollected impression of that period at Aberdeen, in 1796."

The malformation of his foot was, even at this childish age, a subject on which he showed peculiar sensitiveness. I have been told by a gentleman of Glasgow, that the person who nursed his wife, and who still lives in his family, used often to join the nurse of Byron when they were out with their respective charges, and one day said to her, as they walked together, "What a pretty boy Byron is! what a pity he has such a leg!" On hearing this allusion to his infirmity, the child's eyes flashed with anger, and striking at her with a little whip which he held in his hand, he exclaimed impatiently, "Dinna speak of it!" Sometimes, however, as in after life, he could talk indifferently and even jestingly of this lameness; and there being another little boy in the neighbourhood, who had a similar defect in one of his feet, Byron would say, laughingly, "Come and see the twa laddies with the twa club feet going up the

Broad Street."

Among many instances of his quickness and energy at this age, his nurse mentioned a little incident that one night occurred, on her taking him to the theatre to see the "Taming of the Shrew." He had attended to the performance, for some time, with silent interest; but, in the scene between Catherine and Petruchio, where the following dialogue takes place,—

Cath. I know it is the moon.
Pet. Nay, then, you lie,— it is the blessed sun,—

little Geordie (as they called the child), starting from his seat, cried out boldly, "But I say it is the moon, sir."

The short visit of Captain Byron to Aberdeen has already been mentioned, and he again passed two or three months in that city, before his last departure for France. On both occasions, his chief object was to extract still more money, if possible, from the unfortunate woman whom he had beggared; and so far was he successful, that, during his last visit, narrow as were her means, she contrived to furnish him with the money necessary for his journey to Valenciennes, where, in the following year, 1791, he died. Though latterly Mrs. Byron would not see her husband, she entertained, it is said, a strong affection for him to the last; and on those occasions, when the nurse used to meet him in her walks, would enquire of her with the tenderest anxiety as to his health and looks. When the intelligence of his death, too, arrived, her grief, according to the account of this same attendant, bordered on distraction, and her shrieks were so loud as to be heard in the street. She was, indeed, a woman full of the most passionate extremes, and her grief and affection were bursts as much of temper as of feeling. To mourn at all, however, for such a husband was, it must be allowed, a most gratuitous stretch of generosity. Having married her, as he openly avowed, for her fortune alone, he soon dissipated this, the solitary charm she possessed for him, and was then unmanful enough to taunt her with the inconveniences of that penury which his own extravagance had occasioned.

When not quite five years old, young Byron was sent to a day-school at Aberdeen, taught by Mr. Bowers, and remained there, with some interruptions, during a twelvemonth, as appears by the following extract from the day-book of the school:—

George Gordon Byron.
19th November, 1792.
19th November, 1793—paid one guinea.

The terms of this school for reading were only five shillings a quarter, and it was evidently less with a view to the boy's advance in learning than as a cheap mode of keeping him quiet that his mother had sent him to it. Of the progress of his infantine studies at Aberdeen, as well under Mr. Bowers as under the various other persons that instructed him, we have the following interesting particulars communicated by himself, in a sort of journal which he once began, under the title of "My Dictionary," and which is preserved in one of his manuscript books.

"For several years of my earliest childhood, I was in that city, but have never revisited it since I was ten years old. I was sent, at five years old, or earlier, to a school kept by a Mr. Bowers, who was called '*Bodsy* Bowers,' by reason of his dapperness. It was a school for both sexes. I learned little there except to repeat by rote the first lesson of monosyllables ('God made man'—'Let us love him'), by hearing it often repeated, without acquiring a letter. Whenever proof was made of my progress, at home, I repeated these words with the most rapid fluency; but on turning over a new leaf, I continued to repeat them, so that the narrow boundaries of my first year's accomplishments were detected, my ears boxed, (which they did not deserve, seeing it was by ear only that I had acquired my letters,) and my intellects consigned to a new preceptor. He was a very devout, clever, little clergyman, named Ross, afterwards minister of one of the kirks (*East*, I think). Under him I made astonishing progress; and I recollect to this day his mild manners and good-natured pains-taking. The moment I could read, my grand passion was *history*, and, why I know not, but I was particularly taken with the battle near the Lake Regillus in the Roman History, put into my hands the first. Four years ago, when standing on the heights of Tusculum, and looking down upon the little round lake that was once Regillus, and which dots the immense expanse below, I remembered my young enthusiasm and my old instructor. Afterwards I had a very serious, saturnine, but kind young man, named Paterson, for a tutor. He was the son of my shoemaker, but a good scholar, as is common with the Scotch. He was a rigid Presbyterian also. With him I began Latin in 'Ruddiman's Grammar,' and continued till I went to the 'Grammar School, (*Scoticè*, 'Schule; *Aberdonicè*, 'Squeel,') where I threaded all the classes to the *fourth*, when I was recalled to England (where I had been hatched) by the demise of my uncle. I acquired this handwriting, which I can hardly read myself, under the fair copies of Mr. Duncan of the same city: I don't think he would plume himself much upon my progress. However, I wrote much better then than I have ever done since. Haste and agitation of one kind or another have quite spoilt as pretty a scrawl as ever scratched over a frank. The grammar-school might consist of a hundred and fifty of all ages under age. It was divided into five classes, taught by four masters, the chief teaching the fourth and fifth himself. As in England, the fifth, sixth forms, and monitors, are heard by the head masters."

Of his class-fellows at the grammar-school there are many, of course, still alive, by whom he is well remembered; and the general impression they retain of him is, that he was a lively, warm-hearted, and high-spirited boy—passionate and resentful, but affectionate and companionable with his schoolfellows—to a remarkable degree venturous and fearless, and (as one of them significantly expressed it) "always more ready to give a blow than take one." Among many anecdotes illustrative of this spirit, it is related that once, in returning home from school, he fell in with a boy who had on some former occasion insulted him, but had then got off unpunished—little Byron, however, at the time, promising to "pay him off" whenever they should meet again. Accordingly, on this second encounter, though there were some other boys to take his opponent's part, he succeeded in inflicting upon him a hearty beating. On his return home, breathless, the servant enquired what he had been about, and was answered by him with a mixture of rage and humour, that he had been paying a debt, by beating a boy according to promise; for that he was a Byron, and would never belie his motto, "*Trust Byron*."

He was, indeed, much more anxious to distinguish himself among his schoolfellows by prowess in all sports and exercises, than by advancement in learning. Though quick, when he could be persuaded to attend, or had any study that pleased him, he was in general very low in the class, nor seemed ambitious of being promoted any higher. It is the custom, it seems, in this seminary, to invert, now and then, the order of the class, so as to make the highest and lowest boys change places,—with a view, no doubt, of piquing the ambition of both. On these occasions, and only these, Byron was sometimes at the head, and the master, to banter him, would say, "Now, George, man, let me see how soon you'll be at the foot again."

During this period, his mother and he made, occasionally, visits among their friends, passing some time at Fetteresso, the seat of his godfather, Colonel Duff, (where the child's delight with a humorous old butler, named Ernest Fidler, is still remembered,) and also at Banff, where some near connections of Mrs. Byron resided.

In the summer of the year 1796, after an attack of scarlet-fever, he was removed by his mother for change of air into the Highlands; and it was either at this time, or in the following year, that they took up their residence at a farm-house in the neighbourhood of Ballater, a favourite summer resort for health and gaiety, about forty miles up the Dee from Aberdeen. Though this house, where they still show with much pride the bed in which young Byron slept, has become naturally a place of pilgrimage for the worshippers of genius, neither its own appearance, nor that of the small bleak valley, in which it stands, is at all worthy of being associated with the memory of a poet. Within a short distance of it, however, all those features of wildness and beauty, which mark the course of the Dee through the Highlands, may be commanded. Here the dark summit of Lachin-y-gair stood towering before the eyes of the future bard; and the verses in which, not many years afterwards, he commemorated this sublime object, show that, young as he was, at the time, its "frowning glories" were not unnoticed by him.

Ah, there my young footsteps in infancy wandered,

My cap was the bonnet, my cloak was the plaid;

On chieftains long perish'd my memory ponder'd

As daily I strode through the pine-cover'd glade.

I sought not my home till the day's dying glory

Gave place to the rays of the bright polar-star;

For Fancy was cheer'd by traditional story,

Disclosed by the natives of dark Loch-na-gar.

To the wildness and grandeur of the scenes, among which his childhood was passed, it is not unusual to trace the first awakening of his poetic talent. But it may be questioned whether this faculty was ever so produced. That the charm of scenery, which derives its chief power from fancy and association, should be much felt at an age when fancy is yet hardly awake, and associations but few, can with difficulty, even making every allowance for the prematurity of genius, be conceived. The light which the poet sees around the forms of nature is not so much in the objects themselves as in the eye that contemplates them; and Imagination must first be able to lend a glory to such scenes, before she can derive inspiration *from* them. As materials, indeed, for the poetic faculty, when developed, to work upon, these impressions of the new and wonderful retained from childhood, and retained with all the vividness of recollection which belongs to genius, may form, it is true, the purest and most precious part of that aliment, with which the memory of the poet feeds his imagination. But still, it is the newly-awakened power within him that is the source of the charm;—it is the force of fancy alone that, acting upon his recollections, impregnates, as it were, all the past with poesy. In this respect, such impressions of natural scenery as Lord Byron received in his childhood must be classed with the various other remembrances which that period leaves behind—of its innocence, its sports, its first hopes and affections—all of them reminiscences which the poet afterwards converts to his use, but which no more *make* the poet than—to apply an illustration of Byron's own—the honey can be said to make the bee that treasures it.

When it happens—as was the case with Lord Byron in Greece—that the same peculiar features of nature, over which Memory has shed this reflective charm, are reproduced before the eyes under new and inspiring circumstances, and with all the accessories which an imagination, in its full vigour and wealth, can lend them, then, indeed, do both the past and present combine to make the enchantment complete; and never was there a heart more borne away by this confluence of feelings than that of Byron. In a poem, written about a year or two before his death, he traces all his enjoyment of mountain scenery to the impressions received during his residence in the Highlands; and even attributes the pleasure which he experienced in gazing upon Ida and Parnassus, far less to classic remembrances, than to those fond and deep-felt associations by which they brought back the memory of his boyhood and Lachin-y-gair.

He who first met the Highland's swelling blue,

Will love each peak that shows a kindred hue,

Hail in each crag a friend's familiar face,

And clasp the mountain in his mind's embrace.

Long have I roam'd through lands which are not mine,

Adored the Alp, and loved the Apennine,

Revered Parnassus, and beheld the steep

Jove's Ida and Olympus crown the deep:

But 'twas not all long ages' lore, nor all

Their nature held me in their thrilling thrall;

The infant rapture still survived the boy,

And Loch-na-gar with Ida look'd o'er Troy,

Mix'd Celtic memories with the Phrygian mount,

And Highland linns with Castalie's clear fount.

In a note appended to this passage, we find him falling into that sort of anachronism in the history of his own feelings, which I have above adverted to as not uncommon, and referring to childhood itself that love of mountain prospects, which was but the after result of his imaginative recollections of that period.

"From this period" (the time of his residence in the Highlands) "I date my love of mountainous countries. I can never forget the effect, a few years afterwards in England, of the only thing I had long seen, even in miniature, of a mountain, in the Malvern Hills. After I returned to Cheltenham, I used to watch them every afternoon at sunset, with a sensation which I cannot describe." His love of solitary rambles, and his taste for exploring in all directions, led him not unfrequently so far, as to excite serious apprehensions for his safety. While at Aberdeen, he used often to steal from home unperceived;—sometimes he would find his way to the sea-side; and once, after a long and anxious search, they found the adventurous little rover struggling in a sort of morass or marsh, from which he was unable to extricate himself.

In the course of one of his summer excursions up Dee-side, he had an opportunity of seeing still more of the wild beauties of the Highlands than even the neighbourhood of their residence at Ballatrech afforded, —having been taken by his mother through the romantic passes that lead to Invercauld, and as far up as the small waterfall, called the Linn of Dee. Here his love of adventure had nearly cost him his life. As he was scrambling along a declivity that overhung the fall, some heather caught his lame foot, and he fell. Already he was rolling downward, when the attendant luckily caught hold of him, and was but just in time to save him from being killed. It was about this period, when he was not quite eight years old, that a feeling partaking more of the nature of love than it is easy to believe possible in so young a child, took, according to his own account, entire possession of his thoughts, and showed how early, in this passion, as in most others, the sensibilities of his nature were awakened. The name of the object of this attachment was Mary Duff; and the following passage from a Journal, kept by him in 1813, will show how freshly, after an interval of seventeen years, all the circumstances of this early love still lived in his memory:—

"I have been thinking lately a good deal of Mary Duff. How very odd that I should have been so utterly, devotedly fond of that girl, at an age when I could neither feel passion, nor know the meaning of the word. And the effect!—My mother used always to rally me about this childish amour; and, at last, many years after, when I was sixteen, she told me one day, 'Oh, Byron, I have had a letter from Edinburgh, from Miss Abercromby, and your old sweetheart Mary Duff is married to a Mr. Co^e.' And what was my answer? I really cannot explain or account for my feelings at that moment; but they nearly threw me into convulsions, and alarmed my mother so much, that after I grew better, she generally avoided the subject—to *me*—and contented herself with telling it to all her acquaintance. Now, what could this be? I had never seen her since her mother's faux-pas at Aberdeen had been the cause of her removal to her grandmother's at Banff; we were both the merest children. I had and have been attached fifty times since that period; yet I recollect all we said to each other, all our caresses, her features, my restlessness, sleeplessness, my tormenting my mother's maid to write for me to her, which she at last did, to quiet me. Poor Nancy thought I was wild, and, as I could not write for myself, became my secretary. I remember, too, our walks, and the happiness of sitting by Mary, in the children's apartment, at their house not far from the Plain-stones at Aberdeen, while her lesser sister Helen played with the doll, and we sat gravely making love, in our way.

"How the deuce did all this occur so early? where could it originate? I certainly had no sexual ideas for years afterwards; and yet my misery, my love for that girl were so violent, that I sometimes doubt if I have ever been really attached since. Be that as it may, hearing of her marriage several years after was like a thunder-stroke—it nearly choked me—to the horror of my mother and the astonishment and almost incredulity of every body. And it is a phenomenon in my existence (for I was not eight years old) which has puzzled, and will puzzle me to the latest hour of it; and lately, I know not why, the *recollection* (*not* the attachment) has recurred as forcibly as ever. I wonder if she can have the least remembrance of it or me? or remember her pitying sister Helen for not having an admirer too? How very pretty is the perfect image of her in my memory—her brown, dark hair, and hazel eyes; her very dress! I should be quite grieved to see *her now*; the reality, however beautiful, would destroy, or at least confuse, the features of the lovely Peri which then existed in her, and still lives in my imagination, at the distance of more than sixteen years. I am now twenty-five and odd months....

"I think my mother told the circumstances (on my hearing of her marriage) to the Parkynses, and certainly to the Pigot family, and probably mentioned it in her answer to Miss A., who was well acquainted with my childish *penchant*, and had sent the news on purpose for *me*,—and thanks to her!

"Next to the beginning, the conclusion has often occupied my reflections, in the way of investigation. That the facts are thus, others know as well as I, and my memory yet tells me so, in more than a whisper. But, the more I reflect, the more I am bewildered to assign any cause for this precocity of affection."

Though the chance of his succession to the title of his ancestors was for some time altogether uncertain—there being, so late as the year 1794, a grandson of the fifth lord still alive—his mother had, from his very birth, cherished a strong persuasion that he was destined not only to be a lord, but "a great man." One of the circumstances on which she founded this belief was, singularly enough, his lameness;—for what reason it is difficult to conceive, except that, possibly (having a mind of the most superstitious cast), she had consulted on the subject some village fortune-teller, who, to ennoble this infirmity in her eyes, had linked the future destiny of the child with it.

By the death of the grandson of the old lord at Corsica in 1794, the only claimant, that had hitherto stood between little George and the immediate succession to the peerage, was removed; and the increased importance which this event conferred upon them was felt not only by Mrs. Byron, but by the young future Baron of Newstead himself. In the winter of 1797, his mother having chanced, one day, to read part of a speech spoken in the House of Commons, a friend who was present said to the boy, "We shall have the pleasure, some time or other, of reading your speeches in the House of Commons."—"I hope not," was his answer: "if you read any speeches of mine, it will be in the House of Lords."

The title, of which he thus early anticipated the enjoyment, devolved to him but too soon. Had he been left to struggle on for ten years longer, as plain George Byron, there can be little doubt that his character would have been, in many respects, the better for it. In the following year his grand-uncle, the fifth Lord Byron, died at Newstead Abbey, having passed the latter years of his strange life in a state of austere and almost savage seclusion. It is said, that the day after little Byron's accessionto the title, he ran up to his mother and asked her, "whether she perceived any difference in him since he had been made a lord, as he perceived none himself:"—a quick and natural thought; but the child little knew what a total and talismanic change had been wrought in all his future relations with society, by the simple addition of that word before his name. That the event, as a crisis in his life, affected him, even at that time, may be collected from the agitation which he is said to have manifested on the important morning, when his name was first called out in school with the title of "Dominus" prefixed to it. Unable to give utterance to the usual answer "adsum," he stood silent amid the general stare of his school-fellows, and, at last, burst into tears.

The cloud, which, to a certain degree, undeservedly, his unfortunate affray with Mr. Chaworth had thrown upon the character of the late Lord Byron, was deepened and confirmed by what it, in a great measure, produced,—the eccentric and unsocial course of life to which he afterwards betook himself. Of his cruelty to Lady Byron, before her separation from him, the most exaggerated stories are still current in the neighbourhood; and it is even believed that, in one of his fits of fury, he flung her into the pond at Newstead. On another occasion, it is said, having shot his coachman for some disobedience of orders, he threw the corpse into the carriage to his lady, and, mounting the box, drove off himself. These stories are, no doubt, as gross fictions as some of those of which his illustrious successor was afterwards made the victim; and a female servant of the old lord, still alive, in contradicting both tales as scandalous fabrications, supposes the first to have had its origin in the following circumstance:—A young lady, of the name of Booth, who was on a visit at Newstead, being one evening with a party who were diverting themselves in front of the abbey, Lord Byron by accident pushed her into the basin which receives the cascades; and out of this little incident, as my informant very plausibly conjectures, the tale of his attempting to drown Lady Byron may have been fabricated.

After his lady had separated from him, the entire seclusion in which he lived gave full scope to the inventive faculties of his neighbours. There was no deed, however dark or desperate, that the village gossips were not ready to impute to him; and two grim images of satyrs, which stood in his gloomy garden, were, by the fears of those who had caught a glimpse of them, dignified by the name of "the old lord's devils." He was known always to go armed; and it is related that, on some particular occasion, when his neighbour, the late Sir John Warren, was admitted to dine with him, there was a case of pistols placed, as if forming a customary part of the dinner service, on the table.

During his latter years, the only companions of his solitude—besides that colony of crickets, which he is said to have amused himself with rearing and feeding—were old Murray, afterwards the favourite servant of his successor, and the female domestic, whose authority I have just quoted, and who, from the station she was suspected of being promoted to by her noble master, received generally through the neighbourhood the appellation of "Lady Betty."

Though living in this sordid and solitary style, he was frequently, as it appears, much distressed for money; and one of the most serious of the injuries inflicted by him upon the property was his sale of the family estate of Rochdale in Lancashire, of which the mineral produce was accounted very valuable. He well knew, it is said, at the time of the sale, his inability to make out a legal title; nor is it supposed that the purchasers themselves were unacquainted with the defect of the conveyance. But they contemplated, and, it seems, actually did realise, an indemnity from any pecuniary loss, before they could, in the ordinary course of events, be dispossessed of the property. During the young lord's minority, proceedings were instituted for the recovery of this estate, and as the reader will learn hereafter with success.

At Newstead, both the mansion and the grounds around it were suffered to fall helplessly into decay; and among the few monuments of either care or expenditure which their lord left behind, were some masses of rockwork, on which much cost had been thrown away, and a few castellated buildings on the banks of the lake and in the woods. The forts upon the lake were designed to give a naval appearance to its waters, and frequently, in his more social days, he used to amuse himself with sham fights,—his vessels attacking the forts, and being cannonaded by them in return. The largest of these vessels had been built for him at some seaport on the eastern coast, and, being conveyed on wheels over the Forest to Newstead, was supposed to have fulfilled one of the prophecies of Mother Shipton, which declared that "when a ship laden with *ling* should cross over Sherwood Forest, the Newstead estate would pass from the Byron family." In Nottinghamshire, "ling" is the term used for *heather*; and, in order to bear out Mother Shipton and spite the old lord, the country people, it is said, ran along by the side of the vessel, heaping it with heather all the way.

This eccentric peer, it is evident, cared but little about the fate of his descendants. With his young heir in Scotland he held no communication whatever; and if at any time he happened to mention him, which but rarely occurred, it was never under any other designation than that of "the little boy who lives at Aberdeen."

On the death of his grand-uncle, Lord Byron having become a ward of chancery, the Earl of Carlisle, who was in some degree connected with the family, being the son of the deceased lord's sister, was appointed his guardian; and in the autumn of 1798, Mrs. Byron and her son, attended by their faithful Mary Gray, left Aberdeen for Newstead. Previously to their departure, the furniture of the humble lodgings which they had occupied was, with the exception of the plate and linen, which Mrs. Byron took with her, sold, and the whole sum that the effects of the mother of the Lord of Newstead yielded was 74*l*. 17*s*. 7*d*.

From the early age at which Byron was taken to Scotland, as well as from the circumstance of his mother being a native of that country, he had every reason to consider himself—as, indeed, he boasts in Don Juan—"half a Scot by birth, and bred a whole one." We have already seen how warmly he preserved through life his recollection of the mountain scenery in which he was brought up; and in the passage of Don Juan, to which I have just referred, his allusion to the romantic bridge of Don, and to other localities of Aberdeen, shows an equal fidelity and fondness of retrospect:—

As Auld Lang Syne brings Scotland, one and all,

Scotch plaids, Scotch snoods, the blue hills and clear streams,

The Dee, the Don, Balgounie's brig's black wall,

All my boy feelings, all my gentler dreams

Of what I then dreamt, clothed in their own pall,

Like Banquo's offspring;—floating past me seems

My childhood in this childishness of mine;

I care not—'tis a glimpse of "Auld Lang Syne."

He adds in a note, "The Brig of Don, near the 'auld town' of Aberdeen, with its one arch and its black deep salmon stream, is in my memory as yesterday. I still remember, though perhaps I may misquote the awful proverb which made me pause to cross it, and yet lean over it with a childish delight, being an only son, at least by the mother's side. The saying, as recollected by me, was this, but I have never heard or seen it since I was nine years of age:—

"'Brig of Balgounie, black's your wa',

Wi' a wife's ae son, and a mear's ae foal,

Down ye shall fa'.'"

To meet with an Aberdonian was, at all times, a delight to him; and when the late Mr. Scott, who was a native of Aberdeen, paid him a visit at Venice in the year 1819, in talking of the haunts of his childhood, one of the places he particularly mentioned was Wallace-nook, a spot where there is a rude statue of the Scottish chief still standing. From first to last, indeed, these recollections of the country of his youth never forsook him. In his early voyage into Greece, not only the shapes of the mountains, but the kilts and hardy forms of the Albanese,—all, as he says, "carried him back to Morven;" and, in his last fatal expedition, the dress which he himself chiefly wore at Cephalonia was a tartan jacket.

Cordial, however, and deep as were the impressions which he retained of Scotland, he would sometimes in this, as in all his other amiable feelings, endeavour perversely to belie his own better nature; and, when under the excitement of anger or ridicule, persuade not only others, but even himself, that the whole current of his feelings ran directly otherwise. The abuse with which, in his anger against the Edinburgh Review, he overwhelmed every thing Scotch, is an instance of this temporary triumph of wilfulness; and, at any time, the least association of ridicule with the country or its inhabitants was sufficient, for the moment, to put all his sentiment to flight. A friend of his once described to me the half playful rage, into which she saw him thrown, one day, by a heedless girl, who remarked that she thought he had a little of the Scotch accent. "Good God, I hope not!" he exclaimed. "I'm sure I haven't. I would rather the whole d——d country was sunk in the sea—I the Scotch accent!"

To such sallies, however, whether in writing or conversation, but little weight is to be allowed,—particularly, in comparison with those strong testimonies which he has left on record of his fondness for his early home; and while, on his side, this feeling so indelibly existed, there is, on the part of the people of Aberdeen, who consider him as almost their fellow-townsman, a correspondent warmth of affection for his memory and name. The various houses where he resided in his youth are pointed out to the traveller; to have seen him but once is a recollection boasted of with pride; and the Brig of Don, beautiful in itself, is invested, by his mere mention of it, with an additional charm. Two or three years since, the sum of five pounds was offered to a person in Aberdeen for a letter which he had in his possession, written by Captain Byron a few days before his death; and, among the memorials of the young poet, which are treasured up by individuals of that place, there is one which it would have not a little amused himself to hear of, being no less characteristic a relic than an old china saucer, out of which he had bitten a large piece, in a fit of passion, when a child.

It was in the summer of 1798, as I have already said, that Lord Byron, then in his eleventh year, left Scotland with his mother and nurse, to take possession of the ancient seat of his ancestors. In one of his latest letters, referring to this journey, he says, "I recollect Loch Leven as it were but yesterday—I saw it in my way to England in 1798." They had already arrived at the Newstead toll-bar, and saw the woods of the Abbey stretching out to receive them, when Mrs. Byron, affecting to be ignorant of the place, asked the woman of the toll-house—to whom that seat belonged? She was told that the owner of it, Lord Byron, had been some months dead. "And who is the next heir?" asked the proud and happy mother. "They say," answered the woman, "it is a little boy who lives at Aberdeen."—"And this is he, bless him!" exclaimed the nurse, no longer able to contain herself, and turning to kiss with delight the young lord who was seated on her lap.

Even under the most favourable circumstances, such an early elevation to rank would be but too likely to have a dangerous influence on the character; and the guidance under which young Byron entered upon his new station was, of all others, the least likely to lead him safely through its perils and temptations. His mother, without judgment or self-command, alternately spoiled him by indulgence, and irritated, or—what was still worse—amused him by her violence. That strong sense of the ridiculous, for which he was afterwards so remarkable, and which showed itself thus early, got the better even of his fear of her; and when Mrs. Byron, who was a short and corpulent person, and rolled considerably in her gait, would, in a rage, endeavour to catch him, for the purpose of inflicting punishment, the young urchin, proud of being able to out-strip her, notwithstanding his lameness, would run round the room, laughing like a little Puck, and mocking at all her menaces. In a few anecdotes of his early life which he related in his "Memoranda," though the name of his mother was never mentioned but with respect, it was not difficult to perceive that the recollections she had left behind—at least, those that had made the deepest impression—were of a painful nature. One of the most striking passages, indeed, in the few pages of that Memoir which related to his early days, was where, in speaking of his own sensitiveness, on the subject of his deformed foot, he described the feeling of horror and humiliation that came over him, when his mother, in one of her fits of passion, called him "a lame brat." As all that he had felt strongly through life was, in some shape or other, reproduced in his poetry, it was not likely that an expression such as this should fail of being recorded. Accordingly we find, in the opening of his drama, "The Deformed Transformed,"

Bertha. Out, hunchback!
Arnold. I was born so, mother!

It may be questioned, indeed, whether that whole drama was not indebted for its origin to this single recollection.

While such was the character of the person under whose immediate eye his youth was passed, the counteraction which a kind and watchful guardian might have opposed to such example and influence was almost wholly lost to him. Connected but remotely with the family, and never having had any opportunity of knowing the boy, it was with much reluctance that Lord Carlisle originally undertook the trust; nor can we wonder that, when his duties as a guardian brought him acquainted with Mrs. Byron, he should be deterred from interfering more than was absolutely necessary for the child by his fear of coming into collision with the violence and caprice of the mother.

Had even the character which the last lord left behind been sufficiently popular to pique his young successor into an emulation of his good name, such a salutary rivalry of the dead would have supplied the place of living examples; and there is no mind in which such an ambition would have been more likely to spring up than that of Byron. But unluckily, as we have seen, this was not the case; and not only was so fair a stimulus to good conduct wanting, but a rivalry of a very different nature substituted in its place. The strange anecdotes told of the last lord by the country people, among whom his fierce and solitary habits had procured for him a sort of fearful renown, were of a nature livelily to arrest the fancy of the young poet, and even to waken in his mind a sort of boyish admiration for singularities which he found thus elevated into matters of wonder and record. By some it has been even supposed that in these stories of his eccentric relative his imagination found the first dark outlines of that ideal character, which he afterwards embodied in so many different shapes, and ennobled by his genius. But however this may be, it is at least far from improbable that, destitute as he was of other and better models, the peculiarities of his immediate predecessor should, in a considerable degree, have influenced his fancy and tastes. One habit, which he seems early to have derived from this spirit of imitation, and which he retained through life, was that of constantly having arms of some description about or near him—it being his practice, when quite a boy, to carry, at all times, small loaded pistols in his waistcoat pockets. The affray, indeed, of the late lord with Mr. Chaworth had, at a very early age, by connecting duelling in his mind with the name of his race, led him to turn his attention to this mode of arbitrament; and the mortification which he had, for some time, to endure at school, from insults, as he imagined, hazarded on the presumption of his physical inferiority, found consolation in the thought that a day would yet arrive when the law of the pistol would place him on a level with the strongest.

On their arrival from Scotland, Mrs. Byron, with the hope of having his lameness removed, placed her son under the care of a person, who professed the cure of such cases, at Nottingham. The name of this man, who appears to have been a mere empirical pretender, was Lavender; and the manner in which he is said to have proceeded was by first rubbing the foot over, for a considerable time, with handsful of oil, and then twisting the limb forcibly round, and screwing it up in a wooden machine. That the boy might not lose ground in his education during this interval, he received lessons in Latin from a respectable schoolmaster, Mr. Rogers, who read parts of Virgil and Cicero with him, and represents his proficiency to have been, for his age, considerable. He was often, during his lessons, in violent pain, from the torturing position in which his foot was kept; and Mr. Rogers one day said to him, "It makes me uncomfortable, my Lord, to see you sitting there in such pain as I *know* you must be suffering."—"Never mind, Mr. Rogers," answered the boy; "you shall not see any signs of it in *me*."

This gentleman, who speaks with the most affectionate remembrance of his pupil, mentions several instances of the gaiety of spirit with which he used to take revenge on his tormentor, Lavender, by exposing and laughing at his pompous ignorance. Among other tricks, he one day scribbled down on a sheet of paper all the letters of the alphabet, put together at random, but in the form of words and sentences, and, placing them before this all-pretending person, asked him gravely what language it was. The quack, unwilling to own his ignorance, answered confidently, "Italian,"—to the infinite delight, as it may be supposed, of the little satirist in embryo, who burst into a loud, triumphant laugh at the success of the trap which he had thus laid for imposture.

With that mindfulness towards all who had been about him in his youth, which was so distinguishing a trait in his character, he, many years after, when in the neighbourhood of Nottingham, sent a message, full of kindness, to his old instructor, and bid the bearer of it tell him, that, beginning from a certain line in Virgil which he mentioned, he could recite twenty verses on, which he well remembered having read with this gentleman, when suffering all the time the most dreadful pain.

It was about this period, according to his nurse, May Gray, that the first symptom of any tendency towards rhyming showed itself in him; and the occasion which she represented as having given rise to this childish effort was as follows:—An elderly lady, who was in the habit of visiting his mother, had made use of some expression that very much affronted him; and these slights, his nurse said, he generally resented violently and implacably. The old lady had some curious notions respecting the soul, which, she imagined, took its flight to the moon after death, as a preliminary essay before it proceeded further. One day, after a repetition, it is supposed, of her original insult to the boy, he appeared before his nurse in a violent rage. "Well, my little hero," she asked, "what's the matter with you now?" Upon which the child answered, that "this old woman had put him in a most terrible passion—that he could not bear the sight of her," &c. &c.—and then broke out into the following doggerel, which he repeated over and over, as if delighted with the vent he had found for his rage:—

In Nottingham county there lives at Swan Green,

As curst an old lady as ever was seen;

And when she does die, which I hope will be soon,

She firmly believes she will go to the moon.

It is possible that these rhymes may have been caught up at second-hand; and he himself, as will presently be seen, dated his "first dash into poetry," as he calls it, a year later:—but the anecdote altogether, as containing some early dawnings of character, appeared to me worth preserving.

The small income of Mrs. Byron received at this time the addition—most seasonable, no doubt, though on what grounds accorded, I know not—of a pension on the Civil List, of 300*l.* a year. The following is a copy of the King's warrant for the grant:—(Signed)

"GEORGE R.

"WHEREAS we are graciously pleased to grant unto Catharine Gordon Byron, widow, an annuity of 300*l.*, to commence from 5th July, 1799, and to continue during pleasure: our will and pleasure is, that, by virtue of our general letters of Privy Seal, bearing date 5th November, 1760, you do issue and pay out of our treasure, or revenue in the receipt of the Exchequer, applicable to the uses of our civil government, unto the said Catharine Gordon Byron, widow, or her assignees, the said annuity, to commence from 5th July, 1799, and to be paid quarterly, or otherwise, as the same shall become due, and to continue during our pleasure; and for so doing this shall be your warrant. Given at our Court of St. James's, 2d October, 1799, 39th year of our reign.

"By His Majesty's command,

(Signed) "W. PITT.

"S. DOUGLAS.

"EDW^D. ROBERTS, Dep. Cler^{us}. Pellium."

Finding but little benefit from the Nottingham practitioner, Mrs. Byron, in the summer of the year 1799, thought it right to remove her boy to London, where, at the suggestion of Lord Carlisle, he was put under the care of Dr. Baillie. It being an object, too, to place him at some quiet school, where the means adopted for the cure of his infirmity might be more easily attended to, the establishment of the late Dr. Glennie, at Dulwich, was chosen for that purpose; and as it was thought advisable that he should have a separate apartment to sleep in, Dr. Glennie had a bed put up for him in his own study. Mrs. Byron, who had remained a short time behind him at Newstead, on her arrival in town took a house upon Sloane Terrace; and, under the direction of Dr. Baillie, one of the Messrs. Sheldrake was employed to construct an instrument for the purpose of straightening the limb of the child. Moderation in all athletic exercises was, of course, prescribed; but Dr. Glennie found it by no means easy to enforce compliance with this rule, as, though sufficiently quiet when along with him in his study, no sooner was the boy released for play, than he showed as much ambition to excel in all exercises as the most robust youth of the school;—"an ambition," adds Dr. Glennie, in the communication with which he favoured me a short time before his death, "which I have remarked to prevail in general in young persons labouring under similar defects of nature."

Having been instructed in the elements of Latin grammar according to the mode of teaching adopted at Aberdeen, the young student had now unluckily to retrace his steps, and was, as is too often the case, retarded in his studies and perplexed in his recollections, by the necessity of toiling through the rudiments again in one of the forms prescribed by the English schools. "I found him enter upon his tasks," says Dr. Glennie, "with alacrity and success. He was playful, good-humoured, and beloved by his companions. His reading in history and poetry was far beyond the usual standard of his age, and in my study he found many books open to him, both to please his taste and gratify his curiosity; among others, a set of our poets from Chaucer to Churchill, which I am almost tempted to say he had more than once perused from beginning to end. He showed at this age an intimate acquaintance with the historical parts of the Holy Scriptures, upon which he seemed delighted to converse with me, especially after our religious exercises of a Sunday evening; when he would reason upon the facts contained in the Sacred Volume with every appearance of belief in the divine truths which they unfold. That the impressions," adds the writer, "thus imbibed in his boyhood, had, notwithstanding the irregularities of his after life, sunk deep into his mind, will appear, I think, to every impartial reader of his works in general; and I never have been able to divest myself of the persuasion that, in the strange aberrations which so unfortunately marked his subsequent career, he must have found it difficult to violate the better principles early instilled into him."

It should have been mentioned, among the traits which I have recorded of his still earlier years, that, according to the character given of him by his first nurse's husband, he was, when a mere child, "particularly inquisitive and puzzling about religion."

It was not long before Dr. Glennie began to discover—what instructors of youth must too often experience—that the parent was a much more difficult subject to deal with than the child. Though professing entire acquiescence in the representations of this gentleman, as to the propriety of leaving her son to pursue his studies without interruption, Mrs. Byron had neither sense nor self-denial enough to act up to these professions; but, in spite of the remonstrances of Dr. Glennie, and the injunctions of Lord Carlisle, continued to interfere with and thwart the progress of the boy's education in every way that a fond, wrong-headed, and self-willed mother could devise. In vain was it stated to her that, in all the elemental parts of learning which are requisite for a youth destined to a great public school, young Byron was much behind other youths of his age, and that, to retrieve this deficiency, the undivided application of his whole time would be necessary. Though appearing to be sensible of the truth of these suggestions, she not the less embarrassed and obstructed the teacher in his task. Not content with the interval between Saturday and Monday, which, contrary to Dr. Glennie's wish, the boy generally passed at Sloane Terrace, she would frequently keep him at home a week beyond this time, and, still further to add to the distraction of such interruptions, collected around him a numerous circle of young acquaintances, without exercising, as may be supposed, much discrimination in her choice. "How, indeed, could she?" asks Dr. Glennie—"Mrs. Byron was a total stranger to English society and English manners; with an exterior far from prepossessing, an understanding where nature had not been more bountiful, a mind almost wholly without cultivation, and the peculiarities of northern opinions, northern habits, and northern accent, I trust I do no great prejudice to the memory of my countrywoman, if I say Mrs. Byron was not a Madame de Lambert, endowed with powers to retrieve the fortune, and form the character and manners, of a young nobleman, her son."

The interposition of Lord Carlisle, to whose authority it was found necessary to appeal, had more than once given a check to these disturbing indulgences. Sanctioned by such support, Dr. Glennie even ventured to oppose himself to the privilege, so often abused, of the usual visits on a Saturday; and the scenes which he had to encounter on each new case of refusal were such as would have wearied out the patience of any less zealous and conscientious schoolmaster. Mrs. Byron, whose paroxysms of passion were not, like those of her son, "silent rages," would, on all these occasions, break out into such audible fits of temper as it was impossible to keep from reaching the ears of the scholars and the servants; and Dr. Glennie had, one day, the pain of overhearing a school-fellow of his noble pupil say to him, "Byron, your mother is a fool;" to which the other answered gloomily, "I know it." In consequence of all this violence and impracticability of temper, Lord Carlisle at length ceased to have any intercourse with the mother of his ward; and on a further application from the instructor, for the exertion of his influence, said, "I can have nothing more to do with Mrs. Byron,—you must now manage her as you can."

Among the books that lay accessible to the boys in Dr. Glennie's study was a pamphlet written by the brother of one of his most intimate friends, entitled, "Narrative of the Shipwreck of the Juno on the coast of Arracan, in the year 1795." The writer had been the second officer of the ship, and the account which he had sent home to his friends of the sufferings of himself and his fellow-passengers had appeared to them so touching and strange, that they determined to publish it. The pamphlet attracted but little, it seems, of public attention, but among the young students of Dulwich Grove it was a favourite study; and the impression which it left on the retentive mind of Byron may have had some share, perhaps, in suggesting that curious research through all the various Accounts of Shipwrecks upon record, by which he prepared himself to depict with such power a scene of the same description in Don Juan. The following affecting incident, mentioned by the author of this pamphlet, has been adopted, it will be seen, with but little change either of phrase or circumstance, by the poet:—

"Of those who were not immediately near me I knew little, unless by their cries. Some struggled hard, and died in great agony; but it was not always those whose strength was most impaired that died the easiest, though, in some cases, it might have been so. I particularly remember the following instances. Mr. Wade's servant, a stout and healthy boy, died early and almost without a groan; while another of the same age, but of a less promising appearance, held out much longer. The fate of these unfortunate boys differed also in another respect highly deserving of notice. Their fathers were both in the fore-top when the lads were taken ill. The father of Mr. Wade's boy hearing of his son's illness, answered with indifference, 'that he could do nothing for him,' and left him to his fate. The other, when the accounts reached him, hurried down, and watching for a favourable moment, crawled on all fours along the weather gunwale to his son, who was in the mizen rigging. By that time, only three or four planks of the quarter deck remained, just over the weather-quarter gallery; and to this spot the unhappy man led his son, making him fast to the rail to prevent his being washed away. Whenever the boy was seized with a fit of retching, the father lifted him up and wiped the foam from his lips; and, if a shower came, he made him open his mouth to receive the drops, or gently squeezed them into it from a rag. In this affecting situation both remained four or five days, till the boy expired. The unfortunate parent, as if unwilling to believe the fact, then raised the body, gazed wistfully at it, and, when he could no longer entertain any doubt, watched it in silence till it was carried off by the sea; then, wrapping himself in a piece of canvass, sunk down and rose no more; though he must have lived two days longer, as we judged from the quivering of his limbs, when a wave broke over him."

It was probably during one of the vacations of this year, that the boyish love for his young cousin, Miss Parker, to which he attributes the glory of having first inspired him with poetry, took possession of his fancy. "My first dash into poetry (he says) was as early as 1800. It was the ebullition of a passion for my first cousin, Margaret Parker (daughter and grand-daughter of the two Admirals Parker), one of the most beautiful of evanescent beings. I have long forgotten the verses, but it would be difficult for me to forget her—her dark eyes—her long eye-lashes—her completely Greek cast of face and figure! I was then about twelve—she rather older, perhaps a year. She died about a year or two afterwards, in consequence of a fall, which injured her spine, and induced consumption. Her sister Augusta (by some thought still more beautiful) died of the same malady; and it was, indeed, in attending her, that Margaret met with the accident which occasioned her own death. My sister told me, that when she went to see her, shortly before her death, upon accidentally mentioning my name, Margaret coloured through the paleness of mortality to the eyes, to the great astonishment of my sister, who (residing with her grandmother, Lady Holderness, and seeing but little of me, for family reasons,) knew nothing of our attachment, nor could conceive why my name should affect her at such a time. I knew nothing of her illness, being at Harrow and in the country, till she was gone. Some years after, I made an attempt at an elegy—a very dull one.

"I do not recollect scarcely any thing equal to the *transparent* beauty of my cousin, or to the sweetness of her temper, during the short period of our intimacy. She looked as if she had been made out of a rainbow—all beauty and peace.

"My passion had its usual effects upon me—I could not sleep—I could not eat —I could not rest: and although I had reason to know that she loved me, it was the texture of my life to think of the time which must elapse before we could meet again, being usually about twelve hours of separation! But I was a fool then, and am not much wiser now."

He had been nearly two years under the tuition of Dr. Glennie, when his mother, discontented at the slowness of his progress—though being, herself, as we have seen, the principal cause of it—entreated so urgently of Lord Carlisle to have him removed to a public school, that her wish was at length acceded to; and "accordingly," says Dr. Glennie, "to Harrow he went, as little prepared as it is natural to suppose from two years of elementary instruction, thwarted by every art that could estrange the mind of youth from preceptor, from school, and from all serious study."

This gentleman saw but little of Lord Byron after he left his care; but, from the manner in which both he and Mrs. Glennie spoke of their early charge, it was evident that his subsequent career had been watched by them with interest; that they had seen even his errors through the softening medium of their first feeling towards him, and had never, in his most irregular aberrations, lost the traces of those fine qualities which they had loved and admired in him when a child. Of the constancy, too, of this feeling, Dr. Glennie had to stand no ordinary trial, having visited Geneva in 1817, soon after Lord Byron had left it, when the private character of the poet was in the very crisis of its unpopularity, and when, among those friends who knew that Dr. Glennie had once been his tutor, it was made a frequent subject of banter with this gentleman that he had not more strictly disciplined his pupil, or, to use their own words, "made a better boy of him."

About the time when young Byron was removed, for his education, to London, his nurse May Gray left the service of Mrs. Byron, and returned to her native country, where she died about three years since. She had married respectably, and in one of her last illnesses was attended professionally by Dr. Ewing of Aberdeen, who, having been always an enthusiastic admirer of Lord Byron, was no less surprised than delighted to find that the person tinder his care had for so many years been an attendant on his favourite poet. With avidity, as may be supposed, he noted down from the lips of his patient all the particulars she could remember of his Lordship's early days; and it is to the communications with which this gentleman has favoured me, that I am indebted for many of the anecdotes of that period which I have related.

As a mark of gratitude for her attention to him, Byron had, in parting with May Gray, presented her with his watch,—the first of which he had ever been possessor. This watch the faithful nurse preserved fondly through life, and, when she died, it was given by her husband to Dr. Ewing, by whom, as a relic of genius, it is equally valued. The affectionate boy had also presented her with a full-length miniature of himself, which was painted by Kay of Edinburgh, in the year 1795, and which represents him standing with a bow and arrows in his hand, and a profusion of hair falling over his shoulders. This curious little drawing has likewise passed into the possession of Dr. Ewing.

The same thoughtful gratitude was evinced by Byron towards the sister of this woman, his first nurse, to whom he wrote some years after he left Scotland, in the most cordial terms, making enquiries of her welfare, and informing her, with much joy, that he had at last got his foot so far restored as to be able to put on a common boot,—"an event for which he had long anxiously wished, and which he was sure would give her great pleasure."

In the summer of the year 1801 he accompanied his mother to Cheltenham, and the account which he himself gives of his sensations at that period shows at what an early age those feelings that lead to poetry had unfolded themselves in his heart. A boy, gazing with emotion on the hills at sunset, because they remind him of the mountains among which he passed his childhood, is already, in heart and imagination, a poet. It was during their stay at Cheltenham that a fortune-teller, whom his mother consulted, pronounced a prediction concerning him which, for some time, left a strong impression on his mind. Mrs. Byron had, it seems, in her first visit to this person, (who, if I mistake not, was the celebrated fortune-teller, Mrs. Williams,) endeavoured to pass herself off as a maiden lady. The sibyl, however, was not so easily deceived;— she pronounced her wise consulter to be not only a married woman, but the mother of a son who was lame, and to whom, among other events which she read in the stars, it was predestined that his life should be in danger from poison before he was of age, and that he should be twice married,—the second time, to a foreign lady. About two years afterwards he himself mentioned these particulars to the person from whom I heard the story, and said that the thought of the first part of the prophecy very often occurred to him. The latter part, however, seems to have been the *nearer* guess of the two.

To a shy disposition, such as Byron's was in his youth—and such as, to a certain degree, it continued all his life—the transition from a quiet establishment, like that of Dulwich Grove, to the bustle of a great public school was sufficiently trying. Accordingly, we find from his own account, that, for the first year and a half, he "hated Harrow." The activity, however, and sociableness of his nature soon conquered this repugnance; and, from being, as he himself says, "a most unpopular boy," he rose at length to be a leader in all the sports, schemes, and mischief of the school.

For a general notion of his dispositions and capacities at this period, we could not have recourse to a more trust-worthy or valuable authority than that of the Rev. Dr. Drury, who was at this time head master of the school, and to whom Lord Byron has left on record a tribute of affection and respect, which, like the reverential regard of Dryden for Dr. Busby, will long associate together honourably the names of the poet and the master. From this venerable scholar I have received the following brief, but important statement of the impressions which his early intercourse with the young noble left upon him:—

"Mr. Hanson, Lord Byron's solicitor, consigned him to my care at the age of 13-1/2, with remarks, that his education had been neglected; that he was ill prepared for a public school, but that he thought there was a *cleverness* about him. After his departure I took my young disciple into my study, and endeavoured to bring him forward by enquiries as to his former amusements, employments, and associates, but with little or no effect;—and I soon found that a wild mountain colt had been submitted to my management. But there was mind in his eye. In the first place, it was necessary to attach him to an elder boy, in order to familiarise him with the objects before him, and with some parts of the system in which he was to move. But the information he received from his conductor gave him no pleasure, when he heard of the advances of some in the school, much younger than himself, and conceived by his own deficiency that he should be degraded, and humbled, by being placed below them. This I discovered, and having committed him to the care of one of the masters, as his tutor, I assured him he should not be placed till, by diligence, he might rank with those of his own age. He was pleased with this assurance, and felt himself on easier terms with his associates;—for a degree of shyness hung about him for some time. His manner and temper soon convinced me, that he might be led by a silken string to a point, rather than by a cable;—on that principle I acted. After some continuance at Harrow, and when the powers of his mind had begun to expand, the late Lord Carlisle, his relation, desired to see me in town;—I waited on his Lordship. His object was to inform me of Lord Byron's expectations of property when he came of age, which he represented as contracted, and to enquire respecting his abilities. On the former circumstance I made no remark; as to the latter, I replied, 'He has talents, my Lord, which will *add lustre to his rank.*' 'Indeed!!!' said his Lordship, with a degree of surprise, that, according to my reeling, did not express in it all the satisfaction I expected.

"The circumstance to which you allude, as to his declamatory powers, was as follows. The upper part of the school composed declamations, which, after a revisal by the tutors, were submitted to the master: to him the authors repeated them, that they might be improved in manner and action, before their public delivery. I certainly was much pleased with Lord Byron's attitude, gesture, and delivery, as well as with his composition. All who spoke on that day adhered, as usual, to the letter of their composition, as, in the earlier part of his delivery, did Lord Byron. But to my surprise he suddenly diverged from the written composition, with a boldness and rapidity sufficient to alarm me, lest he should fail in memory as to the conclusion. There was no failure:—he came round to the close of his composition without discovering any impediment and irregularity on the whole. I questioned him, why he had altered his declamation? He declared he had made no alteration, and did not know, in speaking, that he had deviated from it one letter. I believed him; and from a knowledge of his temperament am convinced, that, fully impressed with the sense and substance of the subject, he was hurried on to expressions and colourings more striking than what his pen had expressed."

In communicating to me these recollections of his illustrious pupil, Dr. Drury has added a circumstance which shows how strongly, even in all the pride of his fame, that awe with which he had once regarded the opinions of his old master still hung around the poet's sensitive mind:—

"After my retreat from Harrow, I received from him two very affectionate letters. In my occasional visits subsequently to London, when he had fascinated the public with his productions, I demanded of him; why, as in *duty bound*, he had sent none to me? 'Because,' said he, 'you are the only man I never wish to read them:'—but, in a few moments, he added—'What do you think of the Corsair?'"

I shall now lay before the reader such notices of his school-life as I find scattered through the various note-books he has left behind. Coming, as they do, from his own pen, it is needless to add, that they afford the liveliest and best records of this period that can be furnished.

"Till I was eighteen years old (odd as it may seem) I had never read a review. But while at Harrow, my general information was so great on modern topics as to induce a suspicion that I could only collect so much information from *Reviews,* because I was never *seen* reading, but always idle, and in mischief, or at play. The truth is, that I read eating, read in bed, read when no one else read, and had read all sorts of reading since I was five years old, and yet never *met* with a Review, which is the only reason I know of why I should not have read them. But it is true; for I remember when Hunter and Curzon, in 1804, told me this opinion at Harrow, I made them laugh by my ludicrous astonishment in asking them '*What is* a Review?' To be sure, they were then less common. In three years more, I was better acquainted with that same; but the first I ever read was in 1806-7.

"At school I was (as I have said) remarked for the extent and readiness of my *general* information; but in all other respects idle, capable of great sudden exertions, (such as thirty or forty Greek hexa-meters, of course with such prosody as it pleased God,) but of few continuous drudgeries. My qualities were much more oratorical and martial than poetical, and Dr. Drury, my grand patron, (our head master,) had a great notion that I should turn out an orator, from my fluency, my turbulence, my voice, my copiousness of declamation, and my action. I remember that my first declamation astonished him into some unwonted (for he was economical of such) and sudden compliments, before the declaimers at our first rehearsal. My first Harrow verses, (that is, English, as exercises,) a translation of a chorus from the Prometheus of Æschylus, were received by him but coolly. No one had the least notion that I should subside into poesy.

"Peel, the orator and statesman, ('that was, or is, or is to be,') was my form-fellow, and we were both at the top of our remove (a public-school phrase). We were on good terms, but his brother was my intimate friend. There were always great hopes of Peel, amongst us all, masters and scholars—and he has not disappointed them. As a scholar he was greatly my superior; as a declaimer and actor, I was reckoned at least his equal; as a schoolboy, *out* of school, I was always *in* scrapes, and *he never*; and *in school*, he *always* knew his lesson, and I rarely,—but when I knew it, I knew it nearly as well. In general information, history, &c. &c., I think I was *his* superior, as well as of most boys of my standing.

"The prodigy of our school-days was George Sinclair (son of Sir John); he made exercises for half the school, (*literally*) verses at will, and themes without it.... He was a friend of mine, and in the same remove, and used at times to beg me to let him do my exercise,—a request always most readily accorded upon a pinch, or when I wanted to do something else, which was usually once an hour. On the other hand, he was pacific and I savage; so I fought for him, or thrashed others for him, or thrashed himself to make him thrash others when it was necessary, as a point of honour and stature, that he should so chastise;—or we talked politics, for he was a great politician, and were very good friends. I have some of his letters, written to me from school, still.

"Clayton was another school-monster of learning, and talent, and hope; but what has become of him I do not know. He was certainly a genius.

"My school-friendships were with *me passions*, (for I was always violent,) but I do not know that there is one which has endured (to be sure some have been cut short by death) till now. That with Lord Clare begun one of the earliest, and lasted longest—being only interrupted by distance—that I know of. I never hear the word '*Clare*' without a beating of the heart even *now*, and I write it with the feelings of 1803-4-5, ad infinitum."

The following extract is from another of his manuscript journals:—

"At Harrow I fought my way very fairly. I think I lost but one battle out of seven; and that was to H——;—and the rascal did not win it, but by the unfair treatment of his own boarding-house, where we boxed—I had not even a second. I never forgave him, and I should be sorry to meet him now, as I am sure we should quarrel. My most memorable combats were with Morgan, Rice, Rainsford, and Lord Jocelyn,—but we were always friendly afterwards. I was a most unpopular boy, but *led* latterly, and have retained many of my school friendships, and all my dislikes—except to Dr. Butler, whom I treated rebelliously, and have been sorry ever since. Dr. Drury, whom I plagued sufficiently too, was the best, the kindest (and yet strict, too,) friend I ever had —and I look upon him still as a father.

"P. Hunter, Curzon, Long, and Tatersall, were my principal friends. Clare, Dorset, C^S. Gordon, De Bath, Claridge, and J^{no}. Wingfield, were my juniors and favourites, whom I spoilt by indulgence. Of all human beings, I was, perhaps, at one time, the most attached to poor Wingfield, who died at Coimbra, 1811, before I returned to England."

One of the most striking results of the English system of education is, that while in no country are there so many instances of manly friendships early formed and steadily maintained, so in no other country, perhaps, are the feelings towards the parental home so early estranged, or, at the best, feebly cherished. Transplanted as boys are from the domestic circle, at a time of life when the affections are most disposed to cling, it is but natural that they should seek a substitute for the ties of home in those boyish friendships which they form at school, and which, connected as they are with the scenes and events over which youth threw its charm, retain ever after the strongest hold upon their hearts. In Ireland, and I believe also in France, where the system of education is more domestic, a different result is accordingly observable:—the paternal home comes in for its due and natural share of affection, and the growth of friendships, out of this domestic circle, is proportionably diminished.

To a youth like Byron, abounding with the most passionate feelings, and finding sympathy with only the ruder parts of his nature at home, the little world of school afforded a vent for his affections, which was sure to call them forth in their most ardent form. Accordingly, the friendships which he contracted, both at school and college, were little less than what he himself describes them, "passions." The want he felt at home of those kindred dispositions, which greeted him among "Ida's social band," is thus strongly described in one of his early poems:—

"Is there no cause beyond the common claim,

Endear'd to all in childhood's very name?

Ah! sure some stronger impulse vibrates here,

Which whispers, Friendship will be doubly dear

To one who thus for kindred hearts must roam,

And seek abroad the love denied at home:

Those hearts, dear Ida, have I found in thee,

A home, a world, a paradise to me."

This early volume, indeed, abounds with the most affectionate tributes to his school-fellows. Even his expostulations to one of them, who had given him some cause for complaint, are thus tenderly conveyed:—

"You knew that my soul, that my heart, my existence,

If danger demanded, were wholly your own;

You know me unaltered by years or by distance,

Devoted to love and to friendship alone.

"You knew—but away with the vain retrospection,

The bond of affection no longer endures.

Too late you may droop o'er the fond recollection,

And sigh for the friend who was formerly yours."

The following description of what he felt after leaving Harrow, when he encountered in the world any of his old school-fellows, falls far short of the scene which actually occurred but a few years before his death in Italy,—when, on meeting with his friend, Lord Clare, after a long separation, he was affected almost to tears by the recollections which rushed on him.

"If chance some well remember'd face,

Some old companion of my early race,

Advance to claim his friend with honest joy,

My eyes, my heart proclaim'd me yet a boy;

The glittering scene, the fluttering groups around,

Were all forgotten when my friend was found."

It will be seen, by the extracts from his memorandum-book, which I have given, that Mr. Peel was one of his contemporaries at Harrow; and the following interesting anecdote of an occurrence in which both were concerned, has been related to me by a friend of the latter gentleman, in whose words I shall endeavour as nearly as possible to give it.

While Lord Byron and Mr. Peel were at Harrow together, a tyrant, some few years older, whose name was ———, claimed a right to fag little Peel, which claim (whether rightly or wrongly I know not) Peel resisted. His resistance, however, was in vain:— ——— not only subdued him, but determined also to punish the refractory slave; and proceeded forthwith to put this determination in practice, by inflicting a kind of bastinado on the inner fleshy side of the boy's arm, which, during the operation, was twisted round with some degree of technical skill, to render the pain more acute. While the stripes were succeeding each other, and poor Peel writhing under them, Byron saw and felt for the misery of his friend; and although he knew that he was not strong enough to fight ——— with any hope of success, and that it was dangerouseven to approach him, he advanced to the scene of action, and with a blush of rage, tears in his eyes, and a voice trembling between terror and indignation, asked very humbly if ——— would be pleased to tell him "how many stripes he meant to inflict?"—"Why," returned the executioner, "you little rascal, what is that to you?"—"Because, if you please," said Byron, holding out his arm, "I would take half!"

There is a mixture of simplicity and magnanimity in this little trait which is truly heroic; and however we may smile at the friendships of boys, it is but rarely that the friendship of manhood is capable of any thing half so generous.

Among his school favourites a great number, it may be observed, were nobles or of noble family—Lords Clare and Delaware, the Duke of Dorset and young Wingfield—and that their rank may have had some share in first attracting his regard to them, might appear from a circumstance mentioned to me by one of his school-fellows, who, being monitor one day, had put Lord Delaware on his list for punishment. Byron, hearing of this, came up to him, and said, "Wildman, I find you've got Delaware on your list—pray don't lick him."—"Why not?"—"Why, I don't know—except that he is a brother peer. But pray don't." It is almost needless to add, that his interference, on such grounds, was anything but successful. One of the few merits, indeed, of public schools is, that they level, in some degree, these artificial distinctions, and that, however the peer may have his revenge in the world afterwards, the young plebeian is, for once, at least, on something like an equality with him.

It is true that Lord Byron's high notions of rank were, in his boyish days, so little disguised or softened down, as to draw upon him, at times, the ridicule of his companions; and it was at Dulwich, I think, that from his frequent boast of the superiority of an old English barony over all the later creations of the peerage, he got the nickname, among the boys, of "the Old English Baron." But it is a mistake to suppose that, either at school or afterwards, he was at all guided in the selection of his friends by aristocratic sympathies. On the contrary, like most very proud persons, he chose his intimates in general from a rank beneath his own, and those boys whom he ranked as *friends* at school were mostly of this description; while the chief charm that recommended to him his younger favourites was their inferiority to himself in age and strength, which enabled him to indulge his generous pride by taking upon himself, when necessary, the office of their protector.

Among those whom he attached to himself by this latter tie, one of the earliest (though he has omitted to mention his name) was William Harness, who at the time of his entering Harrow was ten years of age, while Byron was fourteen. Young Harness, still lame from an accident of his childhood, and but just recovered from a severe illness, was ill fitted to struggle with the difficulties of a public school; and Byron, one day, seeing him bullied by a boy much older and stronger than himself, interfered and took his part. The next day, as the little fellow was standing alone, Byron came to him and said, "Harness, if any one bullies you, tell me, and I'll thrash him, if I can." The young champion kept his word, and they were from this time, notwithstanding the difference of their ages, inseparable friends. A coolness, however, subsequently arose between them, to which, and to the juvenile friendship it interrupted, Lord Byron, in a letter addressed to Harness six years afterwards, alludes with so much kindly feeling, so much delicacy and frankness, that I am tempted to anticipate the date of the letter, and give an extract from it here.

"We both seem perfectly to recollect, with a mixture of pleasure and regret, the hours we once passed together, and I assure you, most sincerely, they are numbered among the happiest of my brief chronicle of enjoyment. I am now *getting into years*, that is to say, I was *twenty* a month ago, and another year will send me into the world to run my career of folly with the rest. I was then just fourteen,—you were almost the *first* of my Harrow friends, certainly the first in my esteem, if not in date; but an absence from Harrow for some time, shortly after, and new connections on your side, and the difference in our conduct (an advantage decidedly in your favour) from that turbulent and riotous disposition of mine, which impelled me into every species of mischief, —all these circumstances combined to destroy an intimacy, which affection urged me to continue, and memory compels me to regret. But there is not a circumstance attending that period, hardly a sentence we exchanged, which is not impressed on my mind at this moment. I need not say more,—this assurance alone must convince you, had I considered them as trivial, they would have been less indelible. How well I recollect the perusal of your 'first flights!' There is another circumstance you do not know;—the *first lines* I ever attempted at Harrow were addressed to *you*. You were to have seen them; but Sinclair had the copy in his possession when we went home;—and, on our return, we were *strangers*. They were destroyed, and certainly no great loss; but you will perceive from this circumstance my opinions at an age when we cannot be hypocrites.

"I have dwelt longer on this theme than I intended, and I shall now conclude with what I ought to have begun. We were once friends,—nay, we have always been so, for our separation was the effect of chance, not of dissension. I do not know how far our destinations in life may throw us together, but if opportunity and inclination allow you to waste a thought on such a hare-brained being as myself, you will find me at least sincere, and not so bigoted to my faults as to involve others in the consequences. Will you sometimes write to me? I do not ask it often; and, if we meet, let us be what we *should* be, and what we *were*."

Of the tenaciousness with which, as we see in this letter, he clung to all the impressions of his youth, there can be no stronger proof than the very interesting fact, that, while so little of his own boyish correspondence has been preserved, there were found among his papers almost all the notes and letters which his principal school favourites, even the youngest, had ever addressed to him; and, in some cases, where the youthful writers had omitted to date their scrawls, his faithful memory had, at an interval of years after, supplied the deficiency. Among these memorials, so fondly treasured by him, there is one which it would be unjust not to cite, as well on account of the manly spirit that dawns through its own childish language, as for the sake of the tender and amiable feeling which, it will be seen, the re-perusal of it, in other days, awakened in Byron:—

"TO THE LORD BYRON, &c. &c.

"Harrow on the Hill, July 28. 1805.

"Since you have been so unusually unkind to me, in calling me names whenever you meet me, of late, I must beg an explanation, wishing to know whether you choose to be as good friends with me as ever. I must own that, for this last month, you have entirely cut me,—for, I suppose, your new cronies. But think not that I will (because you choose to take into your head some whim or other) be always going up to you, nor do, as I observe certain other fellows doing, to regain your friendship; nor think that I am your friend either through interest, or because you are bigger and older than I am. No,—it never was so, nor ever shall be so. I was only your friend, and am so still,—unless you go on in this way, calling me names whenever you see me. I am sure you may easily perceive I do not like it; therefore, why should you do it, unless you wish that I should no longer be your friend? And why should I be so, if you treat me unkindly? I have no interest in being so. Though you do not let the boys bully me, yet if *you* treat me unkindly, that is to me a great deal worse.

"I am no hypocrite, Byron, nor will I, for your pleasure, ever suffer you to call me names, if you wish me to be your friend. If not, I cannot help it. I am sure no one can say that I will cringe to regain a friendship that you have rejected.

Why should I do so? Am I not your equal? Therefore, what interest can I have in doing so? When we meet again in the world, (that is, if you choose it,) *you* cannot advance or promote *me*, nor I you. Therefore I beg and entreat of you, if you value my friendship,—which, by your conduct, I am sure I cannot think you do,—not to call me the names you do, nor abuse me. Till that time, it will be out of my power to call you friend. I shall be obliged for an answer as soon as it is convenient; till then

I remain yours,

"I cannot say your friend."

Endorsed on this letter, in the handwriting of Lord Byron, is the following:—

"This and another letter were written at Harrow, by my *then*, and I hope *ever*, beloved friend, Lord ——, when we were both school-boys, and sent to my study in consequence of some childish misunderstanding,—the only one which ever arose between us. It was of short duration, and I retain this note solely for the purpose of submitting it to his perusal, that we may smile over the recollection of the insignificance of our first and last quarrel.

"BYRON."

In a letter, dated two years afterwards, from the same boy, there occurs the following characteristic trait:—"I think, by your last letter, that you are very much piqued with most of your friends; and, if I am not much mistaken, you are a little piqued with me. In one part you say, 'There is little or no doubt a few years, or months, will render us as politely indifferent to each other as if we had never passed a portion of our time together.' Indeed, Byron, you wrong me, and I have no doubt—at least, I hope—you wrong yourself."

As that propensity to self-delineation, which so strongly pervades his maturer works is, to the full, as predominant in his early productions, there needs no better record of his mode of life, as a school-boy, than what these fondly circumstantial effusions supply. Thus the sports he delighted and excelled in are enumerated:—

"Yet when confinement's lingering hour was done,

Our sports, our studies, and our souls were one:

Together we impell'd the flying ball,

Together join'd in cricket's manly toil,

Or shared the produce of the river's spoil;

Or, plunging from the green, declining shore,

Our pliant limbs the buoyant waters bore;

In every element, unchanged, the same,

All, all that brothers should be, but the name."

The danger which he incurred in a fight with some of the neighbouring farmers—an event well remembered by some of his school-fellows—is thus commemorated.—

"Still I remember, in the factious strife,

The rustic's musket aim'd against my life;

High poised in air the massy weapon hung,

A cry of horror burst from every tongue:

Whilst I, in combat with another foe,

Fought on, unconscious of the impending blow.

Your arm, brave boy, arrested his career—

Forward you sprung, insensible to fear;

Disarm'd and baffled by your conquering hand,

The grovelling savage roll'd upon the sand."

Some feud, it appears, had arisen on the subject of the cricket-ground, between these "clods" (as in school-language they are called) and the boys, and one or two skirmishes had previously taken place. But the engagement here recorded was accidentally brought on by the breaking up of school and the dismissal of the volunteers from drill, both happening, on that occasion, at the same hour. This circumstance accounts for the use of the musket, the butt-end of which was aimed at Byron's head, and would have felled him to the ground, but for the interposition of his friend Tatersall, a lively, high-spirited boy, whom he addresses here under the name of Davus.

Notwithstanding these general habits of play and idleness, which might seem to indicate a certain absence of reflection and feeling, there were moments when the youthful poet would retire thoughtfully within himself, and give way to moods of musing uncongenial with the usual cheerfulness of his age. They show a tomb in the churchyard at Harrow, commanding a view over Windsor, which was so well known to be his favourite resting-place, that the boys called it "Byron's tomb;" and here, they say, he used to sit for hours, wrapt up in thought,—brooding lonelily over the first stirrings of passion and genius in his soul, and occasionally, perhaps, indulging in those bright forethoughts of fame, under the influence of which, when little more than fifteen years of age, he wrote these remarkable lines:—

"My epitaph shall be my name alone;

If that with honour fail to crown my clay,

Oh may no other fame my deeds repay;

That, only that, shall single out the spot,

By that remember'd, or with that forgot."

In the autumn of 1802, he passed a short time with his mother at Bath, and entered, rather prematurely, into some of the gaieties of the place. At a masquerade given by Lady Riddel, he appeared in the character of a Turkish boy,—a sort of anticipation, both in beauty and costume, of his own young Selim, in "The Bride." On his entering into the house, some person in the crowd attempted to snatch the diamond crescent from his turban, but was prevented by the prompt interposition of one of the party. The lady who mentioned to me this circumstance, and who was well acquainted with Mrs. Byron at that period, adds the following remark in the communication with which she has favoured me:—"At Bath I saw a good deal of Lord Byron,—his mother frequently sent for me to take tea with her. He was always very pleasant and droll, and, when conversing about absent friends, showed a slight turn for satire, which after-years, as is well known, gave a finer edge to."

We come now to an event in his life which, according to his own deliberate persuasion, exercised a lasting and paramount influence over the whole of his subsequent character and career.

It was in the year 1803 that his heart, already twice, as we have seen, possessed with the childish notion that it loved, conceived an attachment which—young as he was, even then, for such a feeling—sunk so deep into his mind as to give a colour to all his future life. That unsuccessful loves are generally the most lasting, is a truth, however sad, which unluckily did not require this instance to confirm it. To the same cause, I fear, must be traced the perfect innocence and romance which distinguish this very early attachment to Miss Chaworth from the many others that succeeded, without effacing it in his heart;—making it the only one whose details can be entered into with safety, or whose results, however darkening their influence on himself, can be dwelt upon with pleasurable interest by others.

On leaving Bath, Mrs. Byron took up her abode, in lodgings, at Nottingham,— Newstead Abbey being at that time let to Lord Grey de Ruthen,—and during the Harrow vacations of this year, she was joined there by her son. So attached was he to Newstead, that even to be in its neighbourhood was a delight to him; and before he became acquainted with Lord Grey, he used sometimes to sleep, for a night, at the small house near the gate which is still known by the name of "The Hut." An intimacy, however, soon sprang up between him and his noble tenant, and an apartment in the abbey was from thenceforth always at his service. To the family of Miss Chaworth, who resided at Annesley, in the immediate neighbourhood of Newstead, he had been made known, some time before, in London, and now renewed his acquaintance with them. The young heiress herself combined with the many worldly advantages that encircled her, much personal beauty, and a disposition the most amiable and attaching. Though already fully alive to her charms, it was at the period of which we are speaking that the young poet, who was then in his sixteenth year, while the object of his admiration was about two years older, seems to have drunk deepest of that fascination whose effects were to be so lasting;—six short summer weeks which he now passed in her company being sufficient to lay the foundation of a feeling for all life.

He used, at first, though offered a bed at Annesley, to return every night to Newstead, to sleep; alleging as a reason that he was afraid of the family pictures of the Chaworths,—that he fancied "they had taken a grudge to him on account of the duel, and would come down from their frames at night to haunt him." At length, one evening, he said gravely to Miss Chaworth and her cousin, "In going home last night I saw a *bogle*;"—which Scotch term being wholly unintelligible to the young ladies, he explained that he had seen a *ghost*, and would not therefore return to Newstead that evening. From this time he always slept at Annesley during the remainder of his visit, which was interrupted only by a short excursion to Matlock and Castleton, in which he had the happiness of accompanying Miss Chaworth and her party, and of which the following interesting notice appears in one of his memorandum-books:—

"When I was fifteen years of age, it happened that, in a cavern in Derbyshire, I had to cross in a boat (in which two people only could lie down) a stream which flows under a rock, with the rock so close upon the water as to admit the boat only to be pushed on by a ferryman (a sort of Charon) who wades at the stern, stooping all the time. The companion of my transit was M.A.C., with whom I had been long in love, and never told it, though *she* had discovered it without. I recollect my sensations, but cannot describe them, and it is as well. We were a party, a Mr. W., two Miss W.s, Mr. and Mrs. Cl—ke, Miss R. and *my* M.A.C. Alas! why do I say MY? Our union would have healed feuds in which blood had been shed by our fathers,—it would have joined lands broad and rich, it would have joined at least *one* heart, and two persons not ill matched in years (she is two years my elder), and—and—and—*what* has been the result?"

In the dances of the evening at Matlock, Miss Chaworth, of course, joined, while her lover sat looking on, solitary and mortified. It is not impossible, indeed, that the dislike which he always expressed for this amusement may have originated in some bitter pang, felt in his youth, on seeing "the lady of his love" led out by others to the gay dance from which he was himself excluded. On the present occasion, the young heiress of Annesley having had for her partner (as often happens at Matlock) some person with whom she was wholly unacquainted, on her resuming her seat, Byron said to her pettishly, "I hope you like your friend?" The words were scarce out of his lips when he was accosted by an ungainly-looking Scotch lady, who rather boisterously claimed him as "cousin," and was putting his pride to the torture with her vulgarity, when he heard the voice of his fair companion retorting archly in his ear, "I hope *you* like your friend?"

His time at Annesley was mostly passed in riding with Miss Chaworth and her cousin, sitting in idle reverie, as was his custom, pulling at his handkerchief, or in firing at a door which opens upon the terrace, and which still, I believe, bears the marks of his shots. But his chief delight was in sitting to hear Miss Chaworth play; and the pretty Welsh air, "Mary Anne," was (partly, of course, on account of the name) his especial favourite. During all this time he had the pain of knowing that the heart of her he loved was occupied by another;—that, as he himself expresses it,

"Her sighs were not for him; to her he wasEven as a brother—but no more."

Neither is it, indeed, probable, had even her affections been disengaged, that Lord Byron would, at this time, have been selected as the object of them. A seniority of two years gives to a girl, "on the eve of womanhood," an advance into life with which the boy keeps no proportionate pace. Miss Chaworth looked upon Byron as a mere school-boy. He was in his manners, too, at that period, rough and odd, and (as I have heard from more than one quarter) by no means popular among girls of his own age. If, at any moment, however, he had flattered himself with the hope of being loved by her, a circumstance mentioned in his "Memoranda," as one of the most painful of those humiliations to which the defect in his foot had exposed him, must have let the truth in, with dreadful certainty, upon his heart. He either was told of, or overheard, Miss Chaworth saying to her maid, "Do you think I could care any thing for that lame boy?" This speech, as he himself described it, was like a shot through his heart. Though late at night when he heard it, he instantly darted out of the house, and scarcely knowing whither he ran, never stopped till he found himself at Newstead.

The picture which he has drawn of his youthful love, in one of the most interesting of his poems, "The Dream," shows how genius and feeling can elevate the realities of this life, and give to the commonest events and objects an undying lustre. The old hall at Annesley, under the name of "the antique oratory," will long call up to fancy the "maiden and the youth" who once stood in it: while the image of the "lover's steed," though suggested by the unromantic race-ground of Nottingham, will not the less conduce to the general charm of the scene, and share a portion of that light which only genius could shed over it.

He appears already, at this boyish age, to have been so far a proficient in gallantry as to know the use that may be made of the trophies of former triumphs in achieving new ones; for he used to boast, with much pride, to Miss Chaworth, of a locket which some fair favourite had given him, and which probably may have been a present from that pretty cousin, of whom he speaks with such warmth in one of the notices already quoted. He was also, it appears, not a little aware of his own beauty, which, notwithstanding the tendency to corpulence derived from his mother, gave promise, at this time, of that peculiar expression into which his features refined and kindled afterwards.

With the summer holidays ended this dream of his youth. He saw Miss Chaworth once more in the succeeding year, and took his last farewell of her (as he himself used to relate) on that hill near Annesley which, in his poem of "The Dream," he describes so happily as "crowned with a peculiar diadem." No one, he declared, could have told how *much* he felt—for his countenance was calm, and his feelings restrained. "The next time I see you," said he in parting with her, "I suppose you will be Mrs. Chaworth,"—and her answer was, "I hope so." It was before this interview that he wrote, with a pencil, in a volume of Madame de Maintenon's letters, belonging to her, the following verses, which have never, I believe, before been published:—

"Oh Memory, torture me no more,

The present's all o'ercast;

My hopes of future bliss are o'er,

In mercy veil the past.

Why bring those images to view

I henceforth must resign?

Ah! why those happy hours renew,

That never can be mine?

Past pleasure doubles present pain,

To sorrow adds regret,

Regret and hope are both in vain,

I ask but to—forget."

In the following year, 1805, Miss Chaworth was married to his successful rival, Mr. John Musters; and a person who was present when the first intelligence of the event was communicated to him, thus describes the manner in which he received it.—"I was present when he first heard of the marriage. His mother said, 'Byron, I have some news for you.'—'Well, what is it?'—'Take out your handkerchief first, for you will want it.'—'Nonsense!'—Take out your handkerchief, I say.' He did so, to humour her. 'Miss Chaworth is married.' An expression very peculiar, impossible to describe, passed over his pale face, and he hurried his handkerchief into his pocket, saying, with an affected air of coldness and nonchalance, 'Is that all?'—'Why, I expected you would have been plunged in grief!'—He made no reply, and soon began to talk about something else."

His pursuits at Harrow continued to be of the same truant description during the whole of his stay there;—"always," as he says himself, "cricketing, rebelling, *rowing*, and in all manner of mischiefs." The "rebelling," of which he here speaks, (though it never, I believe, proceeded to any act of violence,) took place on the retirement of Dr. Drury from his situation as head master, when three candidates for the vacant chair presented themselves,—Mark Drury, Evans, and Butler. On the first movement to which this contest gave rise in the school, young Wildman was at the head of the party for Mark Drury, while Byron at first held himself aloof from any. Anxious, however, to have him as an ally, one of the Drury faction said to Wildman—"Byron, I know, will not join, because he doesn't choose to act second to any one, but, by giving up the leadership to him, you may at once secure him." This Wildman accordingly did, and Byron took the command of the party.

The violence with which he opposed the election of Dr. Butler on this occasion (chiefly from the warm affection which he had felt towards the last master) continued to embitter his relations with that gentleman during the remainder of his stay at Harrow. Unhappily their opportunities of collision were the more frequent from Byron's being a resident in Dr. Butler's house. One day the young rebel, in a fit of defiance, tore down all the gratings from the window in the hall; and when called upon by his host to say why he had committed this violence, answered, with stern coolness, "Because they darkened the hall." On another occasion he explicitly, and so far manfully, avowed to this gentleman's face the pique he entertained against him. It has long been customary, at the end of a term, for the master to invite the upper boys to dine with him; and these invitations are generally considered as, like royal ones, a sort of command. Lord Byron, however, when asked, sent back a refusal, whichrather surprising Dr. Butler, he, on the first opportunity that occurred, enquired of him, in the presence of the other boys, his motive for this step:—"Have you any other engagement?"—"No, sir."—"But you must have *some* reason, Lord Byron."—"I have."—"What is it?"—"Why, Dr. Butler," replied the young peer, with proud composure, "if you should happen to come into my neighbourhood when I was staying at Newstead, I certainly should not ask you to dine with me, and therefore feel that I ought not to dine with *you*."

The general character which he bore among the masters at Harrow was that of an idle boy, who would never learn anything; and, as far as regarded his tasks in school, this reputation was, by his own avowal, not ill-founded. It is impossible, indeed, to look through the books which he had then in use, and which are scribbled over with clumsy interlined translations, without being struck with the narrow extent of his classical attainments. The most ordinary Greek words have their English signification scrawled under them, showing too plainly that he was not sufficiently familiarised with their meaning to trust himself without this aid. Thus, in his Xenophon we find νεοι, *young*—σωμασιν, *bodies*—ανθρωποις τοις αγαθοις, *good men*, &c. &c.—and even in the volumes of Greek plays which he presented to the library on his departure, we observe, among other instances, the common word χρυσος provided with its English representative in the margin.

But, notwithstanding his backwardness in the mere verbal scholarship, on which so large and precious a portion of life is wasted, in all that general and miscellaneous knowledge which is alone useful in the world, he was making rapid and even wonderful progress. With a mind too inquisitive and excursive to be imprisoned within statutable limits, he flew to subjects that interested his already manly tastes, with a zest which it is in vain to expect that the mere pedantries of school could inspire; and the irregular, but ardent, snatches of study which he caught in this way, gave to a mind like his an impulse forwards, which left more disciplined and plodding competitors far behind. The list, indeed, which he has left on record of the works, in all departments of literature, which he thus hastily and greedily devoured before he was fifteen years of age, is such as almost to startle belief,—comprising, as it does, a range and variety of study, which might make much older "helluones librorum" hide their heads.

Not to argue, however, from the powers and movements of a mind like Byron's, which might well be allowed to take a privileged direction of its own, there is little doubt, that to *any* youth of talent and ambition, the plan of instruction pursued in the great schools and universities of England, wholly inadequate as it is to the intellectual wants of the age, presents an alternative of evils not a little embarrassing. Difficult, nay, utterly impossible, as he will find it, to combine a competent acquisition of useful knowledge with that round of antiquated studies which a pursuit of scholastic honours requires, he must either, by devoting the whole of his attention and ambition to the latter object, remain ignorant on most of those subjects upon which mind grapples with mind in life, or by adopting, as Lord Byron and other distinguished persons have done, the contrary system, consent to pass for a dunce or idler in the schools, in order to afford himself even a chance of attaining eminence in the world.

From the memorandums scribbled by the young poet in his school-books, we might almost fancy that, even at so early an age, he had a sort of vague presentiment that everything relating to him would one day be an object of curiosity and interest. The date of his entrance at Harrow, the names of the boys who were, at that time, monitors, the list of his fellow pupils under Doctor Drury,—all are noted down with a fond minuteness, as if to form points of retrospect in his after-life; and that he sometimes referred to them with this feeling will appear from one touching instance. On the first leaf of his "Scriptores Græci," we find, in his schoolboy hand, the following memorial:—"George Gordon Byron, Wednesday, June 26th, A. D. 1805, 3 quarters of an hour past 3 o'clock in the afternoon, 3d school,—Calvert, monitor; Tom Wildman on my left hand and Long on my right. Harrow on the Hill." On the same leaf, written five years after, appears this comment:—

"Eheu fugaces, Posthume! Posthume!
Labuntur anni."

"B. January 9th, 1809.—Of the four persons whose names are here mentioned, one is dead, another in a distant climate, *all* separated, and not five years have elapsed since they sat together in school, and none are yet twenty-one years of age."

The vacation of 1804 he passed with his mother at Southwell, to which place she had removed from Nottingham, in the summer of this year, having taken the house on the Green called Burgage Manor. There is a Southwell play-bill extant, dated August 8th, 1804, in which the play is announced as bespoke "by Mrs. and Lord Byron." The gentleman, from whom the house where they resided was rented, possesses a library of some extent, which the young poet, he says, ransacked with much eagerness on his first coming to Southwell; and one of the books that most particularly engaged and interested him was, as may be easily believed, the life of Lord Herbert of Cherbury.

In the month of October, 1805, he was removed to Trinity College, Cambridge, and his feelings on the change from his beloved Ida to this new scene of life are thus described by himself:—

"When I first went up to college, it was a new and a heavy-hearted scene for me: firstly, I so much disliked leaving Harrow, that though it was time (I being seventeen), it broke my very rest for the last quarter with counting the days that remained. I always *hated* Harrow till the last year and a half, but then I liked it. Secondly, I wished to go to Oxford, and not to Cambridge. Thirdly, I was so completely alone in this new world, that it half broke my spirits. My companions were not unsocial, but the contrary—lively, hospitable, of rank and fortune, and gay far beyond my gaiety. I mingled with, and dined, and supped, &c., with them; but, I know not how, it was one of the deadliest and heaviest feelings of my life to feel that I was no longer a boy."

But though, for a time, he may have felt this sort of estrangement at Cambridge, to remain long without attaching himself was not in his nature; and the friendship which he now formed with a youth named Eddleston, who was two years younger than himself, even exceeded in warmth and romance all his schoolboy attachments. This boy, whose musical talents first drew them together, was, at the commencement of their acquaintance, one of the choir at Cambridge, though he afterwards, it appears, entered into a mercantile line of life; and this disparity in their stations was by no means without its charm for Byron, as gratifying at once both his pride and good-nature, and founding the tie between them on the mutually dependent relations of protection on the one side, and gratitude and devotion on the other;—the only relations, according to Lord Bacon, in which the little friendship that still remains in the world is to be found. It was upon a gift presented to him by Eddleston, that he wrote those verses entitled "The Cornelian," which were printed in his first, unpublished volume, and of which the following is a stanza:—

"Some, who can sneer at friendship's ties,

Have for my weakness oft reproved me;

Yet still the simple gift I prize,

For I am sure the giver loved me."

Another friendship, of a less unequal kind, which had been begun at Harrow, and which he continued to cultivate during his first year at Cambridge, is thus interestingly dwelt upon in one of his journals:—

"How strange are my thoughts!—The reading of the song of Milton, 'Sabrina fair,' has brought back upon me—I know not how or why—the happiest, perhaps, days of my life (always excepting, here and there, a Harrow holiday in the two latter summers of my stay there) when living at Cambridge with Edward Noel Long, afterwards of the Guards,—who, after having served honourably in the expedition to Copenhagen (of which two or three thousand scoundrels yet survive in plight and pay), was drowned early in 1809, on his passage to Lisbon with his regiment in the St. George transport, which was run foul of in the night by another transport. We were rival swimmers—fond of riding—reading—and of conviviality. We had been at Harrow together; but

—*there*, at least—his was a less boisterous spirit than mine. I was always cricketing—rebelling—fighting—*row*ing (from *row*, not *boat*-rowing, a different practice), and in all manner of mischiefs; while he was more sedate and polished. At Cambridge—both of Trinity—my spirit rather softened, or his roughened, for we became very great friends. The description of Sabrina's seat reminds me of our rival feats in *diving*. Though Cam's is not a very translucent wave, it was fourteen feet deep, where we used to dive for, and pick up—having thrown them in on purpose—plates, eggs, and even shillings. I remember, in particular, there was the stump of a tree (at least ten or twelve feet deep) in the bed of the river, in a spot where we bathed most commonly, round which I used to cling, and 'wonder how the devil I came there.'

"Our evenings we passed in music (he was musical, and played on more than one instrument, flute and violoncello), in which I was audience; and I think that our chief beverage was soda-water. In the day we rode, bathed, and lounged, reading occasionally. I remember our buying, with vast alacrity, Moore's new quarto (in 1806), and reading it together in the evenings.

"We only passed the summer together;—Long had gone into the Guards during the year I passed in Notts, away from college. *His* friendship, and a violent, though*pure*, love and passion—which held me at the same period—were the then romance of the most romantic period of my life.

"I remember that, in the spring of 1809, H—— laughed at my being distressed at Long's death, and amused himself with making epigrams upon his name, which was susceptible of a pun—*Long, short,* &c. But three years after, he had ample leisure to repent it, when our mutual friend and his, H——'s, particular friend, Charles Matthews, was drowned also, and he himself was as much affected by a similar calamity. But *I* did not pay him back in puns and epigrams, for I valued Matthews too much myself to do so; and, even if I had not, I should have respected his griefs.

"Long's father wrote to me to write his son's epitaph. I promised—but I had not the heart to complete it. He was such a good amiable being as rarely remains long in this world; with talent and accomplishments, too, to make him the more regretted. Yet, although a cheerful companion, he had strange melancholy thoughts sometimes. I remember once that we were going to his uncle's, I think—I went to accompany him to the door merely, in some Upper or Lower Grosvenor or Brook Street, I forget which, but it was in a street leading out of some square,—he told me that, the night before, he 'had taken up a pistol—not knowing or examining whether it was loaded or no—and had snapped it at his head, leaving it to chance whether it might or might not be charged.' The letter, too, which he wrote me, on leaving college to join the Guards, was as melancholy in its tenour as it could well be on such an occasion. But he showed nothing of this in his deportment, being mild and gentle;—and yet with much turn for the ludicrous in his disposition. We were both much attached to Harrow, and sometimes made excursions there together from London to revive our schoolboy recollections."

These affecting remembrances are contained in a Journal which he kept during his residence at Ravenna, in 1821, and they are rendered still more touching and remarkable by the circumstances under which they were noted down. Domesticated in a foreign land, and even connected with foreign conspirators, whose arms, at the moment he was writing, were in his house, he could yet thus wholly disengage himself from the scene around him, and, borne away by the current of memory into other times, live over the lost friendships of his boyhood again. An English gentleman (Mr. Wathen) who called upon him, at one of his residences in Italy, having happened to mention in conversation that he had been acquainted with Long, from that moment Lord Byron treated him with the most marked kindness, and talked with him of Long, and of his amiable qualities, till (as this gentleman says) the tears could not be concealed in his eyes.

In the summer of this year (1806) he, as usual, joined his mother at Southwell, —among the small, but select, society of which place he had, during his visits, formed some intimacies and friendships, the memory of which is still cherished there fondly and proudly. With the exception, indeed, of the brief and bewildering interval which he passed, as we have seen, in the company of Miss Chaworth, it was at Southwell alone that an opportunity was ever afforded him of profiting by the bland influence of female society, or of seeing what woman is in the true sphere of her virtues, home. The amiable and intelligent family of the Pigots received him within their circle as one of themselves: and in the Rev. John Becher the youthful poet found not only an acute and judicious critic, but a sincere friend. There were also one or two other families—as the Leacrofts, the Housons—among whom his talents and vivacity made him always welcome; and the proud shyness with which, through the whole of his minority, he kept aloof from all intercourse with the neighbouring gentlemen seems to have been entirely familiarised away by the small, cheerful society of Southwell. One of the most intimate and valued of his friends, at this period, has given me the following account of her first acquaintance with him:—"The first time I was introduced to him was at a party at his mother's, when he was so shy that she was forced to send for him three times before she could persuade him to come into the drawing-room, to play with the young people at a round game. He was then a fat bashful boy, with his hair combed straight over his forehead, and extremely like a miniature picture that his mother had painted by M. de Chambruland. The next morning Mrs. Byron brought him to call at our house, when he still continued shy and formal in his manner. The conversation turned upon Cheltenham, where we had been staying, the amusements there, the plays, &c.; and I mentioned that I had seen the character of Gabriel Lackbrain very well performed. His mother getting up to go, he accompanied her, making a formal bow, and I, in allusion to the play, said, "Good by, Gaby." His countenance lighted up, his handsome mouth displayed a broad grin, all his shyness vanished, never to return, and, upon his mother's saying 'Come, Byron, are you ready?'—no, she might go by herself, he would stay and talk a little longer; and from that moment he used to come in and go out at all hours, as it pleased him, and in our house considered himself perfectly at home."

To this lady was addressed the earliest letter from his pen that has fallen into my hands. He corresponded with many of his Harrow friends,—with Lord Clare, Lord Powerscourt, Mr. William Peel, Mr. William Bankes, and others. But it was then little foreseen what general interest would one day attach to these school-boy letters; and accordingly, as I have already had occasion to lament, there are but few of them now in existence. The letter, of which I have spoken, to his Southwell friend, though containing nothing remarkable, is perhaps for that very reason worth insertion, as serving to show, on comparing it with most of its successors, how rapidly his mind acquired confidence in its powers. There is, indeed, one charm for the eye of curiosity in his juvenile manuscripts, which they necessarily want in their printed form; and that is the strong evidence of an irregular education which they exhibit,—the unformed and childish handwriting, and, now and then, even defective spelling of him who, in a very few years after, was to start up one of the giants of English literature.

LETTER 1.

TO MISS ——.

> Burgage Manor, August 29. 1804.

"I received the arms, my dear Miss ——, and am very much obliged to you for the trouble you have taken. It is impossible I should have any fault to find with them. The sight of the drawings gives me great pleasure for a double reason,— in the first place, they will ornament my books, in the next, they convince me that you have not entirely *forgot* me. I am, however, sorry you do not return sooner—you have already been gone an *age*. I perhaps may have taken my departure for London before you come back; but, however, I will hope not. Do not overlook my watch-riband and purse, as I wish to carry them with me. Your note was given me by Harry, at the play, whither I attended Miss L—— and Dr. S. ——; and now I have set down to answer it before I go to bed. If I am at Southwell when you return,—and I sincerely hope you will soon, for I very much regret your absence,—I shall be happy to hear you sing my favourite, 'The Maid of Lodi.' My mother, together with myself, desires to be affectionately remembered to Mrs. Pigot, and, believe me, my dear Miss ——,

I remain your affectionate friend,

"Byron."

"P.S. If you think proper to send me any answer to this, I shall be extremely happy to receive it. Adieu.

"P.S. 2d. As you say you are a novice in the art of knitting, I hope it don't give you too much trouble. Go on *slowly*, but surely. Once more, adieu."

We shall often have occasion to remark the fidelity to early habits and tastes by which Lord Byron, though in other respects so versatile, was distinguished. In the juvenile letter, just cited, there are two characteristics of this kind which he preserved unaltered during the remainder of his life;—namely, his punctuality in immediately answering letters, and his love of the simplest ballad music. Among the chief favourites to which this latter taste led him at this time were the songs of the Duenna, which he had the good taste to delight in; and some of his Harrow contemporaries still remember the joyousness with which, when dining with his friends at the memorable mother Barnard's, he used to roar out, "This bottle's the sun of our table."

His visit to Southwell this summer was interrupted, about the beginning of August, by one of those explosions of temper on the part of Mrs. Byron, to which, from his earliest childhood, he had been but too well accustomed, and in producing which his own rebel spirit was not always, it may be supposed, entirely blameless. In all his portraits of himself, so dark is the pencil which he employs, that the following account of his own temper, from one of his journals, must be taken with a due portion of that allowance for exaggeration, which his style of self-portraiture, "overshadowing even the shade," requires.

"In all other respects," (he says, after mentioning his infant passion for Mary Duff,) "I differed not at all from other children, being neither tall nor short, dull nor witty, of my age, but rather lively—except in my sullen moods, and then I was always a Devil. They once (in one of my silent rages) wrenched a knife from me, which I had snatched from table at Mrs. B.'s dinner (I always dined earlier), and applied to my breast;—but this was three or four years after, just before the late Lord B.'s decease.

"My *ostensible* temper has certainly improved in later years; but I shudder, and must, to my latest hour, regret the consequence of it and my passions combined. One event—but no matter—there are others not much better to think of also—and to them I give the preference....

"But I hate dwelling upon incidents. My temper is now under management—

rarely *loud*, and *when* loud, never deadly. It is when silent, and I feel my forehead and my cheek paling, that I cannot control it; and then.... but unless there is a woman (and not any or every woman) in the way, I have sunk into tolerable apathy."

Between a temper at all resembling this, and the loud hurricane bursts of Mrs. Byron, the collision, it may be supposed, was not a little formidable; and the age at which the young poet was now arrived; when—as most parents feel— the impatience of youth begins to champ the bit, would but render the occasions for such shocks more frequent. It is told, as a curious proof of their opinion of each other's violence, that, after parting one evening in a tempest of this kind, they were known each to go privately that night to the apothecary's, enquiring anxiously whether the other had been to purchase poison, and cautioning the vender of drugs not to attend to such an application, if made.

It was but rarely, however, that the young lord allowed himself to be provoked into more than a passive share in these scenes. To the boisterousness of his mother he would oppose a civil and, no doubt, provoking silence,—bowing to her but the more profoundly the higher her voice rose in the scale. In general, however, when he perceived that a storm was at hand, in flight lay his only safe resource. To this summary expedient he was driven at the period of which we are speaking; but not till after a scene had taken place between him and Mrs. Byron, in which the violence of her temper had proceeded to lengths, that, however outrageous they may be deemed, were not, it appears, unusual with her. The poet, Young, in describing a temper of this sort, says—

"The cups and saucers, in a whirlwind sent,Just intimate the lady's discontent."

But poker and tongs were, it seems, the missiles which Mrs. Byron preferred, and which she, more than once, sent resounding after her fugitive son. In the present instance, he was but just in time to avoid a blow aimed at him with the former of these weapons, and to make a hasty escape to the house of a friend in the neighbourhood; where, concerting the best means of baffling pursuit, he decided upon an instant flight to London. The letters, which I am about to give, were written, immediately on his arrival in town, to some friends at Southwell, from whose kind interference in his behalf, it may fairly be concluded that the blame of the quarrel, whatever it may have been, did not rest with him. The first is to Mr. Pigot, a young gentleman about the same age as himself, who had just returned, for the vacation, from Edinburgh, where he was, at that time, pursuing his medical studies.

LETTER 2.

TO MR. PIGOT.

"16. Piccadilly, August 9. 1806.

"My dear Pigot,

"Many thanks for your amusing narrative of the last proceedings of ----, who now begins to feel the effects of her folly. I have just received a penitential epistle, to which, apprehensive of pursuit, I have despatched a moderate answer, with a *kind* of promise to return in a fortnight;—this, however (*entre nous*), I never mean to fulfil. Seriously, your mother has laid me under great obligations, and you, with the rest of your family, merit my warmest thanks for your kind connivance at my escape.

"How did S.B. receive the intelligence? How many *puns* did he utter on so *facetious* an event? In your next inform me on this point, and what excuse you made to A. You are probably, by this time, tired of deciphering this hieroglyphical letter;—like Tony Lumpkin, you will pronounce mine to be a d————d up and down hand. All Southwell, without doubt, is involved in amazement. Apropos, how does my blue-eyed nun, the fair ————? is she '*robed in sable garb of woe?*'

"Here I remain at least a week or ten days; previous to my departure you shall receive my address, but what it will be I have not determined. My lodgings must be kept secret from Mrs. B. You may present my compliments to her, and say any attempt to pursue me will fail, as I have taken measures to retreat immediately to Portsmouth, on the first intimation of her removal from Southwell. You may add, I have now proceeded to a friend's house in the country, there to remain a fortnight.

"I have now *blotted* (I must not say written) a complete double letter, and in return shall expect a *monstrous budget*. Without doubt, the dames of Southwell reprobate the pernicious example I have shown, and tremble lest their *babes* should disobey their mandates, and quit, in dudgeon, their mammas on any grievance. Adieu. When you begin your next, drop the 'lordship,' and put 'Byron' in its place.

Believe me yours, &c.

"BYRON."

From the succeeding letters, it will be seen that Mrs. Byron was not behind hand, in energy and decision, with his young Lordship, but immediately on discovering his flight, set off after him.

LETTER 3.

TO MISS ————.

"London, August 10. 1806.

"My dear Bridget,

"As I have already troubled your brother with more than he will find pleasure in deciphering, you are the next to whom I shall assign the employment of perusing this second epistle. You will perceive from my first, that no idea of Mrs. B.'s arrival had disturbed me at the time it was written; *not* so the present, since the appearance of a note from the *illustrious cause* of my *sudden decampment* has driven the 'natural ruby from my cheeks,' and completely blanched my woe-begone countenance. This gun-powder intimation of her arrival breathes less of terror and dismay than you will probably imagine, and concludes with the comfortable assurance of all *present motion* being prevented by the fatigue of her journey, for which my *blessings* are due to the rough roads and restive quadrupeds of his Majesty's highways. As I have not the smallest inclination to be chased round the country, I shall e'en make a merit of necessity; and since, like Macbeth, 'they've tied me to the stake, I cannot fly,' I shall imitate that valorous tyrant, and 'bear-like fight the course,' all escape being precluded. I can now engage with less disadvantage, having drawn the enemy from her intrenchments, though, like the *prototype* to whom I have compared myself, with an excellent chance of being knocked on the head. However, 'lay on, Macduff, and d——d be he who first cries, Hold, enough.'

"I shall remain in town for, at least, a week, and expect to hear from *you* before its expiration. I presume the printer has brought you the offspring of my *poetic mania*. Remember in the first line to 'loud the winds whistle,' instead of 'round,' which that blockhead Ridge has inserted by mistake, and makes nonsense of the whole stanza. Addio!—Now to encounter my *Hydra*.

Yours ever."

LETTER 4.

TO MR. PIGOT.

"London, Sunday, midnight, August 10. 1806.

"Dear Pigot,

"This *astonishing* packet will, doubtless, amaze you; but having an idle hour this evening, I wrote the enclosed stanzas, which I request you will deliver to Ridge, to be printed *separate* from my other compositions, as you will perceive them to be improper for the perusal of ladies; of course, none of the females of your family must see them. I offer 1000 apologies for the trouble I have given you in this and other instances.

Yours truly."

Letter 5.

TO MR. PIGOT.

"Piccadilly, August 16. 1806.

"I cannot exactly say with Cæsar, 'Veni, vidi, vici:' however, the most important part of his laconic account of success applies to my present situation; for, though Mrs. Byron took the *trouble* of '*coming*,' and '*seeing*,' yet your humble servant proved the *victor*. After an obstinate engagement of some hours, in which we suffered considerable damage, from the quickness of the enemy's fire, they at length retired in confusion, leaving behind the artillery, field equipage, and some prisoners: their defeat is decisive for the present campaign. To speak more intelligibly, Mrs. B. returns immediately, but I proceed, with all my laurels, to Worthing, on the Sussex coast; to which place you will address (to be left at the post office) your next epistle. By the enclosure of a second *gingle* of *rhyme*, you will probably conceive my muse to be *vastly prolific*; her inserted production was brought forth a few years ago, and found by accident on Thursday among some old papers. I have recopied it, and, adding the proper date, request it may be printed with the rest of the family. I thought your sentiments on the last bantling would coincide with mine, but it was impossible to give it any other garb, being founded on *facts*. My stay at Worthing will not exceed three weeks, and you may *possibly* behold me again at Southwell the middle of September.

"Will you desire Ridge to suspend the printing of my poems till he hears further from me, as I have determined to give them a new form entirely. This prohibition does not extend to the two last pieces I have sent with my letters to you. You will excuse the *dull vanity* of this epistle, as my brain is a *chaos* of absurd images, and full of business, preparations, and projects.

"I shall expect an answer with impatience;—believe me, there is nothing at this moment could give me greater delight than your letter."

Letter 6.

TO MR. PIGOT.

"London, August 18. 1806.

"I am just on the point of setting off for Worthing, and write merely to request you will send that *idle scoundrel Charles* with my horses immediately; tell him I am excessively provoked he has not made his appearance before, or written to inform me of the cause of his delay, particularly as I supplied him with money for his journey. On *no* pretext is he to postpone his *march* one day longer; and if, in obedience to Mrs. B., he thinks proper to disregard my positive orders, I shall not, in future, consider him as my servant. He must bring the surgeon's bill with him, which I will discharge immediately on receiving it. Nor can I conceive the reason of his not acquainting Frank with the state of my unfortunate quadrupeds. Dear Pigot, forgive this *petulant* effusion, and attribute it to the idle conduct of that *precious* rascal, who, instead of obeying my injunctions, is sauntering through the streets of that *political Pandemonium*, Nottingham. Present my remembrances to your family and the Leacrofts, and believe me, &c.

"P.S. I delegate to *you* the unpleasant task of despatching him on his journey—Mrs. B.'s orders to the contrary are not to be attended to: he is to proceed first to London, and then to Worthing, without delay. Every thing I have *left* must be sent to London. My *Poetics you* will *pack up* for the same place, and not even reserve a copy for yourself and sister, as I am about to give them an *entire new form*: when they are complete, you shall have the *first fruits*. Mrs. B. on no account is to *see* or touch them. Adieu."

Letter 7.

TO MR. PIGOT.

"Little Hampton, August 26. 1806.

"I this morning received your epistle, which I was obliged to send for to Worthing, whence I have removed to this place, on the same coast, about eight miles distant from the former. You will probably not be displeased with this letter, when it informs you that I am 30,000*l*. richer than I was at our parting, having just received intelligence from my lawyer that a cause has been gained at Lancaster assizes, which will be worth that sum by the time I come of age. Mrs. B. is, doubtless, acquainted of this acquisition, though not apprised of its exact *value*, of which she had better be ignorant. You may give my compliments to her, and say that her detaining my servant's things shall only lengthen my absence; for unless they are immediately despatched to 16. Piccadilly, together with those which have been so long delayed, belonging to myself, she shall never again behold my *radiant countenance* illuminating her gloomy mansion. If they are sent, I may probably appear in less than two years from the date of my present epistle.

"Metrical compliment is an ample reward for my strains; you are one of the few votaries of Apollo who unite the sciences over which that deity presides. I wish you to send my poems to my lodgings in London immediately, as I have several alterations and some additions to make; *every* copy must be sent, as I am about to *amend*them, and you shall soon behold them in all their glory. *Entre nous,*—you may expect to see me soon. Adieu.

Yours ever."

From these letters it will be perceived that Lord Byron was already engaged in preparing a collection of his poems for the press. The idea of printing them first occurred to him in the parlour of that cottage which, during his visits to Southwell, had become his adopted home. Miss Pigot, who was not before aware of his turn for versifying, had been reading aloud the poems of Burns, when young Byron said that "he, too, was a poet sometimes, and would write down for her some verses of his own which he remembered." He then, with a pencil, wrote those lines, beginning "In thee I fondly hoped to clasp," which were printed in his first unpublished volume, but are not contained in the editions that followed. He also repeated to her the verses I have already referred to, "When in the hall my father's voice," so remarkable for the anticipations of his future fame that glimmer through them.

From this moment the desire of appearing in print took entire possession of him;—though, for the present, his ambition did not extend its views beyond a small volume for private circulation. The person to whom fell the honour of receiving his first manuscripts was Ridge, the bookseller, at Newark; and while the work was printing, the young author continued to pour fresh materials into his hands, with the same eagerness and rapidity that marked the progress of all his maturer works.

His return to Southwell, which he announced in the last letter we have given was but for a very short time. In a week or two after he again left that place, and, accompanied by his young friend Mr. Pigot, set out for Harrowgate. The following extracts are from a letter written by the latter gentleman, at the time to his sister.

"Harrowgate is still extremely full; Wednesday (to-day) is our ball-night, and I meditate going into the room for an hour, although I am by no means fond of strange faces. Lord B., you know, is even more shy than myself; but for an hour this evening I will shake it off.... How do our theatricals proceed? Lord Byron can say *all* his part, and I *most* of mine. He certainly acts it inimitably. Lord B. is now *poetising,* and, since he has been here, has written some very pretty verses. He is very good in trying to amuse me as much as possible, but it is not in my nature to be happy without either female society or study.... There are many pleasant rides about here, which I have taken in company with Bo'swain, who, with Brighton, is universally admired. *You* must read this to Mrs. B., as it is a little *Tony Lumpkinish.* Lord B. desires some space left: therefore, with respect to all the comedians *elect,* believe me to be," &c. &c.

To this letter the following note from Lord Byron was appended:—

"My dear Bridget,

"I have only just dismounted from my *Pegasus*, which has prevented me from descending to *plain* prose in an epistle of greater length to your *fair* self. You regretted, in a former letter, that my poems were not more extensive; I now for your satisfaction announce that I have nearly doubled them, partly by the discovery of some I conceived to be lost, and partly by some new productions. We shall meet on Wednesday next; till then believe me yours affectionately,

"BYRON."

"P.S.—Your brother John is seized with a poetic mania, and is now rhyming away at the rate of three lines *per hour*—so much for *inspiration*! Adieu!"

By the gentleman, who was thus early the companion and intimate of Lord Byron, and who is now pursuing his profession with the success which his eminent talents deserve, I have been favoured with some further recollections of their visit together to Harrowgate, which I shall take the liberty of giving in his own words:—

"You ask me to recall some anecdotes of the time we spent together at Harrowgate in the summer of 1806, on our return from college, he from Cambridge, and I from Edinburgh; but so many years have elapsed since then, that I really feel myself as if recalling a distant dream. We, I remember, went in Lord Byron's own carriage, with post-horses; and he sent his groom with two saddle-horses, and a beautifully formed, very ferocious, bull-mastiff, called Nelson, to meet us there. Boatswain went by the side of his valet Frank on the box, with us.

"The bull-dog, Nelson, always wore a muzzle, and was occasionally sent for into our private room, when the muzzle was taken off, much to my annoyance, and he and his master amused themselves with throwing the room into disorder. There was always a jealous feud between this Nelson and Boatswain; and whenever the latter came into the room while the former was there, they instantly seized each other: and then, Byron, myself, Frank, and all the waiters that could be found, were vigorously engaged in parting them,—which was in general only effected by thrusting poker and tongs into the mouths of each. But, one day, Nelson unfortunately escaped out of the room without his muzzle, and going into the stable-yard fastened upon the throat of a horse, from which he could not be disengaged. The stable-boys ran in alarm to find Frank, who taking one of his Lord's Wogdon's pistols, always kept loaded in his room, shot poor Nelson through the head, to the great regret of Byron.

"We were at the Crown Inn, at Low Harrowgate. We always dined in the public room, but retired very soon after dinner to our private one; for Byron was no more a friend to drinking than myself. We lived retired, and made few acquaintance; for he was naturally shy, *very* shy, which people who did not know him mistook for pride. While at Harrowgate he accidentally met with

Professor Hailstone from Cambridge, and appeared much delighted to see him. The professor was at Upper Harrowgate: we called upon him one evening to take him to the theatre, I think,—and Lord Byron sent his carriage for him, another time, to a ball at the Granby. This desire to show attention to one of the professors of his college is a proof that, though he might choose to satirise the mode of education in the university, and to abuse the antiquated regulations and restrictions to which under-graduates are subjected, he had yet a due discrimination in his respect for the individuals who belonged to it. I have always, indeed, heard him speak in high terms of praise of Hailstone, as well as of his master, Bishop Mansel, of Trinity College, and of others whose names I have now forgotten.

"Few people understood Byron; but I know that he had naturally a kind and feeling heart, and that there was not a single spark of malice in his composition."

The private theatricals alluded to in the letters from Harrowgate were, both in prospect and performance, a source of infinite delight to him, and took place soon after his return to Southwell. How anxiously he was expected back by all parties, may be judged from the following fragment of a letter which was received by his companion during their absence from home:—

"Tell Lord Byron that, if any accident should retard his return, his mother desires he will write to her, as she shall be miserable if he does not arrive the day he fixes. Mr. W. B. has written a card to Mrs. H. to offer for the character of 'Henry Woodville,'—Mr. and Mrs. —— not approving of their son's taking a part in the play: but I believe he will persist in it. Mr. G. W. says, that sooner than the party should be disappointed, *he* will take any part,—sing—dance—in short, do any thing to oblige. Till Lord Byron returns, nothing can be done; and positively he must not be later than Tuesday or Wednesday."

We have already seen that, at Harrow, his talent for declamation was the only one by which Lord Byron was particularly distinguished; and in one of his note-books he adverts, with evident satisfaction, both to his school displays and to the share which he took in these representations at Southwell:—

"When I was a youth, I was reckoned a good actor. Besides Harrow speeches (in which I shone), I enacted Penruddock in the Wheel of Fortune, and Tristram Fickle in Allingham's farce of the Weathercock, for three nights (the duration of our compact), in some private theatricals at Southwell, in 1806, with great applause. The occasional prologue for our volunteer play was also of my composition. The other performers were young ladies and gentlemen of the neighbourhood, and the whole went off with great effect upon our good-natured audience."

It may, perhaps, not be altogether trifling to observe, that, in thus personating with such success two heroes so different, the young poet displayed both that love and power of versatility by which he was afterwards impelled, on a grander scale, to present himself under such opposite aspects to the world;—the gloom of Penruddock, and the whim of Tristram, being types, as it were, of the two extremes, between which his own character, in after-life, so singularly vibrated.

These representations, which form a memorable era at Southwell, took place about the latter end of September, in the house of Mr. Leacroft, whose drawing-room was converted into a neat theatre on the occasion, and whose family contributed some of the fair ornaments of its boards. The prologue which Lord Byron furnished, and which may be seen in his "Hours of Idleness," was written by him between stages, on his way from Harrowgate. On getting into the carriage at Chesterfield, he said to his companion, "Now, Pigot, I'll spin a prologue for our play;" and before they reached Mansfield, he had completed his task,—interrupting, only once, his rhyming reverie, to ask the proper pronunciation of the French word *début*, and, on being told it, exclaiming, in the true spirit of Byshe, "Ay, that will do for rhyme to *new*."

The epilogue on the occasion was from the pen of Mr. Becher; and for the purpose of affording to Lord Byron, who was to speak it, an opportunity of displaying his powers of mimicry, consisted of good-humoured portraits of all the persons concerned in the representation. Some intimation of this design having got among the actors, an alarm was felt instantly at the ridicule thus in store for them; and to quiet their apprehensions, the author was obliged to assure them that if, after having heard his epilogue at rehearsal, they did not, of themselves, pronounce it harmless, and even request that it should be preserved, he would most willingly withdraw it. In the mean time, it was concerted between this gentleman and Lord Byron that the latter should, on the morning of rehearsal, deliver the verses in a tone as innocent and as free from all point as possible,—reserving his mimicry, in which the whole sting of the pleasantry lay, for the evening of representation. The desired effect was produced;—all the personages of the green-room were satisfied, and even wondered how a suspicion of waggery could have attached itself to so well-bred a production. Their wonder, however, was of a different nature a night or two after, when, on hearing the audience convulsed with laughter at this same composition, they discovered, at last, the trick which the unsuspected mimic had played on them, and had no other resource than that of joining in the laugh which his playful imitation of the whole dramatis personæ excited.

The small volume of poems, which he had now for some time been preparing, was, in the month of November, ready for delivery to the select few among whom it was intended to circulate; and to Mr. Becher the first copy of the work was presented. The influence which this gentleman had, by his love of poetry, his sociability and good sense, acquired at this period over the mind of Lord Byron, was frequently employed by him in guiding the taste of his young friend, no less in matters of conduct than of literature; and the ductility with which this influence was yielded to, in an instance I shall have to mention, will show how far from untractable was the natural disposition of Byron, had he more frequently been lucky enough to fall into hands that "knew the stops" of the instrument, and could draw out its sweetness as well as its strength.

In the wild range which his taste was now allowed to take through the light and miscellaneous literature of the day, it was but natural that he should settle with most pleasure on those works from which the feelings of his age and temperament could extract their most congenial food; and, accordingly, Lord Strangford's Camoëns and Little's Poems are said to have been, at this period, his favourite study. To the indulgence of such a taste his reverend friend very laudably opposed himself,—representing with truth, (as far, at least, as the latter author is concerned,) how much more worthy models, both in style and thought, he might find among the established names of English literature. Instead of wasting his time on the ephemeral productions of his contemporaries, he should devote himself, his adviser said, to the pages of Milton and of Shakspeare, and, above all, seek to elevate his fancy and taste by the contemplation of the sublimer beauties of the Bible. In the latter study, this gentleman acknowledges that his advice had been, to a great extent, anticipated, and that with the poetical parts of the Scripture he found Lord Byron deeply conversant:—a circumstance which corroborates the account given by his early master, Dr. Glennie, of his great proficiency in scriptural knowledge while yet but a child under his care.

To Mr. Becher, as I have said, the first copy of his little work was presented; and this gentleman, in looking over its pages, among many things to commend and admire, as well as some almost too boyish to criticise, found one poem in which, as it appeared to him, the imagination of the young bard had indulged itself in a luxuriousness of colouring beyond what even youth could excuse. Immediately, as the most gentle mode of conveying his opinion, he sat down and addressed to Lord Byron some expostulatory verses on the subject, to which an answer, also in verse, was returned by the noble poet as promptly, with, at the same time, a note in plain prose, to say that he felt fully the justice of his reverend friend's censure, and that, rather than allow the poem in question to be circulated, he would instantly recall all the copies that had been sent out, and cancel the whole impression. On the very same evening this prompt sacrifice was carried into effect;—Mr. Becher saw every copy of the edition burned, with the exception of that which he retained in his own possession, and another which had been despatched to Edinburgh, and could not be recalled.

This trait of the young poet speaks sufficiently for itself;—the sensibility, the temper, the ingenuous pliableness which it exhibits, show a disposition capable, by nature, of every thing we most respect and love.

Of a no less amiable character were the feelings that, about this time, dictated the following letter;—a letter which it is impossible to peruse without acknowledging the noble candour and conscientiousness of the writer:—

LETTER 8.

TO THE EARL OF CLARE.

"Southwell, Notts, February 6. 1807.

"My dearest Clare,

"Were I to make all the apologies necessary to atone for my late negligence, you would justly say you had received a petition instead of a letter, as it would be filled with prayers for forgiveness; but instead of this, I will acknowledge my *sins* at once, and I trust to your friendship and generosity rather than to my own excuses. Though my health is not perfectly re-established, I am out of all danger, and have recovered every thing but my spirits, which are subject to depression. You will be astonished to hear I have lately written to Delawarre, for the purpose of explaining (as far as possible without involving some *old friends* of mine in the business) the cause of my behaviour to him during my last residence at Harrow (nearly two years ago), which you will recollect was rather '*en cavalier*.' Since that period, I have discovered he was treated with injustice both by those who misrepresented his conduct, and by me in consequence of their suggestions. I have therefore made all the reparation in my power, by apologising for my mistake, though with very faint hopes of success; indeed I never expected any answer, but desired one for form's sake;*that* has not yet arrived, and most probably never will. However, I have *eased* my own *conscience* by the atonement, which is humiliating enough to one of my disposition; yet I could not have slept satisfied with the reflection of having, *even unintentionally*, injured any individual. I have done all that could be done to repair the injury, and there the affair must end. Whether we renew our intimacy or not is of very trivial consequence.

"My time has lately been much occupied with very different pursuits. I have been *transporting* a servant, who cheated me,—rather a disagreeable event;— performing in private theatricals;—publishing a volume of poems (at the request of my friends, for their perusal);—making *love*,—and taking physic. The two last amusements have not had the best effect *in the world*; for my attentions have been divided amongst so many *fair damsels,* and the drugs I swallow are of such variety in their composition, that between Venus and Aesculapius I am harassed to death. However, I have still leisure to devote some hours to the recollections of past, regretted friendships, and in the interval to take the advantage of the moment, to assure you how much I am, and ever will be, my dearest Clare,

"Your truly attached and sincere

"BYRON."

Considering himself bound to replace the copies of his work which he had withdrawn, as well as to rescue the general character of the volume from the stigma this one offender might bring upon it, he set instantly about preparing a second edition for the press, and, during the ensuing six weeks, continued busily occupied with his task. In the beginning of January we find him forwarding a copy to his friend, Dr. Pigot, in Edinburgh:—

LETTER 9.

TO MR. PIGOT.

"Southwell, Jan. 13. 1807.

"I ought to begin with *sundry* apologies, for my own negligence, but the variety of my avocations in *prose* and *verse* must plead my excuse. With this epistle you will receive a volume of all my *Juvenilia*, published since your departure: it is of considerably greater size than the *copy* in your possession, which I beg you will destroy, as the present is much more complete. That *unlucky* poem to my poor Mary has been the cause of some animadversion from *ladies in years*. I have not printed it in this collection, in consequence of my being pronounced a most *profligate sinner*, in short, a '*young Moore*,' by ——, your —— friend. I believe, in general, they have been favourably received, and surely the age of their author will preclude *severe* criticism. The adventures of my life from sixteen to nineteen, and the dissipation into which I have been thrown in London, have given a voluptuous tint to my ideas; but the occasions which called forth my muse could hardly admit any other colouring. This volume is *vastly* correct and miraculously chaste. Apropos, talking of love,...

"If you can find leisure to answer this farrago of unconnected nonsense, you need not doubt what gratification will accrue from your reply to yours ever," &c.

To his young friend, Mr. William Bankes, who had met casually with a copy of the work, and wrote him a letter conveying his opinion of it, he returned the following answer:—

Letter 10.

TO MR. WILLIAM BANKES.

"Southwell, March 6. 1807.

"Dear Bankes,

"Your critique is valuable for many reasons: in the first place, it is the only one in which flattery has borne so slight a part; in the *next*, I am *cloyed* with insipid compliments. I have a better opinion of your judgment and ability than your *feelings*. Accept my most sincere thanks for your kind decision, not less welcome, because totally unexpected. With regard to a more exact estimate, I need not remind you how few of the *best poems*, in our language, will stand the test of *minute* or *verbal*criticism: it can, therefore, hardly be expected the effusions of a boy (and most of these pieces have been produced at an early period) can derive much merit either from the subject or composition. Many of them were written under great depression of spirits, and during severe indisposition:—hence the gloomy turn of the ideas. We coincide in opinion that the '*poësies érotiques*' are the most exceptionable; they were, however, grateful to the *deities*, on whose altars they were offered—more I seek not.

"The portrait of Pomposus was drawn at Harrow, after a *long sitting*; this accounts for the resemblance, or rather the *caricatura*. He is *your* friend, he *never was mine*—for both our sakes I shall be silent on this head. *The collegiate* rhymes are not personal—one of the notes may appear so, but could not be omitted. I have little doubt they will be deservedly abused—a just punishment for my unfilial treatment of so excellent an Alma Mater. I sent you no copy, lest *we* should be placed in the situation of *Gil Blas* and the *Archbishop* of Grenada; though running some hazard from the experiment, I wished your *verdict* to be unbiassed. Had my '*Libellus*' been presented previous to your letter, it would have appeared a species of bribe to purchase compliment. I feel no hesitation in saying, I was more anxious to hear your critique, however severe, than the praises of the *million*. On the same day I was honoured with the encomiums of *Mackenzie*, the celebrated author of the 'Man of Feeling.' Whether *his* approbation or *yours* elated me most, I cannot decide.

"You will receive my *Juvenilia*,—at least all yet published. I have a large volume in manuscript, which may in part appear hereafter; at present I have neither time nor inclination to prepare it for the press. In the spring I shall return to Trinity, to dismantle my rooms, and bid you a final adieu. The *Cam* will not be much increased by my *tears* on the occasion. Your further remarks, however *caustic* or bitter, to a palate vitiated with the *sweets of adulation*, will be of service. Johnson has shown us that*no poetry* is perfect;

but to correct mine would be an Herculean labour. In fact I never looked beyond the moment of composition, and published merely at the request of my friends. Notwithstanding so much has been said concerning the 'Genus irritabile vatum,' we shall never quarrel on the subject—poetic fame is by no means the 'acme' of my wishes. Adieu.

"Yours ever,

"BYRON."

This letter was followed by another, on the same subject, to Mr. Bankes, of which, unluckily, only the annexed fragment remains:—

"For my own part, I have suffered severely in the decease of my two greatest friends, the only beings I ever loved (females excepted); I am therefore a solitary animal, miserable enough, and so perfectly a citizen of the world, that whether I pass my days in Great Britain or Kamschatka, is to me a matter of perfect indifference. I cannot evince greater respect for your alteration than by immediately adopting it—this shall be done in the next edition. I am sorry your remarks are not more frequent, as I am certain they would be equally beneficial. Since my last, I have received two critical opinions from Edinburgh, both too flattering for me to detail. One is from Lord Woodhouselee, at the head of the Scotch literati, and a most *voluminous* writer (his last work is a life of Lord Kaimes); the other from Mackenzie, who sent his decision a second time, more at length. I am not personally acquainted with either of these gentlemen, nor ever requested their sentiments on the subject: their praise is voluntary, and transmitted through the medium of a friend, at whose house they read the productions.

"Contrary to my former intention, I am now preparing a volume for the public at large: my amatory pieces will be exchanged, and others substituted in their place. The whole will be considerably enlarged, and appear the latter end of May. This is a hazardous experiment; but want of better employment, the encouragement I have met with, and my own vanity, induce me to stand the test, though not without *sundry palpitations*. The book will circulate fast enough in this country, from mere curiosity, what I prin—"

The following modest letter accompanied a copy which he presented to Mr. Falkner, his mother's landlord:—

LETTER 11.

TO MR. FALKNER.

"Sir,

"The volume of little pieces which accompanies this, would have been presented before, had I not been apprehensive that Miss Falkner's indisposition might render such trifles unwelcome. There are some errors of the printer which I have not had time to correct in the collection: you have it thus, with 'all its imperfections on its head,' a heavy weight, when joined with the faults of its author. Such 'Juvenilia,' as they can claim no great degree of approbation, I may venture to hope, will also escape the severity of uncalled for, though perhaps *not* undeserved, criticism.

"They were written on many and various occasions, and are now published merely for the perusal of a friendly circle. Believe me, sir, if they afford the slightest amusement to yourself and the rest of my *social* readers, I shall have gathered all the *bays* I ever wish to adorn the head of yours,

very truly,

"BYRON.

"P.S.—I hope Miss F. is in a state of recovery."

Notwithstanding this unambitious declaration of the young author, he had that within which would not suffer him to rest so easily; and the fame he had now reaped within a limited circle made him but more eager to try his chance on a wider field. The hundred copies of which this edition consisted were hardly out of his hands, when with fresh activity he went to press again,—and his first published volume, "The Hours of Idleness," made its appearance. Some new pieces which he had written in the interim were added, and no less than twenty of those contained in the former volume omitted;—for what reason does not very clearly appear, as they are, most of them, equal, if not superior, to those retained.

In one of the pieces, reprinted in the "Hours of Idleness," there are some alterations and additions, which, as far as they may be supposed to spring from the known feelings of the poet respecting birth, are curious. This poem, which is entitled "Epitaph on a Friend," appears, from the lines I am about to give, to have been, in its original state, intended to commemorate the death of the same lowly born youth, to whom some affectionate verses, cited in a preceding page, were addressed:—

"Though low thy lot, since in a cottage born,

No titles did thy humble name adorn;

To me, far dearer was thy artless love

Than all the joys wealth, fame, and friends could prove."

But, in the altered form of the epitaph, not only this passage, but every other containing an allusion to the low rank of his young companion, is omitted;

while, in the added parts, the introduction of such language as

"What, though thy sire lament his failing line,"

seems calculated to give an idea of the youth's station in life, wholly different from that which the whole tenour of the original epitaph warrants. The other poem, too, which I have mentioned, addressed evidently to the same boy, and speaking in similar terms, of the "lowness" of his "lot," is, in the "Hours of Idleness," altogether omitted. That he grew more conscious of his high station, as he approached to manhood, is not improbable; and this wish to sink his early friendship with the young cottager may have been a result of that feeling.

As his visits to Southwell were, after this period, but few and transient, I shall take the present opportunity of mentioning such miscellaneous particulars respecting his habits and mode of life, while there, as I have been able to collect.

Though so remarkably shy, when he first went to Southwell, this reserve, as he grew more acquainted with the young people of the place, wore off; till, at length, he became a frequenter of their assemblies and dinner-parties, and even felt mortified if he heard of a rout to which he was not invited. His horror, however, at new faces still continued; and if, while at Mrs. Pigot's, he saw strangers approaching the house, he would instantly jump out of the window to avoid them. This natural shyness concurred with no small degree of pride to keep him aloof from the acquaintance of the gentlemen in the neighbourhood, whose visits, in more than one instance, he left unreturned;—some under the plea that their ladies had not visited his mother; others, because they had neglected to pay him this compliment sooner. The true reason, however, of the haughty distance, at which, both now and afterwards, he stood apart from his more opulent neighbours, is to be found in his mortifying consciousness of the inadequacy of his own means to his rank, and the proud dread of being made to feel this inferiority by persons to whom, in every other respect, he knew himself superior. His friend, Mr. Becher, frequently expostulated with him on this unsociableness; and to his remonstrances, on one occasion, Lord Byron returned a poetical answer, so remarkably prefiguring the splendid burst, with which his own volcanic genius opened upon the world, that as the volume containing the verses is in very few hands, I cannot resist the temptation of giving a few extracts here:—

"Dear Becher, you tell me to mix with mankind,—

I cannot deny such a precept is wise;

But retirement accords with the tone of my mind,

And I will not descend to a world I despise.

"Did the Senate or Camp my exertions require,

Ambition might prompt me at once to go forth;

And, when infancy's years of probation expire,

Perchance, I may strive to distinguish my birth.

"The fire, in the cavern of Ætna concealed,

Still mantles unseen, in its secret recess;—

At length, in a volume terrific revealed,

No torrent can quench it, no bounds can repress.

"Oh thus, the desire in my bosom for fame

Bids me live but to hope for Posterity's praise;

Could I soar, with the Phoenix, on pinions of flame,

With him I would wish to expire in the blaze.

"For the life of a Fox, of a Chatham the death,

What censure, what danger, what woe would I brave?

Their lives did not end when they yielded their breath,—

Their glory illumines the gloom of the grave!"

In his hours of rising and retiring to rest he was, like his mother, always very late; and this habit he never altered during the remainder of his life. The night, too, was at this period, as it continued afterwards, his favourite time for composition; and his first visit in the morning was generally paid to the fair friend who acted as his amanuensis, and to whom he then gave whatever new products of his brain the preceding night might have inspired. His next visit was usually to his friend Mr. Becher's, and from thence to one or two other houses on the Green, after which the rest of the day was devoted to his favourite exercises. The evenings he usually passed with the same family, among whom he began his morning, either in conversation, or in hearing Miss Pigot play upon the piano-forte, and singing over with her a certain set of songs which he admired,—among which the "Maid of Lodi," (with the words, "My heart with love is beating,") and "When Time who steals our years away," were, it seems, his particular favourites. He appears, indeed, to have, even thus early, shown a decided taste for that sort of regular routine of life,—bringing round the same occupations at the stated periods,—which formed so much the system of his existence during the greater part of his residence abroad.

Those exercises, to which he flew for distraction in less happy days, formed his enjoyment now; and between swimming, sparring, firing at a mark, and riding, the greater part of his time was passed. In the last of these accomplishments he was by no means very expert. As an instance of his little knowledge of horses, it is told, that, seeing a pair one day pass his window, he exclaimed, "What beautiful horses! I should like to buy them."—"Why, they are your own, my Lord," said his servant. Those who knew him, indeed, at that period, were rather surprised, in after-life, to hear so much of his riding;—and the truth is, I am inclined to think, that he was at no time a very adroit horseman.

In swimming and diving we have already seen, by his own accounts, he excelled; and a lady in Southwell, among other precious relics of him, possesses a thimble which he borrowed of her one morning, when on his way to bathe in the Greet, and which, as was testified by her brother, who accompanied him, he brought up three times successively from the bottom of the river. His practice of firing at a mark was the occasion, once, of some alarm to a very beautiful young person, Miss H.,—one of that numerous list of fair ones by whom his imagination was dazzled while at Southwell. A poem relating to this occurrence, which may be found in his unpublished volume, is thus introduced:—"As the author was discharging his pistols in a garden, two ladies, passing near the spot, were alarmed by the sound of a bullet hissing near them, to one of whom the following stanzas were addressed the next morning."

Such a passion, indeed, had he for arms of every description, that there generally lay a small sword by the side of his bed, with which he used to amuse himself, as he lay awake in the morning, by thrusting it through his bed-hangings. The person who purchased this bed at the sale of Mrs. Byron's furniture, on her removal to Newstead, gave out—with the view of attaching a stronger interest to the holes in the curtains—that they were pierced by the same sword with which the old lord had killed Mr. Chaworth, and which his descendant always kept as a memorial by his bedside. Such is the ready process by which fiction is often engrafted upon fact;—the sword in question being a most innocent and bloodless weapon, which Lord Byron, during his visits at Southwell, used to borrow of one of his neighbours.

His fondness for dogs—another fancy which accompanied him through life—may be judged from the anecdotes already given, in the account of his expedition to Harrowgate. Of his favourite dog Boatswain, whom he has immortalised in verse, and by whose side it was once his solemn purpose to be buried, some traits are told, indicative, not only of intelligence, but of a generosity of spirit, which might well win for him the affections of such a master as Byron. One of these I shall endeavour to relate as nearly as possible as it was told to me. Mrs. Byron had a fox-terrier, called Gilpin, with whom her son's dog, Boatswain, was perpetually at war, taking every opportunity of attacking and worrying him so violently, that it was very much apprehended he would kill the animal. Mrs. Byron therefore sent off her terrier to a tenant at Newstead; and on the departure of Lord Byron for Cambridge, his "friend" Boatswain, with two other dogs, was intrusted to the care of a servant till his return. One morning the servant was much alarmed by the disappearance of Boatswain, and throughout the whole of the day he could hear no tidings of him. At last, towards evening, the stray dog arrived, accompanied by Gilpin, whom he led immediately to the kitchen fire, licking him and lavishing upon him every possible demonstration of joy. The fact was, he had been all the way to Newstead to fetch him; and having now established his former foe under the roof once more, agreed so perfectly well with him ever after, that he even protected him against the insults of other dogs (a task which the quarrelsomeness of the little terrier rendered no sinecure), and, if he but heard Gilpin's voice in distress, would fly instantly to his rescue.

In addition to the natural tendency to superstition, which is usually found connected with the poetical temperament, Lord Byron had also the example and influence of his mother, acting upon him from infancy, to give his mind this tinge. Her implicit belief in the wonders of second sight, and the strange tales she told of this mysterious faculty, used to astonish not a little her sober English friends; and it will be seen, that, at so late a period as the death of his friend Shelley, the idea of fetches and forewarnings impressed upon him by his mother had not wholly lost possession of the poet's mind. As an instance of a more playful sort of superstition I may be allowed to mention a slight circumstance told me of him by one of his Southwell friends. This lady had a large agate bead with a wire through it, which had been taken out of a barrow, and lay always in her work-box. Lord Byron asking one day what it was, she told him that it had been given her as an amulet, and the charm was, that as long as she had this bead in her possession, she should never be in love. "Then give it to me," he cried, eagerly, "for that's just the thing I want." The young lady refused;—but it was not long before the bead disappeared. She taxed him with the theft, and he owned it; but said, she never should see her amulet again.

Of his charity and kind-heartedness he left behind him at Southwell—as, indeed, at every place, throughout life, where he resided any time—the most cordial recollections. "He never," says a person, who knew him intimately at this period, "met with objects of distress without affording them succour." Among many little traits of this nature, which his friends delight to tell, I select the following,—less as a proof of his generosity, than from the interest which the simple incident itself, as connected with the name of Byron, presents. While yet a school-boy, he happened to be in a bookseller's shop at

Southwell, when a poor woman came in to purchase a Bible. The price, she was told by the shopman, was eight shillings. "Ah, dear sir," she exclaimed, "I cannot pay such a price; I did not think it would cost half the money." The woman was then, with a look of disappointment, going away,—when young Byron called her back, and made her a present of the Bible.

In his attention to his person and dress, to the becoming arrangement of his hair, and to whatever might best show off the beauty with which nature had gifted him, he manifested, even thus early, his anxiety to make himself pleasing to that sex who were, from first to last, the ruling stars of his destiny. The fear of becoming, what he was naturally inclined to be, enormously fat, had induced him, from his first entrance at Cambridge, to adopt, for the purpose of reducing himself, a system of violent exercise and abstinence, together with the frequent use of warm baths. But the embittering circumstance of his life,—that, which haunted him like a curse, amidst thebuoyancy of youth, and the anticipations of fame and pleasure, was, strange to say, the trifling deformity of his foot. By that one slight blemish (as in his moments of melancholy he persuaded himself) all the blessings that nature had showered upon him were counterbalanced. His reverend friend, Mr. Becher, finding him one day unusually dejected, endeavoured to cheer and rouse him, by representing, in their brightest colours, all the various advantages with which Providence had endowed him,—and, among the greatest, that of "a mind which placed him above the rest of mankind."—"Ah, my dear friend," said Byron, mournfully,—"if this (laying his hand on his forehead) places me above the rest of mankind, that (pointing to his foot) places me far, far below them."

It sometimes, indeed, seemed as if his sensitiveness on this point led him to fancy that he was the only person in the world afflicted with such an infirmity. When that accomplished scholar and traveller, Mr. D. Baillie, who was at the same school with him at Aberdeen, met him afterwards at Cambridge, the young peer had then grown so fat that, though accosted by him familiarly as his school-fellow, it was not till he mentioned his name that Mr. Baillie could recognise him. "It is odd enough, too, that you shouldn't know me," said Byron—"I thought nature had set such a mark upon me, that I could never be forgot."

But, while this defect was such a source of mortification to his spirit, it was also, and in an equal degree, perhaps, a stimulus:—and more especially in whatever depended upon personal prowess or attractiveness, he seemed to feel himself piqued by this stigma, which nature, as he thought, had set upon him, to distinguish himself above those whom she had endowed with her more "fair proportion." In pursuits of gallantry he was, I have no doubt, a good deal actuated by this incentive; and the hope of astonishing the world, at some future period, as a chieftain and hero, mingled little less with his young dreams than the prospect of a poet's glory. "I will, some day or other," he used to say, when a boy, "raise a troop,—the men of which shall be dressed in black, and ride on black horses. They shall be called 'Byron's Blacks,' and you will hear of their performing prodigies of valour."

I have already adverted to the exceeding eagerness with which, while at Harrow, he devoured all sorts of learning,—excepting only that which, by the regimen of the school, was prescribed for him. The same rapid and multifarious course of study he pursued during the holidays; and, in order to deduct as little as possible from his hours of exercise, he had given himself the habit, while at home, of reading all dinner-time. In a mind so versatile as his, every novelty, whether serious or light, whether lofty or ludicrous, found a welcome and an echo; and I can easily conceive the glee—as a friend of his once described it to me—with which he brought to her, one evening, a copy of Mother Goose's Tales, which he had bought from a hawker that morning, and read, for the first time, while he dined.

I shall now give, from a memorandum-book begun by him this year, the account, as I find it hastily and promiscuously scribbled out, of all the books in various departments of knowledge, which he had already perused at a period of life when few of his school-fellows had yet travelled beyond their *longs* and *shorts*. The list is, unquestionably, a remarkable one;—and when we recollect that the reader of all these volumes was, at the same time, the possessor of a most retentive memory, it may be doubted whether, among what are called the regularly educated, the contenders for scholastic honours and prizes, there could be found a single one who, at the same age, has possessed any thing like the same stock of useful knowledge.

"LIST OF HISTORICAL WRITERS WHOSE WORKS I HAVE PERUSED IN DIFFERENT LANGUAGES."

"*History of England.*—Hume, Rapin, Henry, Smollet, Tindal, Belsham, Bisset, Adolphus, Holinshed, Froissart's Chronicles (belonging properly to France).

"*Scotland.*—Buchanan, Hector Boethius, both in the Latin.

"*Ireland.*—Gordon.

"*Rome.*—Hooke, Decline and Fall by Gibbon, Ancient History by Rollin (including an account of the Carthaginians, &c.), besides Livy, Tacitus, Eutropius, Cornelius Nepos, Julius Cæsar, Arrian. Sallust.

"*Greece.*—Mitford's Greece, Leland's Philip, Plutarch, Potter's Antiquities,

Xenophon, Thucydides, Herodotus.

"*France.*—Mezeray, Voltaire.

"*Spain.*—I chiefly derived my knowledge of old Spanish History from a book called the Atlas, now obsolete. The modern history, from the intrigues of Alberoni down to the Prince of Peace, I learned from its connection with European politics.

"*Portugal.*—From Vertot; as also his account of the Siege of Rhodes,—though the last is his own invention, the real facts being totally different.—So much for his Knights of Malta.

"*Turkey.*—I have read Knolles, Sir Paul Rycaut, and Prince Cantemir, besides a more modern history, anonymous. Of the Ottoman History I know every event, from Tangralopi, and afterwards Othman I., to the peace of Passarowitz, in 1718,—the battle of Cutzka, in 1739, and the treaty between Russia and Turkey in 1790.

"*Russia.*—Tooke's Life of Catherine II., Voltaire's Czar Peter.

"*Sweden.*—Voltaire's Charles XII., also Norberg's Charles XII.—in my opinion the best of the two.—A translation of Schiller's Thirty Years' War, which contains the exploits of Gustavus Adolphus, besides Harte's Life of the same Prince. I have somewhere, too, read an account of Gustavus Vasa, the deliverer of Sweden, but do not remember the author's name.

"*Prussia.*—I have seen, at least, twenty Lives of Frederick II., the only prince worth recording in Prussian annals. Gillies, his own Works, and Thiebault,—none very amusing. The last is paltry, but circumstantial.

"*Denmark*—I know little of. Of Norway I understand the natural history, but not the chronological.

"*Germany.*—I have read long histories of the house of Suabia, Wenceslaus, and, at length, Rodolph of Hapsburgh and his *thick-lipped* Austrian descendants.

"*Switzerland.*—Ah! William Tell, and the battle of Morgarten, where Burgundy was slain.

"*Italy.*—Davila, Guicciardini, the Guelphs and Ghibellines, the battle of Pavia, Massaniello, the revolutions of Naples, &c. &c.

"*Hindostan*—Orme and Cambridge.

"*America.*—Robertson, Andrews' American War.

"*Africa*—merely from travels, as Mungo Park, Bruce.

"BIOGRAPHY.

"Robertson's Charles V.—Cæsar, Sallust (Catiline and Jugurtha), Lives of Marlborough and Eugene, Tekeli, Bonnard, Buonaparte, all the British Poets, both by Johnson and Anderson, Rousseau's Confessions, Life of Cromwell, British Plutarch, British Nepos, Campbell's Lives of the Admirals, Charles XII., Czar Peter, Catherine II., Henry Lord Kaimes, Marmontel, Teignmouth's Sir William Jones, Life of Newton, Belisaire, with thousands not to be detailed.

"LAW.

"Blackstone, Montesquieu.

"PHILOSOPHY.

"Paley, Locke, Bacon, Hume, Berkeley, Drummond, Beattie, and Bolingbroke. Hobbes I detest.

"GEOGRAPHY.

"Strabo, Cellarius, Adams, Pinkerton, and Guthrie.

"POETRY.

"All the British Classics as before detailed, with most of the living poets, Scott, Southey, &c.—Some French, in the original, of which the Cid is my favourite.—Little Italian.—Greek and Latin without number;—these last I shall give up in future.—I have translated a good deal from both languages, verse as well as prose.

"ELOQUENCE.

"Demosthenes, Cicero, Quintilian, Sheridan, Austin's Chironomia, and Parliamentary Debates from the Revolution to the year 1742.

"DIVINITY.

"Blair, Porteus, Tillotson, Hooker,—all very tiresome. I abhor books of religion, though I reverence and love my God, without the blasphemous notions of sectaries, or belief in their absurd and damnable heresies, mysteries, and Thirty-nine Articles.

"MISCELLANIES.

"Spectator, Rambler, World, &c. &c.—Novels by the thousand.

"All the books here enumerated I have taken down from memory. I recollect reading them, and can quote passages from any mentioned. I have, of course, omitted several in my catalogue; but the greater part of the above I perused before the age of fifteen. Since I left Harrow, I have become idle and conceited, from scribbling rhyme and making love to women.   B.—Nov. 30. 1807.

"I have also read (to my regret at present) above four thousand novels, including the works of Cervantes, Fielding, Smollet, Richardson, Mackenzie, Sterne, Rabelais, and Rousseau, &c. &c. The book, in my opinion, most useful to a man who wishes to acquire the reputation of being well read, with the least trouble, is "Burton's Anatomy of Melancholy," the most amusing and instructive medley of quotations and classical anecdotes I ever perused. But a superficial reader must take care, or his intricacies will bewilder him. If, however, he has patience to go through his volumes, he will be more improved for literary conversation than by the perusal of any twenty other works with which I am acquainted,—at least, in the English language."

To this early and extensive study of English writers may be attributed that mastery over the resources of his own language with which Lord Byron came furnished into the field of literature, and which enabled him, as fast as his youthful fancies sprung up, to clothe them with a diction worthy of their strength and beauty. In general, the difficulty of young writers, at their commencement, lies far less in any lack of thoughts or images, than in that want of a fitting organ to give those conceptions vent, to which their unacquaintance with the great instrument of the man of genius, his native language, dooms them. It will be found, indeed, that the three most remarkable examples of early authorship, which, in their respective lines, the history of literature affords—Pope, Congreve, and Chatterton—were all of them persons self-educated, according to their own intellectual wants and tastes, and left, undistracted by the worse than useless pedantries of the schools, to seek, in the pure "well of English undefiled," those treasures of which they accordingly so very early and intimately possessed themselves. To these three instances may now be added, virtually, that of Lord Byron, who, though a disciple of the schools, was, intellectually speaking, *in* them, not *of* them, and who, while his comrades were prying curiously into the graves of dead languages, betook himself to the fresh, living sources of his own, and from thence drew those rich, varied stores of diction, which have placed his works, from the age of two-and-twenty upwards, among the most precious depositories of the strength and sweetness of the English language that our whole literature supplies.

In the same book that contains the above record of his studies, he has written out, also from memory, a "List of the different poets, dramatic or otherwise, who have distinguished their respective languages by their productions." After enumerating the various poets, both ancient and modern, of Europe, he thus proceeds with his catalogue through other quarters of the world:—

"*Arabia.*—Mahomet, whose Koran contains most sublime poetical passages, far surpassing European poetry.

"*Persia.*—Ferdousi, author of the Shah Nameh, the Persian Iliad—Sadi, and Hafiz, the immortal Hafiz, the oriental Anacreon. The last is reverenced beyond any bard of ancient or modern times by the Persians, who resort to his tomb near Shiraz, to celebrate his memory. A splendid copy of his works is chained to his monument.

"*America.*—An epic poet has already appeared in that hemisphere, Barlow, author of the Columbiad,—not to be compared with the works of more polished nations.

"*Iceland, Denmark, Norway,* were famous for their Skalds. Among these Lodburgh was one of the most distinguished. His Death Song breathes ferocious sentiments, but a glorious and impassioned strain of poetry.

"*Hindostan* is undistinguished by any great bard,—at least the Sanscrit is so imperfectly known to Europeans, we know not what poetical relics may exist.

"*The Birman Empire.*—Here the natives are passionately fond of poetry, but their bards are unknown.

"*China.*—I never heard of any Chinese poet but the Emperor Kien Long, and his ode to *Tea*. What a pity their philosopher Confucius did not write poetry, with his precepts of morality!

"*Africa.*—In Africa some of the native melodies are plaintive, and the words simple and affecting; but whether their rude strains of nature can be classed with poetry, as the songs of the bards, the Skalds of Europe, &c. &c., I know not.

"This brief list of poets I have written down from memory, without any book of reference; consequently some errors may occur, but I think, if any, very trivial. The works of the European, and some of the Asiatic, I have perused, either in the original or translations. In my list of English, I have merely mentioned the greatest;—to enumerate the minor poets would be useless, as well as tedious. Perhaps Gray, Goldsmith, and Collins, might have been added, as worthy of mention, in a *cosmopolite* account. But as for the others, from Chaucer down to Churchill, they are 'voces et præterea nihil;'—sometimes spoken of, rarely read, and never with advantage. Chaucer, notwithstanding the praises bestowed on him, I think obscene and contemptible:—he owes his celebrity merely to his antiquity, which he does not deserve so well as Pierce Plowman, or Thomas of Ercildoune. English living poets I have avoided mentioning;—we have none who will not survive their productions. Taste is over with us; and another century will sweep our empire, our literature, and our name, from all but a place in the annals of mankind.

"November 30. 1807.

BYRON."

Among the papers of his in my possession are several detached poems (in all nearly six hundred lines), which he wrote about this period, but never printed—having produced most of them after the publication of his "Hours of Idleness." The greater number of these have little, besides his name, to recommend them; but there are a few that, from the feelings and circumstances that gave rise to them, will, I have no doubt, be interesting to the reader. When he first went to Newstead, on his arrival from Aberdeen, he planted, it seems, a young oak in some part of the grounds, and had an idea that as it flourished so should he. Some six or seven years after, on revisiting the spot, he found his oak choked up by weeds, and almost destroyed. In this circumstance, which happened soon after Lord Grey de Ruthen left Newstead, originated one of these poems, which consists of five stanzas, but of which the few opening lines will be a sufficient specimen:—

"Young Oak, when I planted thee deep in the ground,

I hoped that thy days would be longer than mine;

That thy dark-waving branches would flourish around,

And ivy thy trunk with its mantle entwine.

"Such, such was my hope, when, in infancy's years,

On the land of my fathers I rear'd thee with pride;

They are past, and I water thy stem with my tears,—

Thy decay, not the weeds that surround thee can hide.

"I left thee, my Oak, and, since that fatal hour,

A stranger has dwelt in the hall of my sire," &c. &c.

The subject of the verses that follow is sufficiently explained by the notice which he has prefixed to them; and, as illustrative of the romantic and almost lovelike feeling which he threw into his school friendships, they appeared to me, though rather quaint and elaborate, to be worth preserving.

"Some years ago, when at H———, a friend of the author engraved on a particular spot the names of both, with a few additional words as a memorial. Afterwards, on receiving some real or imagined injury, the author destroyed the frail record before he left H———. On revisiting the place in 1807, he wrote under it the following stanzas:—

"Here once engaged the stranger's view
Young Friendship's record simply traced;
Few were her words,—but yet though few,
Resentment's hand the line defaced.

"Deeply she cut—but, not erased,
The characters were still so plain,
That Friendship once return'd, and gazed,—
Till Memory hail'd the words again.

"Repentance placed them as before;
Forgiveness join'd her gentle name;
So fair the inscription seem'd once more
That Friendship thought it still the same.

"Thus might the record now have been;
But, ah, in spite of Hope's endeavour,
Or Friendship's tears, Pride rush'd between,
And blotted out the line for ever!"

The same romantic feeling of friendship breathes throughout another of these poems, in which he has taken for the subject the ingenious thought "L'Amitié est l'Amour sans ailes," and concludes every stanza with the words, "Friendship is Love without his wings." Of the nine stanzas of which this poem consists, the three following appear the most worthy of selection:—

"Why should my anxious breast repine,
Because my youth is fled?
Days of delight may still be mine,
Affection is not dead.
In tracing back the years of youth,
One firm record, one lasting truth
Celestial consolation brings;
Bear it, ye breezes, to the seat,
Where first my heart responsive beat,—

'Friendship is Love without his wings!'

"Seat of my youth! thy distant spire
Recalls each scene of joy;
My bosom glows with former fire,—
In mind again a boy.
Thy grove of elms, thy verdant hill,
Thy every path delights me still,
Each flower a double fragrance flings;
Again, as once, in converse gay,
Each dear associate seems to say,
'Friendship is Love without his wings!'

"My Lycus! wherefore dost thou weep?
Thy falling tears restrain;
Affection for a time may sleep,
But, oh, 'twill wake again.
Think, think, my friend, when next we meet,
Our long-wish'd intercourse, how sweet!
From this my hope of rapture springs,
While youthful hearts thus fondly swell,
Absence, my friend, can only tell,
'Friendship is Love without his wings!'"

"My Lycus! wherefore dost thou weep?Thy falling tears restrain;Affection for a time may sleep,But, oh, 'twill wake again.Think, think, my friend, when next we meet,Our long-wish'd intercourse, how sweet!From this my hope of rapture springs,While youthful hearts thus fondly swell,Absence, my friend, can only tell,'Friendship is Love without his wings!'"

Whether the verses I am now about to give are, in any degree, founded on fact, I have no accurate means of determining. Fond as he was of recording every particular of his youth, such an event, or rather era, as is here commemorated, would have been, of all others, the least likely to pass unmentioned by him;— and yet neither in conversation nor in any of his writings do I remember even an allusion to it. On the other hand, so entirely was all that he wrote,—making allowance for the embellishments of fancy,—the transcript of his actual life and feelings, that it is not easy to suppose a poem, so full of natural tenderness, to have been indebted for its origin to imagination alone.

"TO MY SON!

"Those flaxen locks, those eyes of blue,

Bright as thy mother's in their hue;

Those rosy lips, whose dimples play

And smile to steal the heart away,

Recall a scene of former joy,

And touch thy Father's heart, my Boy!

"And thou canst lisp a father's name—

Ah, William, were thine own the same,

No self-reproach—but, let me cease—

My care for thee shall purchase peace;

Thy mother's shade shall smile in joy,

And pardon all the past, my Boy!

"Her lowly grave the turf has prest,

And thou hast known a stranger's breast.

Derision sneers upon thy birth,

And yields thee scarce a name on earth;

Yet shall not these one hope destroy,—

A Father's heart is thine, my Boy!

"Why, let the world unfeeling frown,

Must I fond Nature's claim disown?

Ah, no—though moralists reprove,

I hail thee, dearest child of love,

Fair cherub, pledge of youth and joy—

A Father guards thy birth, my Boy!

"Oh, 'twill be sweet in thee to trace,

Ere age has wrinkled o'er my face,

Ere half my glass of life is run,

At once a brother and a son;

And all my wane of years employ

In justice done to thee, my Boy!

"Although so young thy heedless sire,

Youth will not damp parental fire;

And, wert thou still less dear to me,

While Helen's form revives in thee,

The breast, which beat to former joy,

Will ne'er desert its pledge, my Boy!

"B——, 1807."

But the most remarkable of these poems is one of a date prior to any I have given, being written in December, 1806, when he was not yet nineteen years old. It contains, as will be seen, his religious creed at that period, and shows how early the struggle between natural piety and doubt began in his mind.

"THE PRAYER OF NATURE.

"Father of Light! great God of Heaven!

Hear'st thou the accents of despair?

Can guilt like man's be e'er forgiven?

Can vice atone for crimes by prayer?

Father of Light, on thee I call!

Thou see'st my soul is dark within;

Thou who canst mark the sparrow's fall,

Avert from me the death of sin.

No shrine I seek, to sects unknown,

Oh point to me the path of truth!

Thy dread omnipotence I own,

Spare, yet amend, the faults of youth.

Let bigots rear a gloomy fane,

Let superstition hail the pile,

Let priests, to spread their sable reign,

With tales of mystic rites beguile.

Shall man confine his Maker's sway

To Gothic domes of mouldering stone?

Thy temple is the face of day;

Earth, ocean, heaven, thy boundless throne.

Shall man condemn his race to hell

Unless they bend in pompous form;

Tell us that all, for one who fell,

Must perish in the mingling storm?

Shall each pretend to reach the skies,

Yet doom his brother to expire,

Whose soul a different hope supplies,

Or doctrines less severe inspire?

Shall these, by creeds they can't expound,

Prepare a fancied bliss or woe?

Shall reptiles, grovelling on the ground,

Their great Creator's purpose know?

Shall those who live for self alone,

Whose years float on in daily crime—

Shall they by Faith for guilt atone,

And live beyond the bounds of Time?

Father! no prophet's laws I seek,—

Thy laws in Nature's works appear;—

I own myself corrupt and weak,

Yet will I pray, for thou wilt hear!

Thou, who canst guide the wandering star

Through trackless realms of Æther's space;

Who calm'st the elemental war,

Whose hand from pole to pole I trace:

Thou, who in wisdom placed me here,

Who, when thou wilt, can take me hence,

Ah! whilst I tread this earthly sphere,

Extend to me thy wide defence.

To Thee, my God, to Thee I call!

Whatever weal or woe betide,

By thy command I rise or fall,

In thy protection I confide.

If, when this dust to dust restored,

My soul shall float on airy wing,

How shall thy glorious name adored,

Inspire her feeble voice to sing!

But, if this fleeting spirit share

With clay the grave's eternal bed,

While life yet throbs, I raise my prayer,

Though doom'd no more to quit the dead.

To Thee I breathe my humble strain,

Grateful for all thy mercies past,

And hope, my God, to thee again

This erring life may fly at last.

"29th Dec. 1806.

Byron."

In another of these poems, which extends to about a hundred lines, and which he wrote under the melancholy impression that he should soon die, we find him concluding with a prayer in somewhat the same spirit. After bidding adieu to all the favourite scenes of his youth, he thus continues,—

"Forget this world, my restless sprite,

Turn, turn thy thoughts to Heav'n:

There must thou soon direct thy night,

If errors are forgiven.

To bigots and to sects unknown.

Bow down beneath the Almighty's throne;—

To him address thy trembling prayer;

He, who is merciful and just,

Will not reject a child of dust,

Although his meanest care.

Father of Light, to thee I call,

My soul is dark within;

Thou, who canst mark the sparrow fall,

Avert the death of sin.

Thou, who canst guide the wandering star,

Who calm'st the elemental war,

Whose mantle is yon boundless sky,

My thoughts, my words, my crimes forgive;

And, since I soon must cease to live,

Instruct me how to die.

1807."

We have seen, by a former letter, that the law proceedings for the recovery of his Rochdale property had been attended with success in some trial of the case at Lancaster. The following note to one of his Southwell friends, announcing a second triumph of the cause, shows how sanguinely and, as it turned out, erroneously, he calculated on the results.

"Feb. 9. 1807.

Dear ——,

"I have the pleasure to inform you we have gained the Rochdale cause a second time, by which I am, £60,000 plus. Yours ever,

"BYRON."

In the month of April we find him still at Southwell, and addressing to his friend, Dr. Pigot, who was at Edinburgh, the following note:—

"Southwell, April, 1807.

"My dear Pigot,

"Allow me to congratulate you on the success of your first examination —'*Courage*, mon ami.' The title of Doctor will do wonders with the damsels. I shall most probably be in Essex or London when you arrive at this d——d place, where I am detained by the publication of my rhymes.

"Adieu.—Believe me yours very truly,

"BYRON.

"P.S. Since we met, I have reduced myself by violent exercise, much physic, and hot bathing, from 14 stone 6 lb. to 12 stone 7 lb. In all I have lost 27 pounds. Bravo!—what say you?"

His movements and occupations for the remainder of this year will be best collected from a series of his own letters, which I am enabled, by the kindness of the lady to whom they were addressed, to give. Though these letters are boyishly written, and a good deal of their pleasantry is of that conventional kind which depends more upon phrase than thought, they will yet, I think, be found curious and interesting, not only as enabling us to track him through this period of his life, but as throwing light upon various little traits of character, and laying open to us the first working of his hopes and fears while waiting, in suspense, the opinions that were to decide, as he thought, his future fame. The first of the series, which is without date, appears to have been written before he had left Southwell. The other letters, it will be seen, are dated from Cambridge and from London.

LETTER 12.

TO MISS ———.

"June 11. 1807.

"Dear Queen Bess,

"*Savage* ought to be *immortal*:—though not a *thorough-bred bull-dog*, he is the finest puppy I ever *saw*, and will answer much better; in his great and manifold kindness he has already bitten my fingers, and disturbed the *gravity* of old Boatswain, who is *grievously discomposed*. I wish to be informed what he *costs*, his*expenses*, &c. &c., that I may indemnify Mr. G ——. My thanks are *all* I can give for the trouble he has taken, make a *long speech*, and conclude it with 1 2 3 4 5 6 7. I am out of practice, so *deputize* you as legate,—*ambassador* would not do in a matter concerning the *Pope*, which I presume this must, as the *whole* turns upon a*Bull*.

"Yours,

"Byron.

"P.S. I write in bed."

LETTER 13.

TO MISS ——.

"Cambridge, June 30. 1807.

"'Better late than never, Pal,'" is a saying of which you know the origin, and as it is applicable on the present occasion, you will excuse its conspicuous place in the front of my epistle. I am almost superannuated here. My old friends (with the exception of a very few) all departed, and I am preparing to follow them, but remain till Monday to be present at three *Oratorios*, two *Concerts*, a *Fair*, and a Ball. I find I am not only *thinner* but *taller* by an inch since my last visit. I was obliged to tell every body my *name*, nobody having the least recollection of my *visage*, or person. Even the hero of *my Cornelian* (who is now sitting *vis-à-vis*, reading a volume of my *Poetics*) passed me in Trinity walks without recognising me in the least, and was thunderstruck at the alteration which had taken place in my countenance, &c. &c. Some say I look *better*, others *worse*, but all agree I am *thinner*—more I do not require. I have lost two pounds in my weight since I left your *cursed, detestable,* and*abhorred* abode of *scandal*, where, excepting yourself and John Becher, I care not if the whole race were consigned to the *Pit of Acheron*, which I would visit in person rather than contaminate my *sandals* with the polluted dust of Southwell. *Seriously*, unless obliged by the *emptiness* of my purse to revisit Mrs. B., you will see me no more.

"On Monday I depart for London. I quit Cambridge with little regret, because our *set* are *vanished*, and my *musical protégé* before mentioned has left the choir, and is stationed in a mercantile house of considerable eminence in the metropolis. You may have heard me observe he is exactly to an hour two years younger than myself. I found him grown considerably, and, as you will suppose, very glad to see his former *Patron*. He is nearly my height, very *thin*, very fair complexion, dark eyes, and light locks. My opinion of his mind you already know;—I hope I shall never have occasion to change it. Every body here conceives me to be an *invalid*. The University at present is very gay from the fêtes of divers kinds. I supped out last night, but eat (or ate) nothing, sipped a bottle of claret, went to bed at two, and rose at eight. I have commenced early rising, and find it agrees with me. The Masters and the Fellows all very *polite*, but look a little *askance*—don't much admire *lampoons*—truth always disagreeable.

"Write, and tell me how the inhabitants of your *Menagerie* go *on*, and if my publication goes *off* well: do the quadrupeds *growl?* Apropos, my bull-dog is deceased—'Flesh both of cur and man is grass.' Address your answer to Cambridge. If I am gone, it will be forwarded. Sad news just arrived—Russians beat—a bad set, eat nothing but *oil*, consequently must melt before a *hard fire*. I get awkward in my academic habiliments for want of practice. Got up in a window to hear the oratorio at St. Mary's, popped down in the middle of the *Messiah*, tore a *woeful* rent in the back of my best black silk gown, and damaged an egregious pair of breeches. Mem.—never tumbled from a church window during service. Adieu, dear ——! do not remember me to any body:—to *forget* and be forgotten by the people of Southwell is all I aspire to."

LETTER 14.

TO MISS ——.

"Trin. Coll. Camb. July 5. 1807.

"Since my last letter I have determined to reside *another year* at Granta, as my rooms, &c. &c. are finished in great style, several old friends come up again, and many new acquaintances made; consequently my inclination leads me forward, and I shall return to college in October if still *alive*. My life here has been one continued routine of dissipation—out at different places every day, engaged to more dinners, &c. &c. than my *stay* would permit me to fulfil. At this moment I write with a bottle of claret in my *head* and *tears* in my *eyes*; for I have just parted with my '*Cornelian*,' who spent the evening with me. As it was our last interview, I postponed my engagement to devote the hours of the *Sabbath* to friendship:—Edleston and I have separated for the present, and my mind is a chaos of hope and sorrow. To-morrow I set out for London: you will address your answer to 'Gordon's Hotel, Albemarle Street,' where I *sojourn* during my visit to the metropolis.

"I rejoice to hear you are interested in my *protégé*; he has been my *almost constant* associate since October, 1805, when I entered Trinity College. His *voice* first attracted my attention, his *countenance* fixed it, and his *manners* attached me to him for ever. He departs for a *mercantile house* in *town* in October, and we shall probably not meet till the expiration of my minority, when I shall leave to his decision either entering as a *partner* through my interest, or residing with me altogether. Of course he would in his present frame of mind prefer the *latter*, but he may alter his opinion previous to that period;—however, he shall have his choice. I certainly love him more than any human being, and neither time nor distance have had the least effect on my (in general) changeable disposition. In short, we shall put *Lady E. Butler* and *Miss Ponsonby* to the blush, *Pylades* and *Orestes* out of countenance, and want nothing but a catastrophe like *Nisus* and *Euryalus*, to give *Jonathan* and *David* the 'go by.' He certainly is perhaps more attached to *me* than even I am in return. During the whole of my residence at Cambridge we met every day, summer and winter, without passing *one* tiresome moment, and separated each time with increasing reluctance. I hope you will one day see us together, he is the only being I esteem, though I *like* many.

"The Marquis of Tavistock was down the other day; I supped with him at his tutor's—entirely a Whig party. The opposition muster strong here now, and Lord Hartington, the Duke of Leinster, &c. &c. are to join us in October, so every thing will be *splendid*. The *music* is all over at present. Met with another '*accidency*'—upset a butter-boat in the lap of a lady—look'd very *blue*—*spectators* grinned—'curse 'em!' Apropos, sorry to say, been *drunk* every day, and not quite *sober* yet—however, touch no meat, nothing but fish, soup, and vegetables, consequently it does me no harm—sad dogs all the *Cantabs*. Mem.—*we mean* to reform next January. This place is a *monotony of endless variety*—like it—hate Southwell. Has Ridge sold well? or do the ancients demur? What ladies have bought?

"Saw a girl at St. Mary's the image of Anne ———, thought it was her—all in the wrong—the lady stared, so did I—I *blushed,* so did *not* the lady,—sad thing—wish women had *more modesty*. Talking of women, puts me in mind of my terrier Fanny—how is she? Got a headache, must go to bed, up early in the morning to travel. My *protégé* breakfasts with me; parting spoils my appetite—excepting from Southwell. Mem. *I hate Southwell.*

Yours, &c."

Letter 15.

TO MISS ———.

"Gordon's Hotel, July 13, 1807.

"You write most excellent epistles—a fig for other correspondents, with their nonsensical apologies for *'knowing nought about it,'*—you send me a delightful budget. I am here in a perpetual vortex of dissipation (very pleasant for all that), and, strange to tell, I get thinner, being now below eleven stone considerably. Stay in town a *month,* perhaps six weeks, trip into Essex, and then, as a favour, *irradiate* Southwell for three days with the light of my countenance; but nothing shall ever make me *reside* there again. I positively return to Cambridge in October; we are to be uncommonly gay, or in truth I should *cut* the University. An extraordinary circumstance occurred to me at Cambridge; a girl so very like —— made her appearance, that nothing but the most *minute inspection* could have undeceived me. I wish I had asked if *she* had ever been at H——.

"What the devil would Ridge have? is not fifty in a fortnight, before the advertisements, a sufficient sale? I hear many of the London booksellers have them, and Crosby has sent copies to the principal watering places. Are they liked or not in Southwell?... I wish Boatswain had *swallowed* Damon! How is Bran? by the immortal gods, Bran ought to be a *Count* of the *Holy Roman Empire.*

"The intelligence of London cannot be interesting to you, who have rusticated all your life—the annals of routs, riots, balls and boxing-matches, cards and crim. cons., parliamentary discussion, political details, masquerades, mechanics, Argyle Street Institution and aquatic races, love and lotteries, Brookes's and Buonaparte, opera-singers and oratorios, wine, women, wax-work, and weather-cocks, can't accord with your *insulated* ideas of decorum and other *silly expressions* not inserted in *our vocabulary.*

"Oh! Southwell, Southwell, how I rejoice to have left thee, and how I curse the heavy hours I dragged along, for so many months, among the Mohawks who inhabit your kraals!—However, one thing I do not regret, which is having *pared off* a sufficient quantity of flesh to enable me to slip into 'an eel skin,' and vie with the *slim*beaux of modern times; though I am sorry to say, it seems to be the mode amongst *gentlemen* to grow *fat,* and I am told I am at least fourteen pound below the fashion. However, I *decrease* instead of enlarging, which is extraordinary, as *violent* exercise in London is impracticable; but I attribute the phenomenon to our *evening squeezes*at public and private parties. I heard from Ridge this morning (the 14th, my letter was begun yesterday): he says the poems go on as well as can be wished; the seventy-five sent to town are circulated, and a demand for fifty more complied with, the day he dated his epistle, though the advertisements are not yet half published. Adieu.

"P.S. Lord Carlisle, on receiving my poems, sent, before he opened the book, a tolerably handsome letter:—I have not heard from him since. His opinions I neither know nor care about: if he is the least insolent, I shall enrol him with *Butler* and the other worthies. He is in Yorkshire, poor man! and very ill!

He said he had not had time to read the contents, but thought it necessary to acknowledge the receipt of the volume immediately. Perhaps the Earl '*bears no brother near the throne,*'—*if so,* I will make his *sceptre* totter *in his hands.* —Adieu!"

LETTER **16.**

TO MISS ——.

"August 2. 1807.

"London begins to disgorge its contents—town is empty—consequently I can scribble at leisure, as occupations are less numerous. In a fortnight I shall depart to fulfil a country engagement; but expect two epistles from you previous to that period. Ridge does not proceed rapidly in Notts—very possible. In town things wear a more promising aspect, and a man whose works are praised by *reviewers,* admired by *duchesses,* and sold by every bookseller of the metropolis, does not dedicate much consideration to *rustic readers.* I have now a review before me, entitled 'Literary Recreations,' where my *hardship* is applauded far beyond my deserts. I know nothing of the critic, but think *him* a very discerning gentleman, and *myself* a devilish *clever* fellow. His critique pleases me particularly, because it is of great length, and a proper quantum of censure is administered, just to give an agreeable *relish* to the praise. You know I hate insipid, unqualified, common-place compliment. If you would wish to see it, order the 13th Number of 'Literary Recreations' for the last month. I assure you I have not the most distant idea of the writer of the article—it is printed in a periodical publication—and though I have written a paper (a review of Wordsworth), which appears in the same work, I am ignorant of every other person concerned in it—even the editor, whose name I have not heard. My cousin, Lord Alexander Gordon, who resided in the same hotel, told me his mother, her Grace of Gordon, requested he would introduce my *Poetical* Lordship to her *Highness,* as she had bought my volume, admired it exceedingly, in common with the rest of the fashionable world, and wished to claim her relationship with the author. I was unluckily engaged on an excursion for some days afterwards, and as the Duchess was on the eve of departing for Scotland, I have postponed my introduction till the winter, when I shall favour the lady, *whose taste I shall not dispute,* with my most sublime and edifying conversation. She is now in the Highlands, and Alexander took his departure, a few days ago, for the same *blessed* seat of *'dark rolling winds.'*

"Crosby, my London publisher, has disposed of his second importation, and has sent to Ridge for a *third*—at least so he says. In every bookseller's window I see my*own name,* and *say nothing,* but enjoy my fame in secret. My last reviewer kindly requests me to alter my determination of writing no more; and 'A Friend to the Cause of Literature' begs I will *gratify* the *public* with some new work 'at no very distant period.' Who would not be a bard?—that is to say, if all critics would be so polite. However, the others will pay me off, I doubt not, for this *gentle* encouragement. If so, have at 'em? By the by, I have written at my intervals of leisure, after two in the morning, 380 lines in blank verse, of Bosworth Field. I have luckily got Hutton's account. I shall extend the poem to eight or ten books, and shall have finished it in a year. Whether it will be published or not must depend on circumstances. So much for *egotism*! My *laurels* have turned my brain, but the *cooling acids* of forthcoming criticisms will probably restore me to *modesty*.

"Southwell is a damned place—I have done with it—at least in all probability: excepting yourself, I esteem no one within its precincts. You were my only *rational*companion; and in plain truth, I had more respect for you than the whole *bevy*, with whose foibles I amused myself in compliance with their prevailing propensities. You gave yourself more trouble with me and my manuscripts than a thousand *dolls* would have done. Believe me, I have not forgotten your good nature in *this circle of sin*, and one day I trust I shall be able to evince my gratitude. Adieu,

yours, &c.

"P.S. Remember me to Dr. P."

Letter 17.

TO MISS ———.

"London, August 11, 1807.

"On Sunday next I set off for the Highlands. A friend of mine accompanies me in my carriage to Edinburgh. There we shall leave it, and proceed in a *tandem* (a species of open carriage) through the western passes to Inverary, where we shall purchase *shelties*, to enable us to view places inaccessible to *vehicular conveyances.* On the coast we shall hire a vessel, and visit the most remarkable of the Hebrides; and, if we have time and favourable weather, mean to sail as far as Iceland, only 300 miles from the northern extremity of Caledonia, to peep at *Hecla*. This last intention you will keep a secret, as my nice *mamma* would imagine I was on a Voyage of Discovery, and raise the accustomed *maternal warwhoop*.

"Last week I swam in the Thames from Lambeth through the two bridges, Westminster and Blackfriars, a distance, including the different turns and tacks made on the way, of three miles! You see I am in excellent training in case of a *squall* at sea. I mean to collect all the Erse traditions, poems, &c. &c., and translate, or expand the subject to fill a volume, which may appear next spring under the denomination of *'The Highland Harp,'* or some title equally *picturesque*. Of Bosworth Field, one book is finished, another just began. It will be a work of three or four years, and most probably never conclude. What would you say to some stanzas on Mount Hecla? they would be written at least with *fire*. How is the immortal Bran? and the Phoenix of canine quadrupeds, Boatswain? I have lately purchased a thorough-bred bull-dog, worthy to be the coadjutor of the aforesaid celestials—his name is *Smut*! —'Bear it, ye breezes, on your *balmy* wings.'

"Write to me before I set off, I conjure you, by the fifth rib of your grandfather. Ridge goes on well with the books—I thought that worthy had not done much in the country. In town they have been very successful; Carpenter (Moore's publisher) told me a few days ago they sold all theirs immediately, and had several enquiries made since, which, from the books being gone, they could not supply. The Duke of York, the Marchioness of Headfort, the Duchess of Gordon, &c. &c., were among the purchasers; and Crosby says, the circulation will be still more extensive in the winter, the summer season being very bad for a sale, as most people are absent from London. However, they have gone off extremely well altogether. I shall pass very near you on my journey through Newark, but cannot approach. Don't tell this to Mrs. B., who supposes I travel a different road. If you have a letter, order it to be left at Ridge's shop, where I shall call, or the post-office, Newark, about six or eight in the evening. If your brother would ride over, I should be devilish glad to see him—he can return the same night, or sup with us and go home the next morning—the Kingston Arms is my inn.

"Adieu, yours ever,

"BYRON."

LETTER 18.

TO MISS ———.

"Trinity College, Cambridge, October 26. 1807.

"My dear Elizabeth,

"Fatigued with sitting up till four in the morning for the last two days at hazard, I take up my pen to enquire how your highness and the rest of my female acquaintance at the seat of archiepiscopal grandeur go on. I know I deserve a scolding for my negligence in not writing more frequently; but racing up and down the country for these last three months, how was it possible to fulfil the duties of a correspondent? Fixed at last for six weeks, I write, as *thin* as ever (not having gained an ounce since my reduction), and rather in better humour;—but, after all, Southwell was a detestable residence. Thank St. Dominica, I have done with it: I have been twice within eight miles of it, but could not prevail on myself to *suffocate* in its heavy atmosphere. This place is wretched enough—a villanous chaos of din and drunkenness, nothing but hazard and burgundy, hunting, mathematics, and Newmarket, riot and racing. Yet it is a paradise compared with the eternal dulness of Southwell. Oh! the misery of doing nothing but make love, enemies, and *verses*.

"Next January, (but this is *entre nous only*, and pray let it be so, or my maternal persecutor will be throwing her tomahawk at any of my curious projects,) I am going to *sea* for four or five months, with my cousin Capt. Bettesworth, who commands the Tartar, the finest frigate in the navy. I have seen most scenes, and wish to look at a naval life. We are going probably to the Mediterranean, or to the West Indies, or—to the d——l; and if there is a possibility of taking me to the latter, Bettesworth will do it; for he has received four and twenty wounds in different places, and at this moment possesses a letter from the late Lord Nelson, stating Bettesworth as the only officer in the navy who had more wounds than himself.

"I have got a new friend, the finest in the world, a *tame bear*. When I brought him here, they asked me what I meant to do with him, and my reply was, 'he should *sit for a fellowship*.' Sherard will explain the meaning of the sentence, if it is ambiguous. This answer delighted them not. We have several parties here, and this evening a large assortment of jockeys, gamblers, boxers, authors, parsons, and poets, sup with me,—a precious mixture, but they go on well together; and for me, I am a *spice* of every thing except a jockey; by the by, I was dismounted again the other day.

Thank your brother in my name for his treatise. I have written 214 pages of a novel,—one poem of 380 lines, to be published (without my name) in a few weeks, with notes,—560 lines of Bosworth Field, and 250 lines of another poem in rhyme, besides half a dozen smaller pieces. The poem to be published is a Satire. *Apropos*, I have been praised to the skies in the Critical Review, and abused greatly in another publication. So much the better, they tell me, for the sale of the book: it keeps up controversy, and prevents it being forgotten. Besides, the first men of all ages have had their share, nor do the humblest escape;—so I bear it like a philosopher. It is odd two opposite critiques came out on the same day, and out of five pages of abuse, my censor only quotes *two lines* from different poems, in support of his opinion. Now, the proper way to *cut up*, is to quote long passages, and make them appear absurd, because simple allegation is no proof. On the other hand, there are seven pages of praise, and more than *my modesty* will allow, said on the subject. Adieu.

"P.S. Write, write, write!!!"

It was at the beginning of the following year that an acquaintance commenced between Lord Byron and a gentleman, related to his family by marriage, Mr. Dallas,—the author of some novels, popular, I believe, in their day, and also of a sort of Memoir of the noble Poet, published soon after his death, which, from being founded chiefly on original correspondence, is the most authentic and trust-worthy of any that have yet appeared. In the letters addressed by Lord Byron to this gentleman, among many details, curious in a literary point of view, we find, what is much more important for our present purpose, some particulars illustrative of the opinions which he had formed, at this time of his life, on the two subjects most connected with the early formation of character —morals and religion.

It is but rarely that infidelity or scepticism finds an entrance into youthful minds. That readiness to take the future upon trust, which is the charm of this period of life, would naturally, indeed, make it the season of belief as well as of hope. There are also then, still fresh in the mind, the impressions of early religious culture, which, even in those who begin soonest to question their faith, give way but slowly to the encroachments of doubt, and, in the mean time, extend the benefit of their moral restraint over a portion of life when it is acknowledged such restraints are most necessary. If exemption from the checks of religion be, as infidels themselves allow, a state of freedom from responsibility dangerous at all times, it must be peculiarly so in that season of temptation, youth, when the passions are sufficiently disposed to usurp a latitude for themselves, without taking a licence also from infidelity to enlarge their range. It is, therefore, fortunate that, for the causes just stated, the inroads of scepticism and disbelief should be seldom felt in the mind till a period of life when the character, already formed, is out of the reach of their disturbing influence,—when, being the result, however erroneous, of thought and reasoning, they are likely to partake of the sobriety of the process by which they were acquired, and, being considered but as matters of pure speculation, to have as little share in determining the mind towards evil as, too often, the most orthodox creed has, at the same age, in influencing it towards good.

While, in this manner, the moral qualities of the unbeliever himself are guarded from some of the mischiefs that might, at an earlier age, attend such doctrines, the danger also of his communicating the infection to others is, for reasons of a similar nature, considerably diminished. The same vanity or daring which may have prompted the youthful sceptic's opinions, will lead him likewise, it is probable, rashly and irreverently to avow them, without regard either to the effect of his example on those around him, or to the odium which, by such an avowal, he entails irreparably on himself. But, at a riper age, these consequences are, in general, more cautiously weighed. The infidel, if at all considerate of the happiness of others, will naturally pause before he chases from their hearts a hope of which his own feels the want so desolately.

If regardful only of himself, he will no less naturally shrink from the promulgation of opinions which, in no age, have men uttered with impunity. In either case there is a tolerably good security for his silence;—for, should benevolence not restrain him from making converts of others, prudence may, at least, prevent him from making a martyr of himself.

Unfortunately, Lord Byron was an exception to the usual course of such lapses. With him, the canker showed itself "in the morn and dew of youth," when the effect of such "blastments" is, for every reason, most fatal,—and, in addition to the real misfortune of being an unbeliever at any age, he exhibited the rare and melancholy spectacle of an unbelieving schoolboy. The same prematurity of developement which brought his passions and genius so early into action, enabled him also to anticipate this worst, dreariest result of reason; and at the very time of life when a spirit and temperament like his most required control, those checks, which religious pre-possessions best supply, were almost wholly wanting.

We have seen, in those two Addresses to the Deity which I have selected from among his unpublished poems, and still more strongly in a passage of the Catalogue of his studies, at what a boyish age the authority of all systems and sects was avowedly shaken off by his enquiring spirit. Yet, even in these, there is a fervour of adoration mingled with his defiance of creeds, through which the piety implanted in his nature (as it is deeply in all poetic natures) unequivocally shows itself; and had he then fallen within the reach of such guidance and example as would have seconded and fostered these natural dispositions, the licence of opinion into which he afterwards broke loose might have been averted. His scepticism, if not wholly removed, might have been softened down into that humble doubt, which, so far from being inconsistent with a religious spirit, is, perhaps, its best guard against presumption and uncharitableness; and, at all events, even if his own views of religion had not been brightened or elevated, he would have learned not wantonly to cloud or disturb those of others. But there was no such monitor near him. After his departure from Southwell, he had not a single friend or relative to whom he could look up with respect; but was thrown alone on the world, with his passions and his pride, to revel in the fatal discovery which he imagined himself to have made of the nothingness of the future, and the all-paramount claims of the present. By singular ill fortune, too, the individual who, among all his college friends, had taken the strongest hold on his admiration and affection, and whose loss he afterwards lamented with brotherly tenderness, was, to the same extent as himself, if not more strongly, a sceptic. Of this remarkable young man, Matthews, who was so early snatched away, and whose career in after-life, had it been at all answerable to the extraordinary promise of his youth, must have placed him upon a level with the first men of his day, a Memoir was, at one time, intended to be published by his relatives; and to Lord Byron, among others of his college friends, application, for assistance in the task, was addressed. The letter which this circumstance drew forth from the noble poet, besides containing many amusing traits of his friend, affords such an insight into his own habits of life at this period, that, though infringing upon the chronological order of his correspondence, I shall insert it here.

LETTER 19.

TO MR. MURRAY.

"Ravenna, 9bre 12. 1820.

"What you said of the late Charles Skinner Matthews has set me to my recollections; but I have not been able to turn up any thing which would do for the purposed Memoir of his brother,—even if he had previously done enough during his life to sanction the introduction of anecdotes so merely personal. He was, however, a very extraordinary man, and would have been a great one. No one ever succeeded in a more surpassing degree than he did, as far as he went. He was indolent, too; but whenever he stripped, he overthrew all antagonists. His conquests will be found registered at Cambridge, particularly his *Downing* one, which was hotly and highly contested, and yet easily *won*. Hobhouse was his most intimate friend, and can tell you more of him than any man. William Bankes also a great deal. I myself recollect more of his oddities than of his academical qualities, for we lived most together at a very idle period of *my* life. When I went up to Trinity, in 1805, at the age of seventeen and a half, I was miserable and untoward to a degree. I was wretched at leaving Harrow, to which I had become attached during the two last years of my stay there; wretched at going to Cambridge instead of Oxford (there were no rooms Vacant at Christ-church); wretched from some private domestic circumstances of different kinds, and consequently about as unsocial as a wolf taken from the troop. So that, although I knew Matthews, and met him often *then* at Bankes's, (who was my collegiate pastor, and master, and patron,) and at Rhode's, Milnes's, Price's, Dick's, Macnamara's, Farrell's, Galley Knight's, and others of that *set* of contemporaries, yet I was neither intimate with him nor with any one else, except my old schoolfellow Edward Long (with whom I used to pass the day in riding and swimming), and William Bankes, who was good-naturedly tolerant of my ferocities.

"It was not till 1807, after I had been upwards of a year away from Cambridge, to which I had returned again to *reside* for my degree, that I became one of Matthews's familiars, by means of H——, who, after hating me for two years, because I wore a *white hat*, and a *grey* coat, and rode a *grey* horse (as he says himself), took me into his good graces because I had written some poetry. I had always lived a good deal, and got drunk occasionally, in their company—but now we became really friends in a morning. Matthews, however, was not at this period resident in College. I met *him* chiefly in London, and at uncertain periods at Cambridge. H——, in the mean time, did great things: he founded the Cambridge 'Whig Club' (which he seems to have forgotten), and the 'Amicable Society,' which was dissolved in consequence of the members constantly quarrelling, and made himself very popular with 'us youth,' and no less formidable to all tutors, professors, and beads of Colleges. William B—— was gone; while he stayed, he ruled the roast—or rather the *roasting*—and was father of all mischiefs.

"Matthews and I, meeting in London, and elsewhere, became great cronies. He was not good tempered—nor am I—but with a little tact his temper was manageable, and I thought him so superior a man, that I was willing to sacrifice something to his humours, which were often, at the same time, amusing and provoking. What became of his *papers* (and he certainly had many), at the time of his death, was never known. I mention this by the way, fearing to skip it over, and *as* he *wrote* remarkably well, both in Latin and English. We went down to Newstead together, where I had got a famous cellar, and *Monks'* dresses from a masquerade warehouse. We were a company of some seven or eight, with an occasional neighbour or so for visitors, and used to sit up late in our friars' dresses, drinking burgundy, claret, champagne, and what not, out of the *skull-cup,* and all sorts of glasses, and buffooning all round the house, in our conventual garments. Matthews always denominated me 'the Abbot,' and never called me by any other name in his good humours, to the day of his death. The harmony of these our symposia was somewhat interrupted, a few days after our assembling, by Matthews's threatening to throw —— out of a *window,* in consequence of I know not what commerce of jokes ending in this epigram. —— came to me and said, that 'his respect and regard for me as host would not permit him to call out any of my guests, and that he should go to town next morning.' He did. It was in vain that I represented to him that the window was not high, and that the turf under it was particularly soft. Away he went.

"Matthews and myself had travelled down from London together, talking all the way incessantly upon one single topic. When we got to Loughborough, I know not what chasm had made us diverge for a moment to some other subject, at which he was indignant. 'Come,' said he, 'don't let us break through —let us go on as we began, to our journey's end;' and so he continued, and was as entertaining as ever to the very end. He had previously occupied, during my year's absence from Cambridge, my rooms in Trinity, with the furniture; and Jones, the tutor, in his odd way, had said, on putting him in, 'Mr. Matthews, I recommend to your attention not to damage any of the movables, for Lord Byron, Sir, is a young man of *tumultuous passions*.' Matthews was delighted with this; and whenever anybody came to visit him, begged them to handle the very door with caution; and used to repeat Jones's admonition in his tone and manner. There was a large mirror in the room, on which he remarked, 'that he thought his friends were grown uncommonly assiduous in coming to see *him*, but he soon discovered that they only came to *see themselves*.' Jones's phrase of '*tumultuous passions*,' and the whole scene, had put him into such good humour, that I verily believe that I owed to it a portion of his good graces.

"When at Newstead, somebody by accident rubbed against one of his white silk stockings, one day before dinner; of course the gentleman apologised. 'Sir,' answered Matthews, 'it may be all very well for you, who have a great many silk stockings, to dirty other people's; but to me, who have only this *one pair*, which I have put on in honour of the Abbot here, no apology can compensate for such carelessness; besides, the expense of washing.' He had the same sort of droll sardonic way about every thing. A wild Irishman, named F——, one evening beginning to say something at a large supper at Cambridge, Matthews roared out 'Silence!' and then, pointing to F——, cried out, in the words of the oracle, '*Orson is endowed with reason*.' You may easily suppose that Orson lost what reason he had acquired, on hearing this compliment. When H—— published his volume of poems, the Miscellany (which Matthews *would* call the '*Miss-sell-any*'), all that could be drawn from him was, that the preface was 'extremely like *Walsh*.' H—— thought this at first a compliment; but we never could make out what it was, for all we know of *Walsh* is his Ode to King William, and Pope's epithet of '*knowing Walsh*.' When the Newstead party broke up for London, H—— and Matthews, who were the greatest friends possible, agreed, for a whim, to *walk together* to town. They quarrelled by the way, and actually walked the latter half of their journey, occasionally passing and repassing, without speaking. When Matthews had got to Highgate, he had spent all his money but three-pence halfpenny, and determined to spend that also in a pint of beer, which I believe he was drinking before a public-house, as H—— passed him (still without speaking) for the last time on their route. They were reconciled in London again.

"One of Matthews's passions was 'the Fancy;' and he sparred uncommonly well. But he always got beaten in rows, or combats with the bare fist. In swimming, too, he swam well; but with *effort* and *labour*, and *too high* out of the water; so that Scrope Davies and myself, of whom he was therein somewhat emulous, always told him that he would be drowned if ever he came to a difficult pass in the water. He was so; but surely Scrope and myself would have been most heartily glad that "'the Dean had lived, And our prediction proved a lie.'

"His head was uncommonly handsome, very like what *Pope*'s was in his youth.

"His voice, and laugh, and features, are strongly resembled by his brother Henry's, if Henry be *he* of *King's College*. His passion for boxing was so great, that he actually wanted me to match him with Dogherty (whom I had backed and made the match for against Tom Belcher), and I saw them spar together at my own lodgings with the gloves on. As he was bent upon it, I would have backed Dogherty to please him, but the match went off. It was of course to have been a private fight, in a private room.

"On one occasion, being too late to go home and dress, he was equipped by a friend (Mr. Baillie, I believe,) in a magnificently fashionable and somewhat exaggerated shirt and neckcloth. He proceeded to the Opera, and took his station in Fops' Alley. During the interval between the opera and the ballet, an acquaintance took his station by him and saluted him: 'Come round,' said Matthews, 'come round.'—'Why should I come round?' said the other; 'you have only to turn your head—I am close by you.'—'That is exactly what I cannot do,' said Matthews; 'don't you see the state I am in?' pointing to his buckram shirt collar and inflexible cravat,—and there he stood with his head always in the same perpendicular position during the whole spectacle.

"One evening, after dining together, as we were going to the Opera, I happened to have a spare Opera ticket (as subscriber to a box), and presented it to Matthews. 'Now, sir,' said he to Hobhouse afterwards, 'this I call *courteous* in the Abbot—another man would never have thought that I might do better with half a guinea than throw it to a door-keeper;—but here is a man not only asks me to dinner, but gives me a ticket for the theatre.' These were only his oddities, for no man was more liberal, or more honourable in all his doings and dealings, than Matthews. He gave Hobhouse and me, before we set out for Constantinople, a most splendid entertainment, to which we did ample justice. One of his fancies was dining at all sorts of out-of-the-way places. Somebody popped upon him in I know not what coffee-house in the Strand—and what do you think was the attraction? Why, that he paid a shilling (I think) to *dine with his hat on*. This he called his '*hat* house,' and used to boast of the comfort of being covered at meal-times.

"When Sir Henry Smith was expelled from Cambridge for a row with a tradesman named 'Hiron,' Matthews solaced himself with shouting under Hiron's windows every evening,

"'Ah me! what perils do environThe man who meddles with *hot Hiron*.'

"He was also of that band of profane scoffers who, under the auspices of ———, used to rouse Lort Mansel (late Bishop of Bristol) from his slumbers in the lodge of Trinity; and when he appeared at the window foaming with wrath, and crying out, 'I know you, gentlemen, I know you!' were wont to reply, 'We beseech thee to hear us, good *Lort*'—'Good *Lort* deliver us!' (Lort was his Christian name.) As he was very free in his speculations upon all kinds of subjects, although by no means either dissolute or intemperate in his conduct, and as I was no less independent, our conversation and correspondence used to alarm our friend Hobhouse to a considerable degree.

"You must be almost tired of my packets, which will have cost a mint of postage.

"Salute Gifford and all my friends.

"Yours, &c."

As already, before his acquaintance with Mr. Matthews commenced, Lord Byron had begun to bewilder himself in the mazes of scepticism, it would be unjust to impute to this gentleman any further share in the formation of his noble friend's opinions than what arose from the natural influence of example and sympathy;—an influence which, as it was felt perhaps equally on both sides, rendered the contagion of their doctrines, in a great measure, reciprocal. In addition, too, to this community of sentiment on such subjects, they were both, in no ordinary degree, possessed by that dangerous spirit of ridicule, whose impulses even the pious cannot always restrain, and which draws the mind on, by a sort of irresistible fascination, to disport itself most wantonly on the brink of all that is most solemn and awful. It is not wonderful, therefore, that, in such society, the opinions of the noble poet should have been, at least, accelerated in that direction to which their bias already leaned; and though he cannot be said to have become thus confirmed in these doctrines,—as neither now, nor at any time of his life, was he a confirmed unbeliever,—he had undoubtedly learned to feel less uneasy under his scepticism, and even to mingle somewhat of boast and of levity with his expression of it. At the very first onset of his correspondence with Mr. Dallas, we find him proclaiming his sentiments on all such subjects with a flippancy and confidence far different from the tone in which he had first ventured on his doubts,—from that fervid sadness, as of a heart loth to part with its illusions, which breathes through every line of those prayers, that, but a year before, his pen had traced.

Here again, however, we should recollect, there must be a considerable share of allowance for his usual tendency to make the most and the worst of his own obliquities. There occurs, indeed, in his first letter to Mr. Dallas, an instance of this strange ambition,—the very reverse, it must be allowed, of hypocrisy,— which led him to court, rather than avoid, the reputation of profligacy, and to put, at all times, the worst face on his own character and conduct. His new correspondent having, in introducing himself to his acquaintance, passed some compliments on the tone of moral and charitable feeling which breathed through one of his poems, had added, that it "brought to his mind another noble author, who was not only a fine poet, orator, and historian, but one of the closest reasoners we have on the truth of that religion of which forgiveness is a prominent principle, the great and good Lord Lyttleton, whose fame will never die. His son," adds Mr. Dallas, "to whom he had transmitted genius, but not virtue, sparkled for a moment and went out like a star,—and with him the title became extinct." To this Lord Byron answers in the following letter:—

LETTER 20.

TO MR. DALLAS.

"Dorant's Hotel, Albemarle Street, Jan. 20. 1808.

"Sir,

"Your letter was not received till this morning, I presume from being addressed to me in Notts., where I have not resided since last June, and as the date is the 6th, you will excuse the delay of my answer.

"If the little volume you mention has given pleasure to the author of *Percival* and *Aubrey*, I am sufficiently repaid by his praise. Though our periodical censors have been uncommonly lenient, I confess a tribute from a man of acknowledged genius is still more flattering. But I am afraid I should forfeit all claim to candour, if I did not decline such praise as I do not deserve; and this is, I am sorry to say, the case in the present instance.

"My compositions speak for themselves, and must stand or fall by their own worth or demerit: *thus far* I feel highly gratified by your favourable opinion. But my pretensions to virtue are unluckily so few, that though I should be happy to merit, I cannot accept, your applause in that respect. One passage in your letter struck me forcibly: you mention the two Lords Lyttleton in a manner they respectively deserve, and will be surprised to hear the person who is now addressing you has been frequently compared to the *latter*. I know I am injuring myself in your esteem by this avowal, but the circumstance was so remarkable from your observation, that I cannot help relating the fact. The events of my short life have been of so singular a nature, that, though the pride commonly called honour has, and I trust ever will, prevent me from disgracing my name by a mean or cowardly action, I have been already held up as the votary of licentiousness, and the disciple of infidelity. How far justice may have dictated this accusation, I cannot pretend to say; but, like the *gentleman* to whom my religious friends, in the warmth of their charity, have already devoted me, I am made worse than I really am. However, to quit myself (the worst theme I could pitch upon), and return to my poems, I cannot sufficiently express my thanks, and I hope I shall some day have an opportunity of rendering them in person. A second edition is now in the press, with some additions and considerable omissions; you will allow me to present you with a copy. The Critical, Monthly, and Anti-Jacobin Reviews have been very indulgent; but the Eclectic has pronounced a furious Philippic, not against the *book* but the *author,* where you will find all I have mentioned asserted by a reverend divine who wrote the critique.

Your name and connection with our family have been long known to me, and I hope your person will be not less so: you will find me an excellent compound of a 'Brainless' and a 'Stanhope.' I am afraid you will hardly be able to read this, for my hand is almost as bad as my character; but you will find me, as legibly as possible,

"Your obliged and obedient servant,

"BYRON."

There is here, evidently, a degree of pride in being thought to resemble the wicked Lord Lyttleton; and, lest his known irregularities should not bear him out in the pretension, he refers mysteriously, as was his habit, to certain untold events of his life, to warrant the parallel. Mr. Dallas, who seems to have been but little prepared for such a reception of his compliments, escapes out of the difficulty by transferring to the young lord's "candour" the praise he had so thanklessly bestowed on his morals in general; adding, that from the design Lord Byron had expressed in his preface of resigning the service of the Muses for a different vocation, he had "conceived him bent on pursuits which lead to the character of a legislator and statesman;—had imagined him at one of the universities, training himself to habits of reasoning and eloquence, and storing up a large fund of history and law." It is in reply to this letter that the exposition of the noble poet's opinions, to which I have above alluded, is contained.

LETTER 21.

TO MR. DALLAS.

"Dorant's, January 21. 1808.

"Sir,

"Whenever leisure and inclination permit me the pleasure of a visit, I shall feel truly gratified in a personal acquaintance with one whose mind has been long known to me in his writings.

"You are so far correct in your conjecture, that I am a member of the University of Cambridge, where I shall take my degree of A. M. this term; but were reasoning, eloquence, or virtue, the objects of my search, Granta is not their metropolis, nor is the place of her situation an 'El Dorado,' far less an Utopia. The intellects of her children are as stagnant as her Cam, and their pursuits limited to the church—not of Christ, but of the nearest benefice.

"As to my reading, I believe I may aver, without hyperbole, it has been tolerably extensive in the historical; so that few nations exist, or have existed, with whose records I am not in some degree acquainted, from Herodotus down to Gibbon. Of the classics, I know about as much as most schoolboys after a discipline of thirteen years; of the law of the land as much as enables me to keep 'within the statute'—to use the poacher's vocabulary. I did study the 'Spirit of Laws' and the Law of Nations; but when I saw the latter violated every month, I gave up my attempts at so useless an accomplishment;—of geography, I have seen more land on maps than I should wish to traverse on foot;—of mathematics, enough to give me the headache without clearing the part affected;—of philosophy, astronomy, and metaphysics, more than I can comprehend; and of common sense so little, that I mean to leave a Byronian prize at each of our 'Almæ Matres' for the first discovery,—though I rather fear that of the longitude will precede it.

"I once thought myself a philosopher, and talked nonsense with great decorum: I defied pain, and preached up equanimity. For some time this did very well, for no one was in *pain* for me but my friends, and none lost their patience but my hearers. At last, a fall from my horse convinced me bodily suffering was an evil; and the worst of an argument overset my maxims and my temper at the same moment: so I quitted Zeno for Aristippus, and conceive that pleasure constitutes the το χαλον. I hold virtue, in general, or the virtues severally, to be only in the disposition, each a *feeling*, not a principle. I believe truth the prime attribute of the Deity, and death an eternal sleep, at least of the body. You have here a brief compendium of the sentiments of the *wicked* George Lord Byron; and, till I get a new suit, you will perceive I am badly clothed.

I remain," &c.

Though such was, doubtless, the general cast of his opinions at this time, it must be recollected, before we attach any particular importance to the details of his creed, that, in addition to the temptation, never easily resisted by him, of displaying his wit at the expense of his character, he was here addressing a person who, though, no doubt, well meaning, was evidently one of those officious, self-satisfied advisers, whom it was the delight of Lord Byron at all times to astonish and *mystify*. The tricks which, when a boy, he played upon the Nottingham quack, Lavender, were but the first of a long series with which, through life, he amused himself, at the expense of all the numerous quacks whom his celebrity and sociability drew around him.

The terms in which he speaks of the university in this letter agree in spirit with many passages both in the "Hours of Idleness," and his early Satire, and prove that, while Harrow was remembered by him with more affection, perhaps, than respect, Cambridge had not been able to inspire him with either. This feeling of distaste to his "nursing mother" he entertained in common with some of the most illustrious names of English literature. So great was Milton's hatred to Cambridge, that he had even conceived, says Warton, a dislike to the face of the country,—to the fields in its neighbourhood. The poet Gray thus speaks of the same university:—"Surely, it was of this place, now Cambridge, but formerly known by the name of Babylon, that the prophet spoke when he said, 'The wild beasts of the deserts shall dwell there, and their houses shall be full of doleful creatures, and owls shall build there, and satyrs shall dance there,'" &c. &c. The bitter recollections which Gibbon retained of Oxford, his own pen has recorded; and the cool contempt by which Locke avenged himself on the bigotry of the same seat of learning is even still more memorable.

In poets, such distasteful recollections of their collegiate life may well be thought to have their origin in that antipathy to the trammels of discipline, which is not unusually observable among the characteristics of genius, and which might be regarded, indeed, as a sort of instinct, implanted in it for its own preservation, if there be any truth in the opinion that a course of learned education is hurtful to the freshness and elasticity of the imaginative faculty. A right reverend writer, but little to be suspected of any desire to depreciate academical studies, not only puts the question, "Whether the usual forms of learning be not rather injurious to the true poet, than really assisting to him?" but appears strongly disposed to answer it in the affirmative,—giving, as an instance, in favour of this conclusion, the classic Addison, who, "as appears," he says, "from some original efforts in the sublime, allegorical way, had no want of natural talents for the greater poetry,—which yet were so restrained and disabled by his constant and superstitious study of the old classics, that he was, in fact, but a very ordinary poet."

It was, no doubt, under some such impression of the malign influence of a collegiate atmosphere upon genius, that Milton, in speaking of Cambridge, gave vent to the exclamation, that it was "a place quite incompatible with the votaries of Phœbus," and that Lord Byron, versifying a thought of his own, in the letter to Mr. Dallas just given, declares,

"Her Helicon is duller than her Cam."

The poet Dryden, too, who, like Milton, had incurred some mark of disgrace at Cambridge, seems to have entertained but little more veneration for his Alma Mater; and the verses in which he has praised Oxford at the expense of his own university were, it is probable, dictated much less by admiration of the one than by a desire to spite and depreciate the other.

Nor is it genius only that thus rebels against the discipline of the schools. Even the tamer quality of Taste, which it is the professed object of classical studies to cultivate, is sometimes found to turn restive under the pedantic *manège* to which it is subjected. It was not till released from the duty of reading Virgil as a task, that Gray could feel himself capable of enjoying the beauties of that poet; and Lord Byron was, to the last, unable to vanquish a similar prepossession, with which the same sort of school association had inoculated him, against Horace.

—"Though Time hath taught

My mind to meditate what then it learn'd,

Yet such the fix'd inveteracy wrought

By the impatience of my early thought,

That, with the freshness wearing out before

My mind could relish what it might have sought,

If free to choose, I cannot now restore

Its health; but what it then detested, still abhor.

"Then farewell, Horace; whom I hated so,

Not for thy faults, but mine; it is a curse

To understand, not feel thy lyric flow,

To comprehend, but never love thy verse."

Childe Harold, Canto IV

To the list of eminent poets, who have thus left on record their dislike and disapproval of the English system of education, are to be added, the distinguished names of Cowley, Addison, and Cowper; while, among the cases which, like those of Milton and Dryden, practically demonstrate the sort of inverse ratio that may exist between college honours and genius, must not be forgotten those of Swift, Goldsmith, and Churchill, to every one of whom some mark of incompetency was affixed by the respective universities, whose annals they adorn. When, in addition, too, to this rather ample catalogue of poets, whom the universities have sent forth either disloyal or dishonoured, we come to number over such names as those of Shakspeare and of Pope, followed by Gay, Thomson, Burns, Chatterton, &c., all of whom have attained their respective stations of eminence, without instruction or sanction from any college whatever, it forms altogether, it must be owned, a large portion of the poetical world, that must be subducted from the sphere of that nursing influence which the universities are supposed to exercise over the genius of the country.

The following letters, written at this time, contain some particulars which will not be found uninteresting.

LETTER 22.

TO MR. HENRY DRURY.

"Dorant's Hotel, Jan. 13. 1808.

"My dear Sir,

"Though the stupidity of my servants, or the porter of the house, in not showing you up stairs (where I should have joined you directly), prevented me the pleasure of seeing you yesterday, I hoped to meet you at some public place in the evening. However, my stars decreed otherwise, as they generally do, when I have any favour to request of them. I think you would have been surprised at my figure, for, since our last meeting, I am reduced four stone in weight. I then weighed fourteen stone seven pound, and now only *ten stone and a half*. I have disposed of my *superfluities* by means of hard exercise and abstinence.

"Should your Harrow engagements allow you to visit town between this and February, I shall be most happy to see you in Albemarle Street. If I am not so fortunate, I shall endeavour to join you for an afternoon at Harrow, though, I fear, your cellar will by no means contribute to my cure. As for my worthy preceptor, Dr. B., our encounter would by no means prevent the *mutual endearments* he and I were wont to lavish on each other. We have only spoken once since my departure from Harrow in 1805, and then he politely told Tatersall I was not a proper associate for his pupils. This was long before my strictures in verse; but, in plain *prose*, had I been some years older, I should have held my tongue on his perfections. But, being laid on my back, when that schoolboy thing was written—or rather dictated—expecting to rise no more, my physician having taken his sixteenth fee, and I his prescription, I could not quit this earth without leaving a memento of my constant attachment to Butler in gratitude for his manifold good offices.

"I meant to have been down in July; but thinking my appearance, immediately after the publication, would be construed into an insult, I directed my steps elsewhere. Besides, I heard that some of the boys had got hold of my Libellus, contrary to my wishes certainly, for I never transmitted a single copy till October, when I gave one to a boy, since gone, after repeated importunities.

You will, I trust, pardon this egotism. As you had touched on the subject I thought some explanation necessary. Defence I shall not attempt, 'Hic murus aheneus esto, nil conscire sibi'—and 'so on' (as Lord Baltimore said on his trial for a rape)—I have been so long at Trinity as to forget the conclusion of the line; but though I cannot finish my quotation, I will my letter, and entreat you to believe me,

gratefully and affectionately, &c.

"P.S. I will not lay a tax on your time by requiring an answer, lest you say, as Butler said to Tatersall (when I had written his reverence an impudent epistle on the expression before mentioned), viz. 'that I wanted to draw him into a correspondence.'"

LETTER 23.

TO MR. HARNESS.

"Dorant's Hotel, Albemarle Street, Feb. 11. 1808.

"My dear Harness,

"As I had no opportunity of returning my verbal thanks, I trust you will accept my written acknowledgments for the compliment you were pleased to pay some production of my unlucky muse last November,—I am induced to do this not less from the pleasure I feel in the praise of an old schoolfellow, than from justice to you, for I had heard the story with some slight variations. Indeed, when we met this morning, Wingfield had not undeceived me, but he will tell you that I displayed no resentment in mentioning what I had heard, though I was not sorry to discover the truth. Perhaps you hardly recollect, some years ago, a short, though, for the time, a warm friendship between us? Why it was not of longer duration, I know not. I have still a gift of yours in my possession, that must always prevent me from forgetting it. I also remember being favoured with the perusal of many of your compositions, and several other circumstances very pleasant in their day, which I will not force upon your memory, but entreat you to believe me, with much regret at their short continuance, and a hope they are not irrevocable,

yours very sincerely, &c.

"BYRON."

I have already mentioned the early friendship that subsisted between this gentleman and Lord Byron, as well as the coolness that succeeded it. The following extract from a letter with which Mr. Harness favoured me, in placing at my disposal those of his noble correspondent, will explain the circumstances that led, at this time, to their reconcilement; and the candid tribute, in the concluding sentences, to Lord Byron, will be found not less honourable to the reverend writer himself than to his friend.

"A coolness afterwards arose, which Byron alludes to in the first of the accompanying letters, and we never spoke during the last year of his remaining at school, nor till after the publication of his 'Hours of Idleness.' Lord Byron was then at Cambridge; I, in one of the upper forms, at Harrow. In an English theme I happened to quote from the volume, and mention it with praise. It was reported to Byron that I had, on the contrary, spoken slightingly of his work and of himself, for the purpose of conciliating the favour of Dr. Butler, the master, who had been severely satirised in one of the poems. Wingfield, who was afterwards Lord Powerscourt, a mutual friend of Byron and myself, disabused him of the error into which he had been led, and this was the occasion of the first letter of the collection. Our conversation was renewed and continued from that time till his going abroad. Whatever faults Lord Byron might have had towards others, to myself he was always uniformly affectionate. I have many slights and neglects towards him to reproach myself with; but I cannot call to mind a single instance of caprice or unkindness, in the whole course of our intimacy, to allege against him."

In the spring of this year (1808) appeared the memorable critique upon the "Hours of Idleness" in the Edinburgh Review. That he had some notice of what was to be expected from that quarter, appears by the following letter to his friend, Mr. Becher.

LETTER 24.

TO MR. BECHER.

"Dorant's Hotel, Feb. 26. 1803.

"My dear Becher,

"Now for Apollo. I am happy that you still retain your predilection, and that the public allow me some share of praise. I am of so much importance, that a most violent attack is preparing for me in the next number of the Edinburgh Review. This I had from the authority of a friend who has seen the proof and manuscript of the critique. You know the system of the Edinburgh gentlemen is universal attack. They praise none; and neither the public nor the author expects praise from them. It is, however, something to be noticed, as they profess to pass judgment only on works requiring the public attention. You will see this when it comes out;—it is, I understand, of the most unmerciful description; but I am aware of it, and hope you will not be hurt by its severity.

"Tell Mrs. Byron not to be out of humour with them, and to prepare her mind for the greatest hostility on their part. It will do no injury whatever, and I trust her mind will not be ruffled. They defeat their object by indiscriminate abuse, and they never praise except the partisans of Lord Holland and Co. It is nothing to be abused when Southey, Moore, Lauderdale, Strangford, and Payne Knight, share the same fate.

"I am sorry—but 'Childish Recollections' must be suppressed during this edition. I have altered, at your suggestion, the *obnoxious allusions* in the sixth stanza of my last ode.

"And now, my dear Becher, I must return my best acknowledgments for the interest you have taken in me and my poetical bantlings, and I shall ever be proud to show how much I esteem the *advice* and the *adviser*.

Believe me, most truly," &c.

Soon after this letter appeared the dreaded article,—an article which, if not "witty in itself," deserved eminently the credit of causing "wit in others." Seldom, indeed, has it fallen to the lot of the justest criticism to attain celebrity such as injustice has procured for this; nor as long as the short, but glorious race of Byron's genius is remembered, can the critic, whoever he may be, that so unintentionally ministered to its first start, be forgotten.

It is but justice, however, to remark,—without at the same time intending any excuse for the contemptuous tone of criticism assumed by the reviewer,—that the early verses of Lord Byron, however distinguished by tenderness and grace, give but little promise of those dazzling miracles of poesy with which he afterwards astonished and enchanted the world; and that, if his youthful verses now have a peculiar charm in our eyes, it is because we read them, as it were, by the light of his subsequent glory.

There is, indeed, one point of view, in which these productions are deeply and intrinsically interesting. As faithful reflections of his character at that period of life, they enable us to judge of what he was in his yet unadulterated state,— before disappointment had begun to embitter his ardent spirit, or the stirring up of the energies of his nature had brought into activity also its defects. Tracing him thus through these natural effusions of his young genius, we find him pictured exactly such, in all the features of his character, as every anecdote of his boyish days proves him really to have been, proud, daring, and passionate,—resentful of slight or injustice, but still more so in the cause of others than in his own; and yet, with all this vehemence, docile and placable, at the least touch of a hand authorised by love to guide him. The affectionateness, indeed, of his disposition, traceable as it is through every page of this volume, is yet but faintly done justice to, even by himself;—his whole youth being, from earliest childhood, a series of the most passionate attachments,—of those overflowings of the soul, both in friendship and love, which are still more rarely responded to than felt, and which, when checked or sent back upon the heart, are sure to turn into bitterness. We have seen also, in some of his early unpublished poems, how apparent, even through the doubts that already clouded them, are those feelings of piety which a soul like his could not but possess, and which, when afterwards diverted out of their legitimate channel, found a vent in the poetical worship of nature, and in that shadowy substitute for religion which superstition offers. When, in addition, too, to these traits of early character, we find scattered through his youthful poems such anticipations of the glory that awaited him,—such, alternately, proud and saddened glimpses into the future, as if he already felt the elements of something great within him, but doubted whether his destiny would allow him to bring it forth,—it is not wonderful that, with the whole of his career present to our imaginations, we should see a lustre round these first puerile attempts not really their own, but shed back upon them from the bright eminence which he afterwards attained; and that, in our indignation against the fastidious blindness of the critic, we should forget that he had not then the aid of this reflected charm, with which the subsequent achievements of the poet now irradiate all that bears his name.

The effect this criticism produced upon him can only be conceived by those who, besides having an adequate notion of what most poets would feel under such an attack, can understand all that there was in the temper and disposition of Lord Byron to make him feel it with tenfold more acuteness than others. We have seen with what feverish anxiety he awaited the verdicts of all the minor Reviews, and, from his sensibility to the praise of the meanest of these censors, may guess how painfully he must have writhed under the sneers of the highest. A friend, who found him in the first moments of excitement after reading the article, enquired anxiously whether he had just received a challenge?—not knowing how else to account for the fierce defiance of his looks. It would, indeed, be difficult for sculptor or painter to imagine a subject of more fearful beauty than the fine countenance of the young poet must have exhibited in the collected energy of that crisis. His pride had been wounded to the quick, and his ambition humbled;—but this feeling of humiliation lasted but for a moment. The very re-action of his spirit against aggression roused him to a full consciousness of his own powers; and the pain and the shame of the injury were forgotten in the proud certainty of revenge.

Among the less sentimental effects of this review upon his mind, he used to mention that, on the day he read it, he drank three bottles of claret to his own share after dinner;—that nothing, however, relieved him till he had given vent to his indignation in rhyme, and that "after the first twenty lines, he felt himself considerably better." His chief care, indeed, afterwards, was amiably devoted,—as we have seen it was, in like manner, *before* the criticism,—to allaying, as far as he could, the sensitiveness of his mother; who, not having the same motive or power to summon up a spirit of resistance, was, of course, more helplessly alive to this attack upon his fame, and felt it far more than, after the first burst of indignation, he did himself. But the state of his mind upon the subject will be best understood from the following letter.

LETTER 25.

TO MR. BECKER.

"Dorant's, March 28. 1808.

"I have lately received a copy of the new edition from Ridge, and it is high time for me to return my best thanks to you for the trouble you have taken in the superintendence. This I do most sincerely, and only regret that Ridge has not seconded you as I could wish,—at least, in the bindings, paper, &c., of the copy he sent to me. Perhaps those for the public may be more respectable in such articles.

You have seen the Edinburgh Review, of course. I regret that Mrs. Byron is so much annoyed. For my own part, these 'paper bullets of the brain' have only taught me to stand fire; and, as I have been lucky enough upon the whole, my repose and appetite are not discomposed. Pratt, the gleaner, author, poet, &c. &c., addressed a long rhyming epistle to me on the subject, by way of consolation; but it was not well done, so I do not send it, though the name of the man might make it go down. The E. R^S. have not performed their task well; at least the literati tell me this; and I think *I* could write a more sarcastic critique on *myself* than any yet published. For instance, instead of the remark, —ill-natured enough, but not keen,—about Macpherson, I (quoad reviewers) could have said, 'Alas, this imitation only proves the assertion of Dr. Johnson, that many men, women, and *children,* could write such poetry as Ossian's.'

"I am *thin* and in exercise. During the spring or summer I trust we shall meet. I hear Lord Ruthyn leaves Newstead in April. As soon as he quits it for ever, I wish much you would take a ride over, survey the mansion, and give me your candid opinion on the most advisable mode of proceeding with regard to the *house. Entre nous,* I am cursedly dipped; my debts, *every* thing inclusive, will be nine or ten thousand before I am twenty-one. But I have reason to think my property will turn out better than general expectation may conceive. Of Newstead I have little hope or care; but Hanson, my agent, intimated my Lancashire property was worth three Newsteads. I believe we have it hollow; though the defendants are protracting the surrender, if possible, till after my majority, for the purpose of forming some arrangement with me, thinking I shall probably prefer a sum in hand to a reversion. Newstead I may *sell;*—

perhaps I will not,—though of that more anon. I will come down in May or June.

"Yours most truly," &c.

The sort of life which he led at this period between the dissipations of London and of Cambridge, without a home to welcome, or even the roof of a single relative to receive him, was but little calculated to render him satisfied either with himself or the world. Unrestricted as he was by deference to any will but his own, even the pleasures to which he was naturally most inclined prematurely palled upon him, for want of those best zests of all enjoyment, rarity and restraint. I have already quoted, from one of his note-books, a passage descriptive of his feelings on first going to Cambridge, in which he says that "one of the deadliest and heaviest feelings of his life was to feel that he was no longer a boy."—"From that moment (he adds) I began to grow old in my own esteem, and in my esteem age is not estimable. I took my gradations in the vices with great promptitude, but they were not to my taste; for my early passions, though violent in the extreme, were concentrated, and hated division or spreading abroad. I could have left or lost the whole world with, or for, that which I loved; but, though my temperament was naturally burning, I could not share in the common-place libertinism of the place and time without disgust. And yet this very disgust, and my heart thrown back upon itself, threw me into excesses perhaps more fatal than those from which I shrunk, as fixing upon one (at a time) the passions which spread amongst many would have hurt only myself."

Though, from the causes here alleged, the irregularities he, at this period, gave way to were of a nature far less gross and miscellaneous than those, perhaps, of any of his associates, yet, partly from the vehemence which this concentration caused, and, still more, from that strange pride in his own errors, which led him always to bring them forth in the most conspicuous light, it so happened that one single indiscretion, in his hands, was made to *go farther*, if I may so express it, than a thousand in those of others. An instance of this, that occurred about the time of which we are speaking, was, I am inclined to think, the sole foundation of the mysterious allusions just cited. An amour (if it may be dignified with such a name) of that sort of casual description which less attachable natures would have forgotten, and more prudent ones at least concealed, was by him converted, at this period, and with circumstances of most unnecessary display, into a connection of some continuance,—the object of it not only becoming domesticated with him in lodgings at Brompton, but accompanied him afterwards, disguised in boy's clothes, to Brighton. He introduced this young person, who used to ride about with him in her male attire, as his younger brother; and the late Lady P——, who was at Brighton at the time, and had some suspicion of the real nature of the relationship, said one day to the poet's companion, "What a pretty horse that is you are riding!"—"Yes," answered the pretended cavalier, "it was *gave* me by my brother!"

Beattie tells us, of his ideal poet,—

"The exploits of strength, dexterity, or speed,To him nor vanity nor joy could bring."

But far different were the tastes of the real poet, Byron; and among the least romantic, perhaps, of the exercises in which he took delight was that of boxing or sparring. This taste it was that, at a very early period, brought him acquainted with the distinguished professor of that art, Mr. Jackson, for whom he continued through life to entertain the sincerest regard, one of his latest works containing a most cordial tribute not only to the professional, but social qualities of this sole prop and ornament of pugilism. During his stay at Brighton this year, Jackson was one of his most constant visiters,—the expense of the professor's chaise thither and back being always defrayed by his noble patron. He also honoured with his notice, at this time, D'Egville, the ballet-master, and Grimaldi; to the latter of whom he sent, as I understand, on one of his benefit nights, a present of five guineas.

Having been favoured by Mr. Jackson with copies of the few notes and letters, which he has preserved out of the many addressed to him by Lord Byron, I shall here lay before the reader one or two, which bear the date of the present year, and which, though referring to matters of no interest in themselves, give, perhaps, a better notion of the actual life and habits of the young poet, at this time, than could be afforded by the most elaborate and, in other respects, important correspondence. They will show, at least, how very little akin to romance were the early pursuits and associates of the author of Childe Harold, and, combined with what we know of the still less romantic youth of Shakspeare, prove how unhurt the vital principle of genius can preserve itself even in atmospheres apparently the most ungenial and noxious to it.

LETTER 26.

TO MR. JACKSON.

"N.A., Notts. September 18. 1808.

"Dear Jack,

"I wish you would inform me what has been done by Jekyll, at No. 40. Sloane Square, concerning the pony I returned as unsound.

"I have also to request you will call on Louch at Brompton, and enquire what the devil he meant by sending such an insolent letter to me at Brighton; and at the same time tell him I by no means can comply with the charge he has made for things pretended to be damaged.

"Ambrose behaved most scandalously about the pony. You may tell Jekyll if he does not refund the money, I shall put the affair into my lawyer's hands. Five and twenty guineas is a sound price for a pony, and by ——, if it costs me five hundred pounds, I will make an example of Mr. Jekyll, and that immediately, unless the cash is returned.

"Believe me, dear Jack," &c.

LETTER 27.

TO MR. JACKSON.

"N.A., Notts. October 4. 1808.

"You will make as good a bargain as possible with this Master Jekyll, if he is not a gentleman. If he is a *gentleman*, inform me, for I shall take very different steps. If he is not, you must get what you can of the money, for I have too much business on hand at present to commence an action. Besides, Ambrose is the man who ought to refund,—but I have done with him. You can settle with L. out of the balance, and dispose of the bidets, &c. as you best can.

"I should be very glad to see you here; but the house is filled with workmen, and undergoing a thorough repair. I hope, however, to be more fortunate before many months have elapsed.

"If you see Bold Webster, remember me to him, and tell him I have to regret Sydney, who has perished, I fear, in my rabbit warren, for we have seen nothing of him for the last fortnight.

"Adieu.—Believe me," &c.

LETTER 28.

TO MR. JACKSON.

"N.A., Notts. December 12. 1808.

"My dear Jack,

"You will get the greyhound from the owner at any price, and as many more of the same breed (male or female) as you can collect.

"Tell D'Egville his dress shall be returned—I am obliged to him for the pattern. I am sorry you should have so much trouble, but I was not aware of the difficulty of procuring the animals in question. I shall have finished part of my mansion in a few weeks, and, if you can pay me a visit at Christmas, I shall be very glad to see you.

"Believe me," &c.

The dress alluded to here was, no doubt, wanted for a private play, which he, at this time, got up at Newstead, and of which there are some further particulars in the annexed letter to Mr. Becher.

LETTER 29.

TO MR. BECHER.

"Newstead Abbey, Notts. Sept. 14. 1808.

"My dear Becher,

"I am much obliged to you for your enquiries, and shall profit by them accordingly. I am going to get up a play here; the hall will constitute a most admirable theatre. I have settled the dram. pers., and can do without ladies, as I have some young friends who will make tolerable substitutes for females, and we only want three male characters, beside Mr. Hobhouse and myself, for the play we have fixed on, which will be the Revenge. Pray direct Nicholson the carpenter to come over to me immediately, and inform me what day you will dine and pass the night here.

"Believe me," &c.

It was in the autumn of this year, as the letters I have just given indicate, that he, for the first time, took up his residence at Newstead Abbey. Having received the place in a most ruinous condition from the hands of its late occupant, Lord Grey de Ruthyn, he proceeded immediately to repair and fit up some of the apartments, so as to render them—more with a view to his mother's accommodation than his own—comfortably habitable. In one of his letters to Mrs. Byron, published by Mr. Dallas, he thus explains his views and intentions on this subject.

LETTER 30.

TO THE HONOURABLE MRS. BYRON.

"Newstead Abbey, Notts. October 7. 1808.

"Dear Madam,

"I have no beds for the H———s or any body else at present. The H———s sleep at Mansfield. I do not know, that I resemble Jean Jacques Rousseau. I have no ambition to be like so illustrious a madman—but this I know, that I shall live in my own manner, and as much alone as possible. When my rooms are ready I shall be glad to see you: at present it would be improper and uncomfortable to both parties. You can hardly object to my rendering my mansion habitable, notwithstanding my departure for Persia in March (or May at farthest), since *you* will be *tenant* till my return; and in case of any accident (for I have already arranged my will to be drawn up the moment I am twenty-one), I have taken care you shall have the house and manor for *life*, besides a sufficient income. So you see my improvements are not entirely selfish. As I have a friend here, we will go to the Infirmary Ball on the 12th; we will drink tea with Mrs. Byron at eight o'clock, and expect to see you at the ball. If that lady will allow us a couple of rooms to dress in, we shall be highly obliged:—if we are at the ball by ten or eleven it will be time enough, and we shall return to Newstead about three or four. Adieu.

"Believe me yours very truly,

"Byron."

The idea, entertained by Mrs. Byron, of a resemblance between her son and Rousseau was founded chiefly, we may suppose, on those habits of solitariness, in which he had even already shown a disposition to follow that self-contemplative philosopher, and which, manifesting themselves thus early, gained strength as he advanced in life. In one of his Journals, to which I frequently have occasion to refer, he thus, in questioning the justice of this comparison between himself and Rousseau, gives,—as usual, vividly,—some touches of his own disposition and habitudes:—

"My mother, before I was twenty, would have it that I was like Rousseau, and Madame de Staël used to say so too in 1813, and the Edinburgh Review has something of the sort in its critique on the fourth Canto of Childe Harold. I can't see any point of resemblance:—he wrote prose, I verse: he was of the people; I of the aristocracy:he was a philosopher; I am none: he published his first work at forty; I mine at eighteen: his first essay brought him universal applause; mine the contrary: he married his housekeeper; I could not keep house with my wife: he thought all the world in a plot against him; my little world seems to think me in a plot against it, if I may judge by their abuse in print and coterie: he liked botany; I like flowers, herbs, and trees, but know nothing of their pedigrees: he wrote music; I limit my knowledge of it to what I catch by *ear*—I never could learn any thing by *study*, not even a *language*—it was all by rote, and ear, and memory: he had a *bad* memory; I *had*, at least, an excellent one (ask Hodgson the poet—a good judge, for he has an astonishing one): he wrote with hesitation and care; I with rapidity, and rarely with pains: *he* could never ride, nor swim, nor 'was cunning of fence;' *I* am an excellent swimmer, a decent, though not at all a dashing, rider, (having staved in a rib at eighteen, in the course of scampering), and was sufficient of fence, particularly of the Highland broadsword,—not a bad boxer, when I could keep my temper, which was difficult, but which I strove to do ever since I knocked down Mr. Purling, and put his knee-pan out (with the gloves on), in Angelo's and Jackson's rooms in 1806, during the sparring,—and I was, besides, a very fair cricketer,—one of the Harrow eleven, when we played against Eton in 1805. Besides, Rousseau's way of life, his country, his manners, his whole character, were so very different, that I am at a loss to conceive how such a comparison could have arisen, as it has done three several times, and all in rather a remarkable manner. I forgot to say that *he* was also short-sighted, and that hitherto my eyes have been the contrary, to such a degree that, in the largest theatre of Bologna, I distinguished and read some busts and inscriptions, painted near the stage, from a box so distant and so *darkly* lighted, that none of the company (composed of young and very bright-eyed people, some of them in the same box,) could make out a letter, and thought it was a trick, though I had never been in that theatre before.

"Altogether, I think myself justified in thinking the comparison not well founded. I don't say this out of pique, for Rousseau was a great man; and the thing, if true, were flattering enough;—but I have no idea of being pleased with the chimera."

In another letter to his mother, dated some weeks after the preceding one, he explains further his plans both with respect to Newstead and his projected travels.

LETTER 31.

TO MRS. BYRON.

"Newstead Abbey, November 2. 1808.

"Dear Mother,

"If you please, we will forget the things you mention. I have no desire to remember them. When my rooms are finished, I shall be happy to see you; as I tell but the truth, you will not suspect me of evasion. I am furnishing the house more for you than myself, and I shall establish you in it before I sail for India, which I expect to do in March, if nothing particularly obstructive occurs. I am now fitting up the *green* drawing-room; the red for a bed-room, and the rooms over as sleeping-rooms. They will be soon completed;—at least I hope so.

"I wish you would enquire of Major Watson (who is an old Indian) what things will be necessary to provide for my voyage. I have already procured a friend to write to the Arabic Professor at Cambridge, for some information I am anxious to procure. I can easily get letters from government to the ambassadors, consuls, &c., and also to the governors at Calcutta and Madras. I shall place my property and my will in the hands of trustees till my return, and I mean to appoint you one. From H—— I have heard nothing—when I do, you shall have the particulars.

"After all, you must own my project is not a bad one. If I do not travel now, I never shall, and all men should one day or other. I have at present no connections to keep me at home; no wife, or unprovided sisters, brothers, &c. I shall take care of you, and when I return I may possibly become a politician. A few years' knowledge of other countries than our own will not incapacitate me for that part. If we see no nation but our own, we do not give mankind a fair chance:—it is from *experience,* not books, we ought to judge of them. There is nothing like inspection, and trusting to our own senses.

"Yours," &c.

In the November of this year he lost his favourite dog, Boatswain,—the poor animal having been seized with a fit of madness, at the commencement of which so little aware was Lord Byron of the nature of the malady, that he more than once, with his bare hand, wiped away the slaver from the dog's lips during the paroxysms. In a letter to his friend, Mr. Hodgson, he thus announces this event:—"Boatswain is dead!—he expired in a state of madness on the 18th, after suffering much, yet retaining all the gentleness of his nature to the last, never attempting to do the least injury to any one near him. I have now lost every thing except old Murray."

The monument raised by him to this dog,—the most memorable tribute of the kind, since the Dog's Grave, of old, at Salamis,—is still a conspicuous ornament of the gardens of Newstead. The misanthropic verses engraved upon it may be found among his poems, and the following is the inscription by which they are introduced:—

"Near this spot
Are deposited the Remains of one
Who possessed Beauty without Vanity,
Strength without Insolence,
Courage without Ferocity,
And all the Virtues of Man without his Vices.
This Praise, which would be unmeaning Flattery
If inscribed over human ashes,
Is but a just tribute to the Memory of
BOATSWAIN, a Dog,
Who was born at Newfoundland, May, 1803,
And died at Newstead Abbey, November 18. 1808."

The poet, Pope, when about the same age as the writer of this inscription, passed a similar eulogy on his dog, at the expense of human nature; adding, that "Histories are more full of examples of the fidelity of dogs than of friends." In a still sadder and bitterer spirit, Lord Byron writes of his favourite,

"To mark a friend's remains these stones arise;
I never knew but one, and here he lies."

Melancholy, indeed, seems to have been gaining fast upon his mind at this period. In another letter to Mr. Hodgson, he says,—"You know laughing is the sign of a rational animal—so says Dr. Smollet. I think so too, but unluckily my spirits don't always keep pace with my opinions."

Old Murray, the servant whom he mentions, in a preceding extract, as the only faithful follower now remaining to him, had long been in the service of the former lord, and was regarded by the young poet with a fondness of affection which it has seldom been the lot of age and dependence to inspire. "I have more than once," says a gentleman who was at this time a constant visiter at Newstead, "seen Lord Byron at the dinner-table fill out a tumbler of Madeira, and hand it over his shoulder to Joe Murray, who stood behind his chair, saying, with a cordiality that brightened his whole countenance, 'Here, my old fellow.'"

The unconcern with which he could sometimes allude to the defect in his foot is manifest from another passage in one of these letters to Mr. Hodgson. That gentleman having said jestingly that some of the verses in the "Hours of Idleness" were calculated to make schoolboys rebellious, Lord Byron answers —"If my songs have produced the glorious effects you mention, I shall be a complete Tyrtæus;—though I am sorry to say I resemble that interesting harper more in his person than in his poesy." Sometimes, too, even an allusion to this infirmity by others, when he could perceive that it was not offensively intended, was borne by him with the most perfect good humour. "I was once present," says the friend I have just mentioned, "in a large and mixed company, when a vulgar person asked him aloud—'Pray, my Lord, how is that foot of yours?'—'Thank you, sir,' answered Lord Byron, with the utmost mildness—'much the same as usual.'"

The following extract, relating to a reverend friend of his Lordship, is from another of his letters to Mr. Hodgson, this year:—

"A few weeks ago I wrote to ——, to request he would receive the son of a citizen of London, well known to me, as a pupil; the family having been particularly polite during the short time I was with them induced me to this application. Now, mark what follows, as somebody sublimely saith. On this day arrives an epistle signed ——, containing not the smallest reference to tuition or *in*tuition, but a *pe*tition for Robert Gregson, of pugilistic notoriety, now in bondage for certain paltry pounds sterling, and liable to take up his everlasting abode in Banco Regis. Had the letter been from any of my *lay* acquaintance, or, in short, from any person but the gentleman whose signature it bears, I should have marvelled not. If —— is serious, I congratulate pugilism on the acquisition of such a patron, and shall be most happy to advance any sum necessary for the liberation of the captive Gregson. But I certainly hope to be certified from you, or some respectable housekeeper, of the fact, before I write to —— on the subject. When I say the *fact*, I mean of the letter being written by ——, not having any doubt as to the authenticity of the statement. The letter is now before me, and I keep it for your perusal."

His time at Newstead during this autumn was principally occupied in enlarging and preparing his Satire for the press; and with the view, perhaps, of mellowing his own judgment of its merits, by keeping it some time before his eyes in a printed form, he had proofs taken off from the manuscript by his former publisher at Newark. It is somewhat remarkable, that, excited as he was by the attack of the reviewers, and possessing, at all times, such rapid powers of composition, he should have allowed so long an interval to elapse between the aggression and the revenge. But the importance of his next move in literature seems to have been fully appreciated by him. He saw that his chances of future eminence now depended upon the effort he was about to make, and therefore deliberately collected all his energies for the spring. Among the preparatives by which he disciplined his talent to the task was a deep study of the writings of Pope; and I have no doubt that from this period may be dated the enthusiastic admiration which he ever after cherished for this great poet,—an admiration which at last extinguished in him, after one or two trials, all hope of pre-eminence in the same track, and drove him thenceforth to seek renown in fields more open to competition.

The misanthropic mood of mind into which he had fallen at this time, from disappointed affections and thwarted hopes, made the office of satirist but too congenial and welcome to his spirit. Yet it is evident that this bitterness existed far more in his fancy than his heart; and that the sort of relief he now found in making war upon the world arose much less from the indiscriminate wounds he dealt around, than from the new sense of power he became conscious of in dealing them, and by which he more than recovered his former station in his own esteem. In truth, the versatility and ease with which, as shall presently be shown, he could, on the briefest consideration, shift from praise to censure, and, sometimes, almost as rapidly, from censure to praise, shows how fanciful and transient were the impressions under which he, in many instances, pronounced his judgments; and though it may in some degree deduct from the weight of his eulogy, absolves him also from any great depth of malice in his Satire.

His coming of age, in 1809, was celebrated at Newstead by such festivities as his narrow means and society could furnish. Besides the ritual roasting of an ox, there was a ball, it seems, given on the occasion,—of which the only particular I could collect, from the old domestic who mentioned it, was, that Mr. Hanson, the agent of her lord, was among the dancers. Of Lord Byron's own method of commemorating the day, I find the following curious record in a letter written from Genoa in 1822:—"Did I ever tell you that the day I came of age I dined on eggs and bacon and a bottle of ale?—For once in a way they are my favourite dish and drinkable; but as neither of them agree with me, I never use them but on great jubilees,—in four or five years or so." The pecuniary supplies necessary towards his outset, at this epoch, were procured from money-lenders at an enormously usurious interest, the payment of which for a long time continued to be a burden to him.

It was not till the beginning of this year that he took his Satire,—in a state ready, as he thought, for publication,—to London. Before, however, he had put the work to press, new food was unluckily furnished to his spleen by the neglect with which he conceived himself to have been treated by his guardian, Lord Carlisle. The relations between this nobleman and his ward had, at no time, been of such a nature as to afford opportunities for the cultivation of much friendliness on either side; and to the temper and influence of Mrs. Byron must mainly be attributed the blame of widening, if not of producing, this estrangement between them. The coldness with which Lord Carlisle had received the dedication of the young poet's first volume was, as we have seen from one of the letters of the latter, felt by him most deeply. He, however, allowed himself to be so far governed by prudential considerations as not only to stifle this displeasure, but even to introduce into his Satire, as originally intended for the press, the following compliment to his guardian:—

"On one alone Apollo deigns to smile,And crowns a new Roscommon in Carlisle."

The crown, however, thus generously awarded, did not long remain where it had been placed. In the interval between the inditing of this couplet and the delivery of the manuscript to the press, Lord Byron, under the impression that it was customary for a young peer, on first taking his seat, to have some friend to introduce him, wrote to remind Lord Carlisle that he should be of age at the commencement of the session. Instead, however, of the sort of answer which he expected, a mere formal, and, as it appeared to him, cold reply, acquainting him with the technical mode of proceeding on such occasions, was all that, in return to this application, he received. Disposed as he had been, by preceding circumstances, to suspect his noble guardian of no very friendly inclinations towards him, this backwardness in proposing to introduce him to the House (a ceremony, however, as it appears, by no means necessary or even usual) was sufficient to rouse in his sensitive mind a strong feeling of resentment. The indignation, thus excited, found a vent, but too temptingly, at hand;—the laudatory couplet I have just cited was instantly expunged, and his Satire went forth charged with those vituperative verses against Lord Carlisle, of which, gratifying as they must have been to his revenge at the moment, he, not long after, with the placability so inherent in his generous nature, repented.

During the progress of his poem through the press, he increased its length by more than a hundred lines; and made several alterations, one or two of which may be mentioned, as illustrative of that prompt susceptibility of new impressions and influences which rendered both his judgment and feelings so variable. In the Satire, as it originally stood, was the following couplet:—

"Though printers condescend the press to soilWith odes by Smythe, and epic songs by Hoyle."

Of the injustice of these lines (unjust, it is but fair to say, to both the writers mentioned,) he, on the brink of publication, repented; and,—as far, at least, as regarded one of the intended victims,—adopted a tone directly opposite in his printed Satire, where the name of Professor Smythe is mentioned honourably, as it deserved, in conjunction with that of Mr. Hodgson, one of the poet's most valued friends:—

"Oh dark asylum of a Vandal race!

At once the boast of learning and disgrace;

So sunk in dulness, and so lost in shame,

That Smythe and Hodgson scarce redeem thy fame."

In another instance we find him "changing his hand" with equal facility and suddenness. The original manuscript of the Satire contained this line,—

"I leave topography to coxcomb Gell;"

but having, while the work was printing, become acquainted with Sir William Gell, he, without difficulty, by the change of a single epithet, converted satire into eulogy, and the line now descends to posterity thus:—

"I leave topography to *classic* Gell."

Among the passages added to the poem during its progress through the press were those lines denouncing the licentiousness of the Opera. "Then let Ausonia," &c. which the young satirist wrote one night, after returning, brimful of morality, from the Opera, and sent them early next morning to Mr. Dallas for insertion. The just and animated tribute to Mr. Crabbe was also among the after-thoughts with which his poem was adorned; nor can we doubt that both this, and the equally merited eulogy on Mr. Rogers, were the disinterested and deliberate result of the young poet's judgment, as he had never at that period seen either of these distinguished persons, and the opinion he then expressed of their genius remained unchanged through life. With the author of the Pleasures of Memory he afterwards became intimate, but with him, whom he had so well designated as "Nature's sternest painter, yet the best," he was never lucky enough to form any acquaintance;—though, as my venerated friend and neighbour, Mr. Crabbe himself, tells me, they were once, without being aware of it, in the same inn together for a day or two, and must have frequently met, as they went in and out of the house, during the time.

Almost every second day, while the Satire was printing, Mr. Dallas, who had undertaken to superintend it through the press, received fresh matter, for the enrichment of its pages, from the author, whose mind, once excited on any subject, knew no end to the outpourings of its wealth. In one of his short notes to Mr. Dallas, he says, "Print soon, or I shall overflow with rhyme;" and it was, in the same manner, in all his subsequent publications,—as long, at least, as he remained within reach of the printer,—that he continued thus to feed the press, to the very last moment, with new and "thick-coming fancies," which the re-perusal of what he had already written suggested to him. It would almost seem, indeed, from the extreme facility and rapidity with which he produced some of his brightest passages during the progress of his works through the press, that there was in the very act of printing an excitement to his fancy, and that the rush of his thoughts towards this outlet gave increased life and freshness to their flow.

Among the passing events from which he now caught illustrations for his poem was the melancholy death of Lord Falkland,—a gallant, but dissipated naval officer, with whom the habits of his town life had brought him acquainted, and who, about the beginning of March, was killed in a duel by Mr. Powell. That this event affected Lord Byron very deeply, the few touching sentences devoted to it in his Satire prove. "On Sunday night (he says) I beheld Lord Falkland presiding at his own table in all the honest pride of hospitality; on Wednesday morning at three o'clock I saw stretched before me all that remained of courage, feeling, and a host of passions." But it was not by words only that he gave proof of sympathy on this occasion. The family of the unfortunate nobleman were left behind in circumstances which needed something more than the mere expression of compassion to alleviate them; and Lord Byron, notwithstanding the pressure of his own difficulties at the time, found means, seasonably and delicately, to assist the widow and children of his friend. In the following letter to Mrs. Byron, he mentions this among other matters of interest,—and in a tone of unostentatious sensibility highly honourable to him.

LETTER 32.

TO MRS. BYRON.

"8. St. James's Street, March 6. 1809.

"Dear Mother,

"My last letter was written under great depression of spirits from poor Falkland's death, who has left without a shilling four children and his wife. I have been endeavouring to assist them, which, God knows, I cannot do as I could wish, from my own embarrassments and the many claims upon me from other quarters.

"What you say is all very true: come what may, *Newstead* and I *stand* or fall together. I have now lived on the spot, I have fixed my heart upon it, and no pressure, present or future, shall induce me to barter the last vestige of our inheritance. I have that pride within me which will enable me to support difficulties. I can endure privations; but could I obtain in exchange for Newstead Abbey the first fortune in the country I would reject the proposition. Set your mind at ease on that score; Mr. H—— talks like a man of business on the subject,—I feel like a man of honour, and I will not sell Newstead.

"I shall get my seat on the return of the affidavits from Carhais, in Cornwall, and will do something in the House soon: I must dash, or it is all over. My Satire must be kept secret for a month; after that you may say what you please on the subject. Lord C. has used me infamously, and refused to state any particulars of my family to the Chancellor. I have *lashed* him in my rhymes, and perhaps his Lordship may regret not being more conciliatory. They tell me it will have a sale; I hope so, for the bookseller has behaved well, as far as publishing well goes.

"Believe me, &c.

"P.S.—You shall have a mortgage on one of the farms."

The affidavits which he here mentions, as expected from Cornwall, were those required in proof of the marriage of Admiral Byron with Miss Trevanion, the solemnisation of which having taken place, as it appears, in a private chapel at Carhais, no regular certificate of the ceremony could be produced. The delay in procuring other evidence, coupled with the refusal of Lord Carlisle to afford any explanations respecting his family, interposed those difficulties which he alludes to in the way of his taking his seat. At length, all the necessary proofs having been obtained, he, on the 13th of March, presented himself in the House of Lords, in a state more lone and unfriended, perhaps, than any youth of his high station had ever before been reduced to on such an occasion,—not having a single individual of his own class either to take him by the hand as friend or acknowledge him as acquaintance. To chance alone was he even indebted for being accompanied as far as the bar of the House by a very distant relative, who had been, little more than a year before, an utter stranger to him. This relative was Mr. Dallas; and the account which he has given of the whole scene is too striking in all its details to be related in any other words than his own:—

"The Satire was published about the middle of March, previous to which he took his seat in the House of Lords, on the 13th of the same month. On that day, passing down St. James's Street, but with no intention of calling, I saw his chariot at his door, and went in. His countenance, paler than usual, showed that his mind was agitated, and that he was thinking of the nobleman to whom he had once looked for a hand and countenance in his introduction to the House. He said to me—'I am glad you happened to come in; I am going to take my seat, perhaps you will go with me.' I expressed my readiness to attend him; while, at the same time, I concealed the shock I felt on thinking that this young man, who, by birth, fortune, and talent, stood high in life, should have lived so unconnected and neglected by persons of his own rank, that there was not a single member of the senate to which he belonged, to whom he could or would apply to introduce him in a manner becoming his birth. I saw that he felt the situation, and I fully partook his indignation.

"After some talk about the Satire, the last sheets of which were in the press, I accompanied Lord Byron to the House. He was received in one of the ante-chambers by some of the officers in attendance, with whom he settled respecting the fees he had to pay. One of them went to apprise the Lord Chancellor of his being there, and soon returned for him. There were very few persons in the House. Lord Eldon was going through some ordinary business. When Lord Byron entered, I thought he looked still paler than before; and he certainly wore a countenance in which mortification was mingled with, but subdued by, indignation. He passed the woolsack without looking round, and advanced to the table where the proper officer was attending to administer the oaths. When he had gone through them, the Chancellor quitted his seat, and went towards him with a smile, putting out his hand warmly to welcome him; and, though I did not catch his words, I saw that he paid him some compliment. This was all thrown away upon Lord Byron, who made a stiff bow, and put the tips of his fingers into the Chancellor's hand. The Chancellor did not press a welcome so received, but resumed his seat; while Lord Byron carelessly seated himself for a few minutes on one of the empty benches to the left of the throne, usually occupied by the lords in opposition. When, on his joining me, I expressed what I had felt, he said—'If I had shaken hands heartily, he would have set me down for one of his party—but I will have nothing to do with any of them, on either side; I have taken my seat, and now I will go abroad.' We returned to St. James's Street, but he did not recover his spirits."

To this account of a ceremonial so trying to the proud spirit engaged in it, and so little likely to abate the bitter feeling of misanthropy now growing upon him, I am enabled to add, from his own report in one of his note-books, the particulars of the short conversation which he held with the Lord Chancellor on the occasion:—

"When I came of age, some delays, on account of some birth and marriage certificates from Cornwall, occasioned me not to take my seat for several weeks. When these were over, and I had taken the oaths, the Chancellor apologised to me for the delay, observing 'that these forms were a part of his *duty*.' I begged him to make no apology, and added (as he certainly had shown no violent hurry), 'Your Lordship was exactly like Tom Thumb' (which was then being acted)—'you did your *duty*, and you did *no more*.'"

In a few days after, the Satire made its appearance; and one of the first copies was sent, with the following letter, to his friend Mr. Harness.

LETTER 33.

TO MR. HARNESS.

"8. St. James's Street, March 18. 1809.

"There was no necessity for your excuses: if you have time and inclination to write, 'for what we receive, the Lord make us thankful,'—if I do not hear from you I console myself with the idea that you are much more agreeably employed.

"I send down to you by this post a certain Satire lately published, and in return for the three and sixpence expenditure upon it, only beg that if you should guess the author, you will keep his name secret; at least for the present. London is full of the Duke's business. The Commons have been at it these last three nights, and are not yet come to a decision. I do not know if the affair will be brought before our House, unless in the shape of an impeachment. If it makes its appearance in a debatable form, I believe I shall be tempted to say something on the subject.—I am glad to hear you like Cambridge: firstly, because, to know that you are happy is pleasant to one who wishes you all possible sub-lunary enjoyment; and, secondly, I admire the morality of the sentiment. *Alma Mater* was to me *injusta noverca*; and the old beldam only gave me my M.A. degree because she could not avoid it.— You know what a farce a noble Cantab. must perform.

"I am going abroad, if possible, in the spring, and before I depart I am collecting the pictures of my most intimate schoolfellows; I have already a few, and shall want yours, or my cabinet will be incomplete. I have employed one of the first miniature painters of the day to take them, of course, at my own expense, as I never allow my acquaintance to incur the least expenditure to gratify a whim of mine. To mention this may seem indelicate; but when I tell you a friend of ours first refused to sit, under the idea that he was to disburse on the occasion, you will see that it is necessary to state these preliminaries to prevent the recurrence of any similar mistake. I shall see you in time, and will carry you to the *limner*. It will be a tax on your patience for a week, but pray excuse it, as it is possible the resemblance may be the sole trace I shall be able to preserve of our past friendship and acquaintance. Just now it seems foolish enough, but in a few years, when some of us are dead, and others are separated by inevitable circumstances, it will be a kind of satisfaction to retain in these images of the living the idea of our former selves, and to contemplate, in the resemblances of the dead, all that remains of judgment, feeling, and a host of passions. But all this will be dull enough for you, and so good night, and to end my chapter, or rather my homily, believe me, my dear H.,

yours most affectionately."

In this romantic design of collecting together the portraits of his school friends, we see the natural working of an ardent and disappointed heart, which, as the future began to darken upon it, clung with fondness to the recollections of the past; and, in despair of finding new and true friends, saw no happiness but in preserving all it could of the old. But even here, his sensibility had to encounter one of those freezing checks, to which feelings, so much above the ordinary temperature of the world, are but too constantly exposed;—it being from one of the very friends thus fondly valued by him, that he experienced, on leaving England, that mark of neglect of which he so indignantly complains in a note on the second Canto of Childe Harold,—contrasting with this conduct the fidelity and devotedness he had just found in his Turkish servant, Dervish. Mr. Dallas, who witnessed the immediate effect of this slight upon him, thus describes his emotion:—

"I found him bursting with indignation. 'Will you believe it?' said he, 'I have just met ——, and asked him to come and sit an hour with me: he excused himself; and what do you think was his excuse? He was engaged with his mother and some ladies to go shopping! And he knows I set out to-morrow, to be absent for years, perhaps never to return!—Friendship! I do not believe I shall leave behind me, yourself and family excepted, and perhaps my mother, a single being who will care what becomes of me.'"

From his expressions in a letter to Mrs. Byron, already cited, that he must "do something in the House soon," as well as from a more definite intimation of the same intention to Mr. Harness, it would appear that he had, at this time, serious thoughts of at once entering on the high political path which his station as an hereditary legislator opened to him. But, whatever may have been the first movements of his ambition in this direction, they were soon relinquished. Had he been connected with any distinguished political families, his love of eminence, seconded by such example and sympathy, would have impelled him, no doubt, to seek renown in the fields of party warfare where it might have been his fate to afford a signal instance of that transmuting process by which, as Pope says, the corruption of a poet sometimes leads to the generation of a statesman. Luckily, however, for the world (though whether luckily for himself may be questioned), the brighter empire of poesy was destined to claim him all its own. The loneliness, indeed, of his position in society at this period, left destitute, as he was, of all those sanctions and sympathies, by which youth at its first start is usually surrounded, was, of itself, enough to discourage him from embarking in a pursuit, where it is chiefly on such extrinsic advantages that any chance of success must depend. So far from taking an active part in the proceedings of his noble brethren, he appears to have regarded even the ceremony of his attendance among them as irksome and mortifying; and in a few days after his admission to his seat, he withdrew himself in disgust to the seclusion of his own Abbey, there to brood over the bitterness of premature experience, or meditate, in the scenes and adventures of other lands, a freer outlet for his impatient spirit than it could command at home.

It was not long, however, before he was summoned back to town by the success of his Satire,—the quick sale of which already rendered the preparation of a new edition necessary. His zealous agent, Mr. Dallas, had taken care to transmit to him, in his retirement, all the favourable opinions of the work he could collect; and it is not unamusing, as showing the sort of steps by which Fame at first mounts, to find the approbation of such authorities as Pratt and the magazine writers put forward among the first rewards and encouragements of a Byron.

"You are already (he says) pretty generally known to be the author. So Cawthorn tells me, and a proof occurred to myself at Hatchard's, the Queen's bookseller. On enquiring for the Satire, he told me that he had sold a great many, and had none left, and was going to send for more, which I afterwards found he did. I asked who was the author? He said it was believed to be Lord Byron's. Did *he* believe it? Yes he did. On asking the ground of his belief, he told me that a lady of distinction had, without hesitation, asked for it as Lord Byron's Satire. He likewise informed me that he had enquired of Mr. Gifford, who frequents his shop, if it was yours. Mr. Gifford denied any knowledge of the author, but spoke very highly of it, and said a copy had been sent to him. Hatchard assured me that all who came to his reading-room admired it. Cawthorn tells me it is universally well spoken of, not only among his own customers, but generally at all the booksellers. I heard it highly praised at my own publisher's, where I have lately called several times. At Phillips's it was read aloud by Pratt to a circle of literary guests, who were unanimous in their applause:—The *Anti-jacobin,* as well as the *Gentleman's Magazine,* has already blown the trump of fame for you. We shall see it in the other Reviews next month, and probably in some severely handled, according to the connection of the proprietors and editors with those whom it lashes."

On his arrival in London, towards the end of April, he found the first edition of his poem nearly exhausted; and set immediately about preparing another, to which he determined to prefix his name. The additions he now made to the work were considerable,—near a hundred new lines being introduced at the very opening,—and it was not till about the middle of the ensuing month that the new edition was ready to go to press. He had, during his absence from town, fixed definitely with his friend, Mr. Hobhouse, that they should leave England together on the following June, and it was his wish to see the last proofs of the volume corrected before his departure.

Among the new features of this edition was a Post-script to the Satire, in prose, which Mr. Dallas, much to the credit of his discretion and taste, most earnestly entreated the poet to suppress. It is to be regretted that the adviser did not succeed in his efforts, as there runs a tone of bravado through this ill-judged effusion, which it is, at all times, painful to see a brave man assume. For instance:—"It may be said," he observes, "that I quit England because I have censured these 'persons of honour and wit about town;' but I am coming back again, and their vengeance will keep hot till my return. Those who know me can testify that my motives for leaving England are very different from fears, literary or personal; those who do not may be one day convinced. Since the publication of this thing, my name has not been concealed; I have been mostly in London, ready to answer for my transgressions, and in daily expectation of sundry cartels; but, alas, 'the age of chivalry is over,' or, in the vulgar tongue, there is no spirit now-a-days."

But, whatever may have been the faults or indiscretions of this Satire, there are few who would now sit in judgment upon it so severely as did the author himself, on reading it over nine years after, when he had quitted England, never to return. The copy which he then perused is now in possession of Mr. Murray, and the remarks which he has scribbled over its pages are well worth transcribing. On the first leaf we find—

"The binding of this volume is considerably too valuable for its contents.

"Nothing but the consideration of its being the property of another prevents me from consigning this miserable record of misplaced anger and indiscriminate acrimony to the flames.

B."

Opposite the passage,

"to be misled By Jeffrey's heart, or Lamb's Bœotian head,"

is written, "This was not just. Neither the heart nor the head of these gentlemen are at all what they are here represented." Along the whole of the severe verses against Mr. Wordsworth he has scrawled "Unjust,"—and the same verdict is affixed to those against Mr. Coleridge. On his unmeasured attack upon Mr. Bowles, the comment is,—"Too savage all this on Bowles;" and down the margin of the page containing the lines, "Health to immortal Jeffrey," &c. he writes,—"Too ferocious—this is mere insanity;"—adding, on the verses that follow ("Can none remember that eventful day?" &c.), "All this is bad, because personal."

Sometimes, however, he shows a disposition to stand by his original decisions. Thus, on the passage relating to a writer of certain obscure Epics (v. 793.), he says,—"All right;" adding, of the same person, "I saw some letters of this fellow to an unfortunate poetess, whose productions (which the poor woman by no means thought vainly of) he attacked so roughly and bitterly, that I could hardly regret assailing him;—even were it unjust, which it is not; for, verily, he *is* an ass." On the strong lines, too (v. 953.), upon Clarke (a writer in a magazine called the Satirist), he remarks,—"Right enough,—this was well deserved and well laid on."

To the whole paragraph, beginning "Illustrious Holland," are affixed the words "Bad enough;—and on mistaken grounds besides." The bitter verses against Lord Carlisle he pronounces "Wrong also:—the provocation was not sufficient to justify such acerbity;"—and of a subsequent note respecting the same nobleman, he says, "Much too savage, whatever the foundation may be." Of Rosa Matilda (v. 738.) he tells us, "She has since married the Morning Post,—an exceeding good match." To the verses, "When some brisk youth, the tenant of a stall," &c., he has appended the following interesting note:—"This was meant at poor Blackett, who was then patronised by A.I.B.;—but *that* I did not know, or this would not have been written; at least I think not."

Farther on, where Mr. Campbell and other poets are mentioned, the following gingle on the names of their respective poems is scribbled:—

"Pretty Miss Jacqueline

Had a nose aquiline;

And would assert rude

Things of Miss Gertrude;

While Mr. Marmion

Led a great army on,

Making Kehama look

Like a fierce Mamaluke."

Opposite the paragraph in praise of Mr. Crabbe he has written, "I consider Crabbe and Coleridge as the first of these times in point of power and genius." On his own line, in a subsequent paragraph, "And glory, like the phoenix mid her fires," he says, comically, "The devil take that phoenix—how came it there?" and his concluding remark on the whole poem is as follows:—

"The greater part of this satire I most sincerely wish had never been written; not only on account of the injustice of much of the critical and some of the personal part of it, but the tone and temper are such as I cannot approve.

BYRON".

"Diodata, Geneva, July 14. 1816."

While engaged in preparing his new edition for the press, he was also gaily dispensing the hospitalities of Newstead to a party of young college friends, whom, with the prospect of so long an absence from England, he had assembled round him at the Abbey, for a sort of festive farewell. The following letter from one of the party, Charles Skinner Matthews, though containing much less of the noble host himself than we could have wished, yet, as a picture, taken freshly and at the moment, of a scene so pregnant with character, will, I have little doubt, be highly acceptable to the reader.

LETTER FROM CHARLES SKINNER MATTHEWS, ESQ. TO MISS I.M.

"London, May 22. 1809.

"My dear ——,

"I must begin with giving you a few particulars of the singular place which I have lately quitted.

"Newstead Abbey is situate 136 miles from London,—four on this side Mansfield. It is so fine a piece of antiquity, that I should think there must be a description, and, perhaps, a picture of it in Grose. The ancestors of its present owner came into possession of it at the time of the dissolution of the monasteries,—but the building itself is of a much earlier date. Though sadly fallen to decay, it is still completely an *abbey*, and most part of it is still standing in the same state as when it was first built. There are two tiers of cloisters, with a variety of cells and rooms about them, which, though not inhabited, nor in an inhabitable state, might easily be made so; and many of the original rooms, amongst which is a fine stone hall, are still in use. Of the abbey church only one end remains; and the old kitchen, with a long range of apartments, is reduced to a heap of rubbish. Leading from the abbey to the modern part of the habitation is a noble room seventy feet in length, and twenty-three in breadth; but every part of the house displays neglect and decay, save those which the present Lord has lately fitted up.

"The house and gardens are entirely surrounded by a wall with battlements. In front is a large lake, bordered here and there with castellated buildings, the chief of which stands on an eminence at the further extremity of it. Fancy all this surrounded with bleak and barren hills, with scarce a tree to be seen for miles, except a solitary clump or two, and you will have some idea of Newstead. For the late Lord being at enmity with his son, to whom the estate was secured by entail, resolved, out of spite to the same, that the estate should descend to him in as miserable a plight as he could possibly reduce it to; for which cause, he took no care of the mansion, and fell to lopping of every tree he could lay his hands on, so furiously, that he reduced immense tracts of woodland country to the desolate state I have just described. However, his son died before him, so that all his rage was thrown away.

"So much for the place, concerning which I have thrown together these few particulars, meaning my account to be, like the place itself, without any order or connection. But if the place itself appear rather strange to you, the ways of the inhabitants will not appear much less so. Ascend, then, with me the hall steps, that I may introduce you to my Lord and his visitants. But have a care how you proceed; be mindful to go there in broad daylight, and with your eyes about you. For, should you make any blunder,—should you go to the right of the hall steps, you are laid hold of by a bear; and should you go to the left, your case is still worse, for you run full against a wolf!—Nor, when you have attained the door, is your danger over; for the hall being decayed, and therefore standing in need of repair, a bevy of inmates are very probably banging at one end of it with their pistols; so that if you enter without giving loud notice of your approach, you have only escaped the wolf and the bear to expire by the pistol-shots of the merry monks of Newstead.

"Our party consisted of Lord Byron and four others, and was, now and then, increased by the presence of a neighbouring parson. As for our way of living, the order of the day was generally this:—for breakfast we had no set hour, but each suited his own convenience,—every thing remaining on the table till the whole party had done; though had one wished to breakfast at the early hour of ten, one would have been rather lucky to find any of the servants up. Our average hour of rising was one. I, who generally got up between eleven and twelve, was always,—even when an invalid,—the first of the party, and was esteemed a prodigy of early rising. It was frequently past two before the breakfast party broke up. Then, for the amusements of the morning, there was reading, fencing, single-stick, or shuttle-cock, in the great room; practising with pistols in the hall; walking—riding—cricket—sailing on the lake, playing with the bear, or teasing the wolf. Between seven and eight we dined; and our evening lasted from that time till one, two, or three in the morning. The evening diversions may be easily conceived.

"I must not omit the custom of handing round, after dinner, on the removal of the cloth, a human skull filled with burgundy. After revelling on choice viands, and the finest wines of France, we adjourned to tea, where we amused ourselves with reading, or improving conversation,—each, according to his fancy,—and, after sandwiches, &c. retired to rest. A set of monkish dresses, which had been provided, with all the proper apparatus of crosses, beads, tonsures, &c. often gave a variety to our appearance, and to our pursuits.

"You may easily imagine how chagrined I was at being ill nearly the first half of the time I was there. But I was led into a very different reflection from that of Dr. Swift, who left Pope's house without ceremony, and afterwards informed him, by letter, that it was impossible for two sick friends to live together; for I found my shivering and invalid frame so perpetually annoyed by the thoughtless and tumultuous health of every one about me, that I heartily wished every soul in the house to be as ill as myself.

"The journey back I performed on foot, together with another of the guests. We walked about twenty-five miles a day; but were a week on the road, from being detained by the rain.

"So here I close my account of an expedition which has somewhat extended my knowledge of this country. And where do you think I am going next? To Constantinople!—at least, such an excursion has been proposed to me. Lord B. and another friend of mine are going thither next month, and have asked me to join the party; but it seems to be but a wild scheme, and requires twice thinking upon.

"Addio, my dear I., yours very affectionately,

"C.S. MATTHEWS."

Having put the finishing hand to his new edition, he, without waiting for the fresh honours that were in store for him, took leave of London (whither he had returned) on the 11th of June, and, in about a fortnight after, sailed for Lisbon.

Great as was the advance which his powers had made, under the influence of that resentment from which he now drew his inspiration, they were yet, even in his Satire, at an immeasurable distance from the point to which they afterwards so triumphantly rose. It is, indeed, remarkable that, essentially as his genius seemed connected with, and, as it were, springing out of his character, the developement of the one should so long have preceded the full maturity of the resources of the other. By her very early and rapid expansion of his sensibilities, Nature had given him notice of what she destined him for, long before he understood the call; and those materials of poetry with which his own fervid temperament abounded were but by slow degrees, and after much self-meditation, revealed to him. In his Satire, though vigorous, there is but little foretaste of the wonders that followed it. His spirit was stirred, but he had not yet looked down into its depths, nor does even his bitterness taste of the bottom of the heart, like those sarcasms which he afterwards flung in the face of mankind. Still less had the other countless feelings and passions, with which his soul had been long labouring, found an organ worthy of them;—the gloom, the grandeur, the tenderness of his nature, all were left without a voice, till his mighty genius, at last, awakened in its strength.

In stooping, as he did, to write after established models, as well in the Satire as in his still earlier poems, he showed how little he had yet explored his own original resources, or found out those distinctive marks by which he was to be known through all times. But, bold and energetic as was his general character, he was, in a remarkable degree, diffident in his intellectual powers. The consciousness of what he could achieve was but by degrees forced upon him, and the discovery of so rich a mine of genius in his soul came with no less surprise on himself than on the world. It was from the same slowness of self-appreciation that, afterwards, in the full flow of his fame, he long doubted, as we shall see, his own aptitude for works of wit and humour,—till the happy experiment of "Beppo" at once dissipated this distrust, and opened a new region of triumph to his versatile and boundless powers.

But, however far short of himself his first writings must be considered, there is in his Satire a liveliness of thought, and still more a vigour and courage, which, concurring with the justice of his cause and the sympathies of the public on his side, could not fail to attach instant celebrity to his name. Notwithstanding, too, the general boldness and recklessness of his tone, there were occasionally mingled with this defiance some allusions to his own fate and character, whose affecting earnestness seemed to answer for their truth, and which were of a nature strongly to awaken curiosity as well as interest. One or two of these passages, as illustrative of the state of his mind at this period, I shall here extract. The loose and unfenced state in which his youth was left to grow wild upon the world is thus touchingly alluded to:—

"Ev'n I, least thinking of a thoughtless throng,

Just skill'd to know the right and choose the wrong,

Freed at that age when Reason's shield is lost

To fight my course through Passion's countless host,

Whom every path of Pleasure's flowery way

Has lured in turn, and all have led astray—

Ev'n I must raise my voice, ev'n I must feel

Such scenes, such men destroy the public weal:

Although some kind, censorious friend will say,

'What art thou better, meddling fool, than they?'

And every brother Rake will smile to see

That miracle, a Moralist, in me."

But the passage in which, hastily thrown off as it is, we find the strongest traces of that wounded feeling, which bleeds, as it were, through all his subsequent writings, is the following:—

"The time hath been, when no harsh sound would fall

From lips that now may seem imbued with gall,

Nor fools nor follies tempt me to despise

The meanest thing that crawl'd beneath my eyes.

But now so callous grown, so changed from youth," &c.

Some of the causes that worked this change in his character have been intimated in the course of the preceding pages. That there was no tinge of bitterness in his natural disposition, we have abundant testimony, besides his own, to prove. Though, as a child, occasionally passionate and headstrong, his docility and kindness towards those who were themselves kind, is acknowledged by all; and "playful" and "affectionate" are invariably the epithets by which those who knew him in his childhood convey their impression of his character.

Of all the qualities, indeed, of his nature, affectionateness seems to have been the most ardent and most deep. A disposition, on his own side, to form strong attachments, and a yearning desire after affection in return, were the feeling and the want that formed the dream and torment of his existence. We have seen with what passionate enthusiasm he threw himself into his boyish friendships. The all-absorbing and unsuccessful love that followed was, if I may so say, the agony, without being the death, of this unsated desire, which lived on through his life, and filled his poetry with the very soul of tenderness, lent the colouring of its light to even those unworthy ties which vanity or passion led him afterwards to form, and was the last aspiration of his fervid spirit in those stanzas written but a few months before his death:—

"'Tis time this heart should be unmoved,

Since others it has ceased to move;

Yet, though I cannot be beloved,

Still let me love!"

It is much, I own, to be questioned, whether, even under the most favourable circumstances, a disposition such as I have here described could have escaped ultimate disappointment, or found any where a resting-place for its imaginings and desires. But, in the case of Lord Byron, disappointment met him on the very threshold of life. His mother, to whom his affections first, naturally with ardour, turned, either repelled them rudely, or capriciously trifled with them. In speaking of his early days to a friend at Genoa, a short time before his departure for Greece, he traced the first feelings of pain and humiliation he had ever known to the coldness with which his mother had received his caresses in infancy, and the frequent taunts on his personal deformity with which she had wounded him.

The sympathy of a sister's love, of all the influences on the mind of a youth the most softening, was also, in his early days, denied to him,—his sister Augusta and he having seen but little of each other while young. A vent through the calm channel of domestic affections might have brought down the high current of his feelings to a level nearer that of the world he had to traverse, and thus saved them from the tumultuous rapids and falls to which this early elevation, in their after-course, exposed them. In the dearth of all home-endearments, his heart had no other resource but in those boyish friendships which he formed at school; and when these were interrupted by his removal to Cambridge, he was again thrown back, isolated, on his own restless desires. Then followed his ill-fated attachment to Miss Chaworth, to which, more than to any other cause, he himself attributed the desolating change then wrought in his disposition.

"I doubt sometimes (he says, in his 'Detached Thoughts,') whether, after all, a quiet and unagitated life would have suited me; yet I sometimes long for it. My earliest dreams (as most boys' dreams are) were martial; but a little later they were all for *love* and retirement, till the hopeless attachment to M—— C —— began and continued (though sedulously concealed) *very* early in my teens; and so upwards for a time. *This* threw me out again 'alone on a wide, wide sea.' In the year 1804 I recollect meeting my sister at General Harcourt's, in Portland Place. I was then *one thing,* and *as* she had always till then found me. When we met again in 1805 (she told me since) that my temper and disposition were so completely altered, that I was hardly to be recognised. I was not then sensible of the change; but I can believe it, and account for it."

I have already described his parting with Miss Chaworth previously to her marriage. Once again, after that event, he saw her, and for the last time,—being invited by Mr. Chaworth to dine at Annesley not long before his departure from England. The few years that had elapsed since their last meeting had made a considerable change in the appearance and manners of the young poet. The fat, unformed schoolboy was now a slender and graceful young man. Those emotions and passions which at first heighten, and then destroy, beauty, had as yet produced only their favourable effects on his features; and, though with but little aid from the example of refined society, his manners had subsided into that tone of gentleness and self-possession which more than any thing marks the well-bred gentleman. Once only was the latter of these qualities put to the trial, when the little daughter of his fair hostess was brought into the room. At the sight of the child he started involuntarily,—it was with the utmost difficulty he could conceal his emotion; and to the sensations of that moment we are indebted for those touching stanzas, "Well—thou art happy," &c., which appeared afterwards in a Miscellany published by one of his friends, and are now to be found in the general collection of his works. Under the influence of the same despondent passion, he wrote two other poems at this period, from which, as they exist only in the Miscellany I have just alluded to, and that collection has for some time been out of print, a few stanzas may, not improperly, be extracted here.

"THE FAREWELL—TO A LADY.

"When man, expell'd from Eden's bowers,

A moment linger'd near the gate,

Each scene recall'd the vanish'd hours,

And bade him curse his future fate.

"But wandering on through distant climes,

He learnt to bear his load of grief;

Just gave a sigh to other times,

And found in busier scenes relief.

"Thus, lady, must it be with me,

And I must view thy charms no more!

For, whilst I linger near to thee,

I sigh for all I knew before," &c. &c.

The other poem is, throughout, full of tenderness; but I shall give only what appear to me the most striking stanzas.

"STANZAS TO —— ON LEAVING ENGLAND.

"'Tis done—and shivering in the gale

The bark unfurls her snowy sail;

And whistling o'er the bending mast,

Loud sings on high the fresh'ning blast;

And I must from this land be gone,

Because I cannot love but one.

"As some lone bird, without a mate,

My weary heart is desolate;

I look around, and cannot trace

One friendly smile or welcome face,

And ev'n in crowds am still alone,

Because I cannot love but one.

"And I will cross the whitening foam,

And I will seek a foreign home;

Till I forget a false fair face,

I ne'er shall find a resting-place;

My own dark thoughts I cannot shun,

But ever love, and love but one.

"I go—but wheresoe'er I flee

There's not an eye will weep for me;

There's not a kind congenial heart,

Where I can claim the meanest part;

Nor thou, who hast my hopes undone,

Wilt sigh, although I love but one.

"To think of every early scene,

Of what we are, and what we've been,

Would whelm some softer hearts with woe—

But mine, alas! has stood the blow;

Yet still beats on as it begun,

And never truly loves but one.

"And who that dear loved one may be

Is not for vulgar eyes to see,

And why that early love was crost,

Thou know'st the best, I feel the most;

But few that dwell beneath the sun

Have loved so long, and loved but one.

"I've tried another's fetters, too,

With charms, perchance, as fair to view;

And I would fain have loved as well,

But some unconquerable spell

Forbade my bleeding breast to own

A kindred care for aught but one.

"'Twould soothe to take one lingering view,

And bless thee in my last adieu;

Yet wish I not those eyes to weep

For him that wanders o'er the deep;

His home, his hope, his youth, are gone,

Yet still he loves, and loves but one."

While thus, in all the relations of the heart, his thirst after affection was thwarted, in another instinct of his nature, not less strong—the desire of eminence and distinction—he was, in an equal degree, checked in his aspirings, and mortified. The inadequacy of his means to his station was early a source of embarrassment and humiliation to him; and those high, patrician notions of birth in which he indulged but made the disparity between his fortune and his rank the more galling. Ambition, however, soon whispered to him that there were other and nobler ways to distinction. The eminence which talent builds for itself might, one day, he proudly felt, be his own; nor was it too sanguine to hope that, under the favour accorded usually to youth, he might with impunity venture on his first steps to fame. But here, as in every other object of his heart, disappointment and mortification awaited him. Instead of experiencing the ordinary forbearance, if not indulgence, with which young aspirants for fame are received by their critics, he found himself instantly the victim of such unmeasured severity as is not often dealt out even to veteran offenders in literature; and, with a heart fresh from the trials of disappointed love, saw those resources and consolations which he had sought in the exercise of his intellectual strength also invaded.

While thus prematurely broken into the pains of life, a no less darkening effect was produced upon him by too early an initiation into its pleasures. That charm with which the fancy of youth invests an untried world was, in his case, soon dissipated. His passions had, at the very onset of their career, forestalled the future; and the blank void that followed was by himself considered as one of the causes of that melancholy, which now settled so deeply into his character.

"My passions" (he says, in his 'Detached Thoughts') "were developed very early—so early that few would believe me if I were to state the period and the facts which accompanied it. Perhaps this was one of the reasons which caused the anticipated melancholy of my thoughts,—having anticipated life. My earlier poems are the thoughts of one at least ten years older than the age at which they were written,—I don't mean for their solidity, but their experience. The two first Cantos of Childe Harold were completed at twenty-two; and they are written as if by a man older than I shall probably ever be."

Though the allusions in the first sentence of this extract have reference to a much earlier period, they afford an opportunity of remarking, that however dissipated may have been the life which he led during the two or three years previous to his departure on his travels, yet the notion caught up by many, from his own allusions, in Childe Harold, to irregularities and orgies of which Newstead had been the scene, is, like most other imputations against him, founded on his own testimony, greatly exaggerated. He describes, it is well known, the home of his poetical representative as a "monastic dome, condemned to uses vile," and then adds,—

"Where Superstition once had made her den,Now Paphian girls were known to sing and smile."

Mr. Dallas, too, giving in to the same strain of exaggeration, says, in speaking of the poet's preparations for his departure, "already satiated with pleasure, and disgusted with those companions who have no other resource, he had resolved on mastering his appetites;—he broke up his harams." The truth, however, is, that the narrowness of Lord Byron's means would alone have prevented such oriental luxuries. The mode of his life at Newstead was simple and unexpensive. His companions, though not averse to convivial indulgences, were of habits and tastes too intellectual for mere vulgar debauchery; and, with respect to the alleged "harams," it appears certain that one or two suspected "*subintroductæ*" (as the ancient monks of the abbey would have styled them), and those, too, among the ordinary menials of the establishment, were all that even scandal itself could ever fix upon to warrant such an assumption.

That gaming was among his follies at this period he himself tells us in the journal I have just cited:—

"I have a notion (he says) that gamblers are as happy as many people, being always *excited*. Women, wine, fame, the table,—even ambition, *sate* now and then; but every turn of the card and cast of the dice keeps the gamester alive: besides, one can game ten times longer than one can do any thing else. I was very fond of it when young, that is to say, of hazard, for I hate all *card* games, —even faro. When macco (or whatever they spell it) was introduced, I gave up the whole thing, for I loved and missed the *rattle* and *dash* of the box and dice, and the glorious uncertainty, not only of good luck or bad luck, but of *any luck at all,* as one had sometimes to throw *often* to decide at all. I have thrown as many as fourteen mains running, and carried off all the cash upon the table occasionally; but I had no coolness, or judgment, or calculation. It was the delight of the thing that pleased me. Upon the whole, I left off in time, without being much a winner or loser. Since one-and-twenty years of age I played but little, and then never above a hundred, or two, or three."

To this, and other follies of the same period, he alludes in the following note: —

TO MR. WILLIAM BANKES.

"Twelve o'clock, Friday night.

"My dear Bankes,

"I have just received your note; believe me I regret most sincerely that I was not fortunate enough to see it before, as I need not repeat to you that your conversation for half an hour would have been much more agreeable to me than gambling or drinking, or any other fashionable mode of passing an evening abroad or at home.—I really am very sorry that I went out previous to the arrival of your despatch: in future pray let me hear from you before six, and whatever my engagements may be, I will always postpone them.—Believe me, with that deference which I have always from my childhood paid to your *talents*, and with somewhat a better opinion of your heart than I have hitherto entertained,

"Yours ever," &c.

Among the causes—if not rather among the results—of that disposition to melancholy, which, after all, perhaps, naturally belonged to his temperament, must not be forgotten those sceptical views of religion, which clouded, as has been shown, his boyish thoughts, and, at the time of which I am speaking, gathered still more darkly over his mind. In general we find the young too ardently occupied with the enjoyments which this life gives or promises to afford either leisure or inclination for much enquiry into the mysteries of the next. But with him it was unluckily otherwise; and to have, at once, anticipated the worst experience both of the voluptuary and the reasoner,—to have reached, as he supposed, the boundary of this world's pleasures, and see nothing but "clouds and darkness" beyond, was the doom, the anomalous doom, which a nature, premature in all its passions and powers, inflicted on Lord Byron.

When Pope, at the age of five-and-twenty, complained of being weary of the world, he was told by Swift that he "had not yet acted or suffered enough in the world to have become weary of it." But far different was the youth of Pope and of Byron;—what the former but anticipated in thought, the latter had drunk deep of in reality;—at an age when the one was but looking forth on the sea of life, the other had plunged in, and tried its depths. Swift himself, in whom early disappointments and wrongs had opened a vein of bitterness that never again closed, affords a far closer parallel to the fate of our noble poet, as well in the untimeliness of the trials he had been doomed to encounter, as in the traces of their havoc which they left in his character.

That the romantic fancy of youth, which courts melancholy as an indulgence, and loves to assume a sadness it has not had time to earn, may have had some share in, at least, fostering the gloom by which the mind of the young poet was overcast, I am not disposed to deny. The circumstance, indeed, of his having, at this time, among the ornaments of his study, a number of skulls highly polished, and placed on light stands round the room, would seem to indicate that he rather courted than shunned such gloomy associations. Being a sort of boyish mimickry, too, of the use to which the poet Young is said to have applied a skull, such a display might well induce some suspicion of the sincerity of his gloom, did we not, through the whole course of his subsequent life and writings, track visibly the deep vein of melancholy which nature had imbedded in his character.

Such was the state of mind and heart,—as, from his own testimony and that of others, I have collected it,—in which Lord Byron now set out on his indefinite pilgrimage; and never was there a change wrought in disposition and character to which Shakspeare's fancy of "sweet bells jangled out of tune" more truly applied. The unwillingness of Lord Carlisle to countenance him, and his humiliating position in consequence, completed the full measure of that mortification towards which so many other causes had concurred. Baffled, as he had been, in his own ardent pursuit of affection and friendship, his sole revenge and consolation lay in doubting that any such feelings really existed. The various crosses he had met with, in themselves sufficiently irritating and wounding, were rendered still more so by the high, impatient temper with which he encountered them. What others would have bowed to, as misfortunes, his proud spirit rose against, as wrongs; and the vehemence of this re-action produced, at once, a revolution throughout his whole character, in which, as in revolutions of the political world, all that was bad and irregular in his nature burst forth with all that was most energetic and grand. The very virtues and excellencies of his disposition ministered to the violence of this change. The same ardour that had burned through his friendships and loves now fed the fierce explosions of his indignation and scorn. His natural vivacity and humour but lent a fresher flow to his bitterness, till he, at last, revelled in it as an indulgence; and that hatred of hypocrisy, which had hitherto only shown itself in a too shadowy colouring of his own youthful frailties, now hurried him, from his horror of all false pretensions to virtue, into the still more dangerous boast and ostentation of vice.

The following letter to his mother, written a few days before he sailed, gives some particulars respecting the persons who composed his suit. Robert Rushton, whom he mentions so feelingly in the postscript, was the boy introduced, as his page, in the first Canto of Childe Harold.

LETTER 34.

TO MRS. BYRON.

"Falmouth, June 22. 1809.

"Dear Mother,

"I am about to sail in a few days; probably before this reaches you. Fletcher begged so hard, that I have continued him in my service. If he does not behave well abroad, I will send him back in a *transport*. I have a German servant, (who has been with Mr. Wilbraham in Persia before, and was strongly recommended to me by Dr. Butler, of Harrow,) Robert and William; they constitute my whole suite. I have letters in plenty:—you shall hear from me at the different ports I touch upon; but you must not be alarmed if my letters miscarry. The Continent is in a fine state—an insurrection has broken out at Paris, and the Austrians are beating Buonaparte—the Tyrolese have risen.

"There is a picture of me in oil, to be sent down to Newstead soon.—I wish the Miss P——s had something better to do than carry my miniatures to Nottingham to copy. Now they have done it, you may ask them to copy the others, which are greater favourites than my own. As to money matters, I am ruined—at least till Rochdale is sold; and if that does not turn out well, I shall enter into the Austrian or Russian service—perhaps the Turkish, if I like their manners. The world is all before me, and I leave England without regret, and without a wish to revisit any thing it contains, except *yourself*, and your present residence.

"P.S—Pray tell Mr. Rushton his son is well and doing well; so is Murray, indeed better than I ever saw him; he will be back in about a month. I ought to add the leaving Murray to my few regrets, as his age perhaps will prevent my seeing him again. Robert I take with me; I like him, because, like myself, he seems a friendless animal."

To those who have in their remembrance his poetical description of the state of mind in which he now took leave of England, the gaiety and levity of the letters I am about to give will appear, it is not improbable, strange and startling. But, in a temperament like that of Lord Byron, such bursts of vivacity on the surface are by no means incompatible with a wounded spirit underneath; and the light, laughing tone that pervades these letters but makes the feeling of solitariness that breaks out in them the more striking and affecting.

LETTER 35.

TO MR. HENRY DRURY.

"Falmouth, June 25. 1809.

My dear Drury,

"We sail to-morrow in the Lisbon packet, having been detained till now by the lack of wind, and other necessaries. These being at last procured, by this time to-morrow evening we shall be embarked on the *v*ide *v*orld of *v*aters, *v*or all the *v*orld like Robinson Crusoe. The Malta vessel not sailing for some weeks, we have determined to go by way of Lisbon, and, as my servants term it, to see 'that there Portingale'—thence to Cadiz and Gibraltar, and so on our old route to Malta and Constantinople, if so be that Captain Kidd, our gallant commander, understands plain sailing and Mercator, and takes us on our voyage all according to the chart.

"Will you tell Dr. Butler that I have taken the treasure of a servant, Friese, the native of Prussia Proper, into my service from his recommendation. He has been all among the Worshippers of Fire in Persia, and has seen Persepolis and all that.

"H—— has made woundy preparations for a book on his return; 100 pens, two gallons of japan ink, and several volumes of best blank, is no bad provision for a discerning public. I have laid down my pen, but have promised to contribute a chapter on the state of morals, &c. &c.

"The cock is crowing,I must be going,And can no more."

GHOST OF GAFFER THUMB.

"Adieu.—Believe me," &c. &c.

LETTER 36.

TO MR. HODGSON.

"Falmouth, June 25. 1809.

"My dear Hodgson,

"Before this reaches you, Hobhouse, two officers' wives, three children, two waiting-maids, ditto subalterns for the troops, three Portuguese esquires and domestics, in all nineteen souls, will have sailed in the Lisbon packet, with the noble Captain Kidd, a gallant commander as ever smuggled an anker of right Nantz.

"We are going to Lisbon first, because the Malta packet has sailed, d'ye see?—from Lisbon to Gibraltar, Malta, Constantinople, and 'all that,' as Orator Henley said, when he put the Church, and 'all that,' in danger.

"This town of Falmouth, as you will partly conjecture, is no great ways from the sea. It is defended on the sea-side by tway castles, St. Maws and Pendennis, extremely well calculated for annoying every body except an enemy. St. Maws is garrisoned by an able-bodied person of fourscore, a widower. He has the whole command and sole management of six most unmanageable pieces of ordnance, admirably adapted for the destruction of Pendennis, a like tower of strength on the opposite side of the Channel. We have seen St. Maws, but Pendennis they will not let us behold, save at a distance, because Hobhouse and I are suspected of having already taken St. Maws by a coup de main.

"The town contains many Quakers and salt fish—the oysters have a taste of copper, owing to the soil of a mining country—the women (blessed be the Corporation therefor!) are flogged at the cart's tail when they pick and steal, as happened to one of the fair sex yesterday noon. She was pertinacious in her behaviour, and damned the mayor.

"I don't know when I can write again, because it depends on that experienced navigator, Captain Kidd, and the 'stormy winds that (don't) blow' at this season. I leave England without regret—I shall return to it without pleasure. I am like Adam, the first convict sentenced to transportation, but I have no Eve, and have eaten no apple but what was sour as a crab;—and thus ends my first, chapter. Adieu.

"Yours," &c.

In this letter the following lively verses were enclosed:—

"Falmouth Roads, June 30. 1809.

"Huzza! Hodgson, we are going,

Our embargo's off at last;

Favourable breezes blowing

Bend the canvass o'er the mast.

From aloft the signal's streaming,

Hark! the farewell gun is fired,

Women screeching, tars blaspheming,

Tell us that our time's expired.

Here 's a rascal,

Come to task all,

Prying from the Custom-house;

Trunks unpacking,

Cases cracking,

Not a corner for a mouse

'Scapes unsearch'd amid the racket,

Ere we sail on board the Packet.

"Now our boatmen quit their mooring.

And all hands must ply the oar;

Baggage from the quay is lowering,

We're impatient—push from shore.

'Have a care! that case holds liquor—

Stop the boat—I'm sick—oh Lord!'

'Sick, ma'am, damme, you'll be sicker

Ere you've been an hour on board.'

Thus are screaming

Men and women,

Gemmen, ladies, servants, Jacks;

Here entangling,

All are wrangling,

Stuck together close as wax.—

Such the general noise and racket,

Ere we reach the Lisbon Packet.

"Now we've reach'd her, lo! the captain,

Gallant Kidd, commands the crew;

Passengers their berths are clapt in,

Some to grumble, some to spew,

'Hey day! call you that a cabin?

Why 'tis hardly three feet square;

Not enough to stow Queen Mab in—

Who the deuce can harbour there?'

'Who, sir? plenty—

Nobles twenty

Did at once my vessel fill'—

'Did they? Jesus,

How you squeeze us!

Would to God they did so still:

Then I'd scape the heat and racket,

Of the good ship, Lisbon Packet.'

"Fletcher! Murray! Bob! where are you?
Stretch'd along the deck like logs—
Bear a hand, you jolly tar, you!
Here's a rope's end for the dogs.
H—— muttering fearful curses,
As the hatchway down he rolls;
Now his breakfast, now his verses,
Vomits forth—and damns our souls.
'Here's a stanza
On Braganza—
Help!'—'A couplet?'—'No, a cup
Of warm water.'—
'What's the matter?'
'Zounds! my liver's coming up;
I shall not survive the racket
Of this brutal Lisbon Packet.'
"Now at length we're off for Turkey,
Lord knows when we shall come back!
Breezes foul and tempests murky
May unship us in a crack.
But, since life at most a jest is,
As philosophers allow,
Still to laugh by far the best is,
Then laugh on—as I do now.
Laugh at all things,
Great and small things,
Sick or well, at sea or shore;
While we're quaffing,

Let's have laughing—

Who the devil cares for more?—

Some good wine! and who would lack it,

Ev'n on board the Lisbon Packet?

"Byron."

On the second of July the packet sailed from Falmouth, and, after a favourable passage of four days and a half, the voyagers reached Lisbon, and took up their abode in that city.

The following letters, from Lord Byron to his friend Mr. Hodgson, though written in his most light and schoolboy strain, will give some idea of the first impressions that his residence in Lisbon made upon him. Such letters, too, contrasted with the noble stanzas on Portugal in "Childe Harold," will show how various were the moods of his versatile mind, and what different aspects it could take when in repose or on the wing.

LETTER 37.

TO MR. HODGSON.

"Lisbon, July 16. 1809.

"Thus far have we pursued our route, and seen all sorts of marvellous sights, palaces, convents, &c.;—which, being to be heard in my friend Hobhouse's forthcoming Book of Travels, I shall not anticipate by smuggling any account whatsoever to you in a private and clandestine manner. I must just observe, that the village of Cintra in Estremadura is the most beautiful, perhaps, in the world.

"I am very happy here, because I loves oranges, and talk bad Latin to the monks, who understand it, as it is like their own,—and I goes into society (with my pocket-pistols), and I swims in the Tagus all across at once, and I rides on an ass or a mule, and swears Portuguese, and have got a diarrhoea and bites from the musquitoes. But what of that? Comfort must not be expected by folks that go a pleasuring.

"When the Portuguese are pertinacious, I say, 'Carracho!'—the great oath of the grandees, that very well supplies the place of 'Damme,'—and, when dissatisfied with my neighbour, I pronounce him 'Ambra di merdo.' With these two phrases, and a third, 'Avra bouro,' which signifieth 'Get an ass,' I am universally understood to be a person of degree and a master of languages. How merrily we lives that travellers be!—if we had food and raiment. But in sober sadness, any thing is better than England, and I am infinitely amused with my pilgrimage as far as it has gone.

"To-morrow we start to ride post near 400 miles as far as Gibraltar, where we embark for Melita and Byzantium. A letter to Malta will find me, or to be forwarded, if I am absent. Pray embrace the Drury and Dwyer, and all the Ephesians you encounter. I am writing with Butler's donative pencil, which makes my bad hand worse. Excuse illegibility.

"Hodgson! send me the news, and the deaths and defeats and capital crimes and the misfortunes of one's friends; and let us hear of literary matters, and the controversies and the criticisms. All this will be pleasant—'Suave mari magno,' &c. Talking of that, I have been sea-sick, and sick of the sea.

"Adieu. Yours faithfully," &c.

LETTER 38.

TO MR. HODGSON.

"Gibraltar, August 6. 1809.

"I have just arrived at this place after a journey through Portugal, and a part of Spain, of nearly 500 miles. We left Lisbon and travelled on horseback to Seville and Cadiz, and thence in the Hyperion frigate to Gibraltar. The horses are excellent—we rode seventy miles a day. Eggs and wine, and hard beds, are all the accommodation we found, and, in such torrid weather, quite enough. My health is better than in England.

"Seville is a fine town, and the Sierra Morena, part of which we crossed, a very sufficient mountain; but damn description, it is always disgusting. Cadiz, sweet Cadiz!—it is the first spot in the creation. The beauty of its streets and mansions is only excelled by the loveliness of its inhabitants. For, with all national prejudice, I must confess the women of Cadiz are as far superior to the English women in beauty as the Spaniards are inferior to the English in every quality that dignifies the name of man. Just as I began to know the principal persons of the city, I was obliged to sail.

"You will not expect a long letter after my riding so far 'on hollow pampered jades of Asia.' Talking of Asia puts me in mind of Africa, which is within five miles of my present residence. I am going over before I go on to Constantinople.

"Cadiz is a complete Cythera. Many of the grandees who have left Madrid during the troubles reside there, and I do believe it is the prettiest and cleanest town in Europe. London is filthy in the comparison. The Spanish women are all alike, their education the same. The wife of a duke is, in information, as the wife of a peasant,—the wife of a peasant, in manner, equal to a duchess.

Certainly they are fascinating; but their minds have only one idea, and the business of their lives is intrigue.

"I have seen Sir John Carr at Seville and Cadiz, and, like Swift's barber, have been down on my knees to beg he would not put me into black and white. Pray remember me to the Drurys and the Davies, and all of that stamp who are yet extant. Send me a letter and news to Malta. My next epistle shall be from Mount Caucasus or Mount Sion. I shall return to Spain before I see England, for I am enamoured of the country.

Adieu, and believe me," &c.

In a letter to Mrs. Byron, dated a few days later, from Gibraltar, he recapitulates the same account of his progress, only dwelling rather more diffusely on some of the details. Thus, of Cintra and Mafra:—"To make amends for this, the village of Cintra, about fifteen miles from the capital, is, perhaps in every respect, the most delightful in Europe; it contains beauties of every description, natural and artificial. Palaces and gardens rising in the midst of rocks, cataracts, and precipices; convents on stupendous heights—a distant view of the sea and the Tagus; and, besides (though that is a secondary consideration), is remarkable as the scene of Sir H.D.'s Convention. It unites in itself all the wildness of the western highlands, with the verdure of the south of France. Near this place, about ten miles to the right, is the palace of Mafra, the boast of Portugal, as it might be of any other country, in point of magnificence without elegance. There is a convent annexed; the monks, who possess large revenues, are courteous enough, and understand Latin, so that we had a long conversation: they have a large library, and asked me if the *English* had *any books* in their country?"

An adventure which he met with at Seville, characteristic both of the country and of himself, is thus described in the same letter to Mrs. Byron:—

"We lodged in the house of two Spanish unmarried ladies, who possess *six* houses in Seville, and gave me a curious specimen of Spanish manners. They are women of character, and the eldest a fine woman, the youngest pretty, but not so good a figure as Donna Josepha. The freedom of manner, which is general here, astonished me not a little; and in the course of further observation, I find that reserve is not the characteristic of the Spanish belles, who are, in general, very handsome, with large black eyes, and very fine forms. The eldest honoured your *unworthy* son with very particular attention, embracing him with great tenderness at parting (I was there but three days), after cutting off a lock of his hair, and presenting him with one of her own, about three feet in length, which I send, and beg you will retain till my return. Her last words were, 'Adios, tu hermoso! me gusto mucho.'—'Adieu, you pretty fellow! you please me much.' She offered me a share of her apartment, which my *virtue* induced me to decline; she laughed, and said I had some English "amante" (lover), and added that she was going to be married to an officer in the Spanish army."

Among the beauties of Cadiz, his imagination, dazzled by the attractions of the many, was on the point, it would appear from the following, of being fixed by *one*:—

"Cadiz, sweet Cadiz, is the most delightful town I ever beheld, very different from our English cities in every respect except cleanliness (and it is as clean as London), but still beautiful and full of the finest women in Spain, the Cadiz belles being the Lancashire witches of their land. Just as I was introduced and began to like the grandees, I was forced to leave it for this cursed place; but before I return to England I will visit it again.

"The night before I left it, I sat in the box at the opera, with admiral ——'s family, an aged wife and a fine daughter, Sennorita ——. The girl is very pretty, in the Spanish style; in my opinion, by no means inferior to the English in charms, and certainly superior in fascination. Long, black hair, dark languishing eyes, clear olive complexions, and forms more graceful in motion than can be conceived by an Englishman used to the drowsy listless air of his countrywomen, added to the most becoming dress, and, at the same time, the most decent in the world, render a Spanish beauty irresistible.

"Miss —— and her little brother understood a little French, and, after regretting my ignorance of the Spanish, she proposed to become my preceptress in that language. I could only reply by a low bow, and express my regret that I quitted Cadiz too soon to permit me to make the progress which would doubtless attend my studies under so charming a directress. I was standing at the back of the box, which resembles our Opera boxes, (the theatre is large and finely decorated, the music admirable,) in the manner which Englishmen generally adopt, for fear of incommoding the ladies in front, when this fair Spaniard dispossessed an old woman (an aunt or a duenna) of her chair, and commanded me to be seated next herself, at a tolerable distance from her mamma. At the close of the performance I withdrew, and was lounging with a party of men in the passage, when, *en passant*, the lady turned round and called me, and I had the honour of attending her to the admiral's mansion. I have an invitation on my return to Cadiz, which I shall accept if I repass through the country on my return from Asia."

To these adventures, or rather glimpses of adventures, which he met with in his hasty passage through Spain, he adverted, I recollect, briefly, in the early part of his "Memoranda;" and it was the younger, I think, of his fair hostesses at Seville, whom he there described himself as making earnest love to, with the help of a dictionary. "For some time," he said, "I went on prosperously both as a linguist and a lover, till at length, the lady took a fancy to a ring which I wore, and set her heart on my giving it to her, as a pledge of my sincerity. This, however, could not be;—anything but the ring, I declared, was at her service, and much more than its value,—but the ring itself I had made a vow never to give away." The young Spaniard grew angry as the contention went on, and it was not long before the lover became angry also; till, at length, the affair ended by their separating unsuccessful on both sides. "Soon after this," said he, "I sailed for Malta, and there parted with both my heart and ring."

In the letter from Gibraltar, just cited, he adds—"I am going over to Africa tomorrow; it is only six miles from this fortress. My next stage is Cagliari in Sardinia, where I shall be presented to his majesty. I have a most superb uniform as a court-dress, indispensable in travelling." His plan of visiting Africa was, however, relinquished. After a short stay at Gibraltar, during which he dined one day with Lady Westmoreland, and another with General Castanos, he, on the 19th of August, took his departure for Malta, in the packet, having first sent Joe Murray and young Rushton back to England,— the latter being unable, from ill health, to accompany him any further. "Pray," he says to his mother, "show the lad every kindness, as he is my great favourite."

He also wrote a letter to the father of the boy, which gives so favourable an impression of his thoughtfulness and kindliness that I have much pleasure in being enabled to introduce it here.

LETTER 39.

TO MR. RUSHTON.

"Gibraltar, August 15. 1809.

"Mr. Rushton,

"I have sent Robert home with Mr. Murray, because the country which I am about to travel through is in a state which renders it unsafe, particularly for one so young. I allow you to deduct five-and-twenty pounds a year for his education for three years, provided I do not return before that time, and I desire he may be considered as in my service. Let every care be taken of him, and let him be sent to school. In case of my death I have provided enough in my will to render him independent. He has behaved extremely well, and has travelled a great deal for the time of his absence. Deduct the expense of his education from your rent.

"BYRON."

It was the fate of Lord Byron, throughout life, to meet, wherever he went, with persons who, by some tinge of the extraordinary in their own fates or characters, were prepared to enter, at once, into full sympathy with his; and to this attraction, by which he drew towards him all strange and eccentric spirits, he owed some of the most agreeable connections of his life, as well as some of the most troublesome. Of the former description was an intimacy which he now cultivated during his short sojourn at Malta. The lady with whom he formed this acquaintance was the same addressed by him under the name of "Florence" in Childe Harold; and in a letter to his mother from Malta, he thus describes her in prose:—"This letter is committed to the charge of a very extraordinary woman, whom you have doubtless heard of, Mrs. S—— S——, of whose escape the Marquis de Salvo published a narrative a few years ago. She has since been shipwrecked, and her life has been from its commencement so fertile in remarkable incidents that in a romance they would appear improbable. She was born at Constantinople, where her father, Baron H——, was Austrian ambassador; married unhappily, yet has never been impeached in point of character; excited the vengeance of Buonaparte by a part in some conspiracy; several times risked her life; and is not yet twenty-five. She is here on her way to England, to join her husband, being obliged to leave Trieste, where she was paying a visit to her mother, by the approach of the French, and embarks soon in a ship of war. Since my arrival here. I have had scarcely any other companion. I have found her very pretty, very accomplished, and extremely eccentric. Buonaparte is even now so incensed against her, that her life would be in some danger if she were taken prisoner a second time."

The tone in which he addresses this fair heroine in Childe Harold is (consistently with the above dispassionate account of her) that of the purest admiration and interest, unwarmed by any more ardent sentiment:—

"Sweet Florence! could another ever share

This wayward, loveless heart, it would be thine:

But, check'd by every tie, I may not dare

To cast a worthless offering at thy shrine,

Nor ask so dear a breast to feel one pang for mine.

"Thus Harold deem'd as on that lady's eye

He look'd, and met its beam without a thought,

Save admiration, glancing harmless by," &c. &c.

In one so imaginative as Lord Byron, who, while he infused so much of his life into his poetry, mingled also not a little of poetry with his life, it is difficult, in unravelling the texture of his feelings, to distinguish at all times between the fanciful and the real. His description here, for instance, of the unmoved and "loveless heart," with which he contemplated even the charms of this attractive person, is wholly at variance, not only with the anecdote from his "Memoranda" which I have recalled, but with the statements in many of his subsequent letters, and, above all, with one of the most graceful of his lesser poems, purporting to be addressed to thissame lady during a thunder-storm, on his road to Zitza.

Notwithstanding, however, these counter evidences, I am much disposed to believe that the representation of the state of heart in the foregoing extract from Childe Harold may be regarded as the true one; and that the notion of his being in love was but a dream that sprung up afterwards, when the image of the fair Florence had become idealised in his fancy, and every remembrance of their pleasant hours among "Calypso's isles" came invested by his imagination with the warm aspect of love. It will be recollected that to the chilled and sated feelings which early indulgence, and almost as early disenchantment, had left behind, he attributes in these verses the calm and passionless regard, with which even attractions like those of Florence were viewed by him. That such was actually his distaste, at this period, to all real objects of love or passion (however his fancy could call up creatures of its own to worship) there is every reason to believe; and the same morbid indifference to those pleasures he had once so ardently pursued still continued to be professed by him on his return to England. No anchoret, indeed, could claim for himself much more apathy towards all such allurements than he did at that period. But to be *thus* saved from temptation was a dear-bought safety, and, at the age of three-and-twenty, satiety and disgust are but melancholy substitutes for virtue.

The brig of war, in which they sailed, having been ordered to convoy a fleet of small merchant-men to Patras and Prevesa, they remained, for two or three days, at anchor off the former place. From thence, proceeding to their ultimate destination, and catching a sunset view of Missolonghi in their way, they landed, on the 29th of September, at Prevesa.

The route which Lord Byron now took through Albania, as well as those subsequent journeys through other parts of Turkey, which he performed in company with his friend Mr. Hobhouse, may be traced, by such as are desirous of details on the subject, in the account which the latter gentleman has given of his travels; an account which, interesting from its own excellence in every merit that should adorn such a work, becomes still more so from the feeling that Lord Byron is, as it were, present through its pages, and that we there follow his first youthful footsteps into the land with whose name he has intertwined his own for ever. As I am enabled, however, by the letters of the noble poet to his mother, as well as by others, still more curious, which are now, for the first time, published, to give his own rapid and lively sketches of his wanderings, I shall content myself, after this general reference to the volume of Mr. Hobhouse, with such occasional extracts from its pages as may throw light upon the letters of his friend.

LETTER 40.

TO MRS. BYRON.

"Prevesa, November 12. 1809.

"My dear Mother,

"I have now been some time in Turkey: this place is on the coast, but I have traversed the interior of the province of Albania on a visit to the Pacha. I left Malta in the Spider, a brig of war, on the 21st of September, and arrived in eight days at Prevesa. I thence have been about 150 miles, as far as Tepaleen, his Highness's country palace, where I stayed three days. The name of the Pacha is *Ali*, and he is considered a man of the first abilities: he governs the whole of Albania (the ancient Illyricum), Epirus, and part of Macedonia. His son, Vely Pacha, to whom he has given me letters, governs the Morea, and has great influence in Egypt; in short, he is one of the most powerful men in the Ottoman empire. When I reached Yanina, the capital, after a journey of three days over the mountains, through a country of the most picturesque beauty, I found that Ali Pacha was with his array in Illyricum, besieging Ibrahim Pacha in the castle of Berat. He had heard that an Englishman of rank was in his dominions, and had left orders in Yanina with the commandant to provide a house, and supply me with every kind of necessary *gratis*; and, though I have been allowed to make presents to the slaves, &c., I have not been permitted to pay for a single article of household consumption.

"I rode out on the vizier's horses, and saw the palaces of himself and grandsons: they are splendid, but too much ornamented with silk and gold. I then went over the mountains through Zitza, a village with a Greek monastery (where I slept on my return), in the most beautiful situation (always excepting Cintra, in Portugal) I ever beheld. In nine days I reached Tepaleen. Our journey was much prolonged by the torrents that had fallen from the mountains and intersected the roads. I shall never forget the singular scene on entering Tepaleen at five in the afternoon, as the sun was going down. It brought to my mind (with some change of *dress*, however) Scott's description of Branksome Castle in his *Lay*, and the feudal system. The Albanians, in their dresses, (the most magnificent in the world, consisting of a long *white kilt*, gold-worked cloak, crimson velvet gold-laced jacket and waistcoat, silver mounted pistols and daggers,) the Tartars with their high caps, the Turks in their vast pelisses and turbans, the soldiers and black slaves with the horses, the former in groups in an immense large open gallery in front of the palace, the latter placed in a kind of cloister below it, two hundred steeds ready caparisoned to move in a moment, couriers entering or passing out with despatches, the kettle-drums beating, boys calling the hour from the minaret of the mosque, altogether, with the singular appearance of the building itself, formed a new and delightful spectacle to a stranger. I was conducted to a very handsome apartment, and my health enquired after by the vizier's secretary, 'a-la-mode Turque!'

"The next day I was introduced to Ali Pacha. I was dressed in a full suit of staff uniform, with a very magnificent sabre, &c. The vizier received me in a large room paved with marble; a fountain was playing in the centre; the apartment was surrounded by scarlet ottomans. He received me standing, a wonderful compliment from a Mussulman, and made me sit down on his right hand. I have a Greek interpreter for general use, but a physician of Ali's, named Femlario, who understands Latin, acted for me on this occasion. His first question was, why, at so early an age, I left my country?—(the Turks have no idea of travelling for amusement.) He then said, the English minister, Captain Leake, had told him I was of a great family, and desired his respects to my mother; which I now, in the name of Ali Pacha, present to you. He said he was certain I was a man of birth, because I had small ears, curling hair, and little white hands, and expressed himself pleased with my appearance and garb. He told me to consider him as a father whilst I was in Turkey, and said he looked on me as his son. Indeed, he treated me like a child, sending me almonds and sugared sherbet, fruit and sweetmeats, twenty times a day. He begged me to visit him often, and at night, when he was at leisure. I then, after coffee and pipes, retired for the first time. I saw him thrice afterwards. It is singular, that the Turks, who have no hereditary dignities, and few great families, except the Sultans, pay so much respect to birth; for I found my pedigree more regarded than my title.

"To-day I saw the remains of the town of Actium, near which Antony lost the world, in a small bay, where two frigates could hardly manœuvre: a broken wall is the sole remnant. On another part of the gulf stand the ruins of Nicopolis, built by Augustus in honour of his victory. Last night I was at a Greek marriage; but this and a thousand things more I have neither time nor space to describe.

"I am going to-morrow, with a guard of fifty men, to Patras in the Morea, and thence to Athens, where I shall winter. Two days ago I was nearly lost in a Turkish ship of war, owing to the ignorance of the captain and crew, though the storm was not violent. Fletcher yelled after his wife, the Greeks called on all the saints, the Mussulmans on Alla; the captain burst into tears and ran below deck, telling us to call on God; the sails were split, the main-yard shivered, the wind blowing fresh, the night setting in, and all our chance was to make Corfu, which is in possession of the French, or (as Fletcher pathetically termed it) 'a watery grave.' I did what I could to console Fletcher, but finding him incorrigible, wrapped myself up in my Albanian capote (an immense cloak), and lay down on deck to wait the worst. I have learnt to philosophise in my travels, and if I had not, complaint was useless. Luckily the wind abated and only drove us on the coast of Suli, on the main land, where we landed, and proceeded, by the help of the natives, to Prevesa again; but I shall not trust Turkish sailors in future, though the Pacha had ordered one of his own galliots to take me to Patras. I am therefore going as far as Missolonghi by land, and there have only to cross a small gulf to get to Patras.

"Fletcher's next epistle will be full of marvels: we were one night lost for nine hours in the mountains in a thunder-storm, and since nearly wrecked. In both cases Fletcher was sorely bewildered, from apprehensions of famine and banditti in the first, and drowning in the second instance. His eyes were a little hurt by the lightning, or crying (I don't know which), but are now recovered. When you write, address to me at Mr. Strané's, English consul, Patras, Morea.

"I could tell you I know not how many incidents that I think would amuse you, but they crowd on my mind as much as they would swell my paper, and I can neither arrange them in the one, nor put them down on the other except in the greatest confusion. I like the Albanians much; they are not all Turks; some tribes are Christians. But their religion makes little difference in their manner or conduct. They are esteemed the best troops in the Turkish service. I lived on my route, two days at once, and three days again in a barrack at Salora, and never found soldiers so tolerable, though I have been in the garrisons of Gibraltar and Malta, and seen Spanish, French, Sicilian, and British troops in abundance. I have had nothing stolen, and was always welcome to their provision and milk. Not a week ago an Albanian chief, (every village has its chief, who is called Primate,) after helping us out of the Turkish galley in her distress, feeding us, and lodging my suite, consisting of Fletcher, a Greek, two Athenians, a Greek priest, and my companion, Mr. Hobhouse, refused any compensation but a written paper stating that I was well received; and when I pressed him to accept a few sequins, 'No,' he replied; 'I wish you to love me, not to pay me.' These are his words.

"It is astonishing how far money goes in this country. While I was in the capital I had nothing to pay by the vizier's order; but since, though I have generally had sixteen horses, and generally six or seven men, the expense has not been *half* as much as staying only three weeks in Malta, though Sir A. Ball, the governor, gave me a house for nothing, and I had only *one servant*. By the by, I expect H———to remit regularly; for I am not about to stay in this province for ever. Let him write to me at Mr. Strané's, English consul, Patras. The fact is, the fertility of the plains is wonderful, and specie is scarce, which makes this remarkable cheapness. I am going to Athens to study modern Greek, which differs much from the ancient, though radically similar. I have no desire to return to England, nor shall *I*, unless compelled by absolute want, and H——'s neglect; but I shall not enter into Asia for a year or two, as I have much to see in Greece, and I may perhaps cross into Africa, at least the Egyptian part. Fletcher, like all Englishmen, is very much dissatisfied, though a little reconciled to the Turks by a present of eighty piastres from the vizier, which, if you consider every thing, and the value of specie here, is nearly worth ten guineas English. He has suffered nothing but from cold, heat, and vermin, which those who lie in cottages and cross mountains in a cold country must undergo, and of which I have equally partaken with himself; but he is not valiant, and is afraid of robbers and tempests. I have no one to be remembered to in England, and wish to hear nothing from it, but that you are well, and a letter or two on business from H——, whom you may tell to write. I will write when I can, and beg you to believe me,

Your affectionate son,

" BYRON."

About the middle of November, the young traveller took his departure from Prevesa (the place where the foregoing letter was written), and proceeded, attended by his guard of fifty Albanians, through Acarnania and Ætolia, towards the Morea.

"And therefore did he take a trusty band

To traverse Acarnania's forest wide,

In war well season'd, and with labours tann'd,

Till he did greet white Achelous' tide,

And from his further bank Ætolia's wolds espied."

Childe Harold, Canto II.

His description of the night-scene at Utraikey (a small place situated in one of the bays of the Gulf of Arta) is, no doubt, vividly in the recollection of every reader of these pages; nor will it diminish their enjoyment of the wild beauties of that picture to be made acquainted with the real circumstances on which it was founded, in the following animated details of the same scene by his fellow-traveller:—

"In the evening the gates were secured, and preparations were made for feeding our Albanians. A goat was killed and roasted whole, and four fires were kindled in the yard, round which the soldiers seated themselves in parties. After eating and drinking, the greater part of them assembled round the largest of the fires, and whilst ourselves and the elders of the party were seated on the ground, danced round the blaze to their own songs, in the manner before described, but with an astonishing energy. All their songs were relations of some robbing exploits. One of them, which detained them more than an hour, began thus:—'When we set out from Parga there were sixty of us:'—then came the burden of the verse,

"'Robbers all at Parga!

Robbers all at Parga!

"'Κλεφτεις ποτε Παργα!

Κλεφτεις ποτε Παργα!'

And as they roared out this stave they whirled round the fire, dropped and rebounded from their knees, and again whirled round as the chorus was again repeated. The rippling of the waves upon the pebbly margin where we were seated filled up the pauses of the song with a milder and not more monotonous music. The night was very dark, but by the flashes of the fires we caught a glimpse of the woods, the rocks, and the lake, which, together with the wild appearance of the dancers, presented us with a scene that would have made a fine picture in the hands of such an artist as the author of the Mysteries of Udolpho."

Having traversed Acarnania, the travellers passed to the Ætolian side of the Achelous, and on the 21st of November reached Missolonghi. And here, it is impossible not to pause, and send a mournful thought forward to the visit which, fifteen years after, he paid to this same spot, when, in the full meridian both of his age and fame, he came to lay down his life as the champion of that land, through which he now wandered a stripling and a stranger. Could some spirit have here revealed to him the events of that interval,—have shown him, on the one side, the triumphs that awaited him, the power his varied genius would acquire over all hearts, alike to elevate or depress, to darken or illuminate them,—and then place, on the other side, all the penalties of this gift, the waste and wear of the heart through the imagination, the havoc of that perpetual fire within, which, while it dazzles others, consumes the possessor, —the invidiousness of such an elevation in the eyes of mankind, and the revenge they take on him who compels them to look up to it,—*would* he, it may be asked, have welcomed glory on such conditions? would he not rather have felt that the purchase was too costly, and that such warfare with an ungrateful world, while living, would be ill recompensed even by the immortality it might award him afterwards?

At Missolonghi he dismissed his whole band of Albanians, with the exception of one, named Dervish, whom he took into his service, and who, with Basilius, the attendant allotted him by Ali Pacha, continued with him during the remainder of his stay in the East. After a residence of near a fortnight at Patras, he next directed his course to Vostizza,—on approaching which town the snowy peak of Parnassus, towering on the other side of the Gulf, first broke on his eyes; and in two days after, among the sacred hollows of Delphi, the stanzas, with which that vision had inspired him, were written.

It was at this time, that, in riding along the sides of Parnassus, he saw an unusually large flight of eagles in the air,—a phenomenon which seems to have affected his imagination with a sort of poetical superstition, as he, more than once, recurs to the circumstance in his journals. Thus, "Going to the fountain of Delphi (Castri) in 1809, I saw a flight of twelve eagles (H. says they were vultures—at least in conversation), and I seised the omen. On the day before I composed the lines to Parnassus (in Childe Harold), and, on beholding the birds, had a hope that Apollo had accepted my homage. I have at least had the name and fame of a poet during the poetical part of life (from twenty to thirty);—whether it will *last* is another matter."

He has also, in reference to this journey from Patras, related a little anecdote of his own sportsmanship, which, by all *but* sportsmen, will be thought creditable to his humanity. "The last bird I ever fired at was an eaglet, on the shore of the Gulf of Lepanto, near Vostizza. It was only wounded, and I tried to save it,—the eye was so bright. But it pined, and died in a few days; and I never did since, and never will, attempt the death of another bird."

To a traveller in Greece, there are few things more remarkable than the diminutive extent of those countries, which have filled such a wide space in fame. "A man might very easily," says Mr. Hobhouse, "at a moderate pace ride from Livadia to Thebes and back again between breakfast and dinner; and the tour of all Bœotia might certainly be made in two days without baggage." Having visited, within a very short space of time, the fountains of Memory and Oblivion at Livadia, and the haunts of the Ismenian Apollo at Thebes, the travellers at length turned towards Athens, the city of their dreams, and, after crossing Mount Cithæron, arrived in sight of the ruins of Phyle, on the evening of Christmas-day, 1809.

Though the poet has left, in his own verses, an ever-during testimony of the enthusiasm with which he now contemplated the scenes around him, it is not difficult to conceive that, to superficial observers, Lord Byron at Athens might have appeared an untouched spectator of much that throws ordinary travellers into, at least, verbal raptures. For pretenders of every sort, whether in taste or morals, he entertained, at all times, the most profound contempt; and if, frequently, his real feelings of admiration disguised themselves under an affected tone of indifference and mockery, it was out of pure hostility to the cant of those, who, he well knew, praised without any feeling at all. It must be owned, too, that while he thus justly despised the raptures of the common herd of travellers, there were some pursuits, even of the intelligent and tasteful, in which he took but very little interest. With the antiquarian and connoisseur his sympathies were few and feeble:—"I am not a collector," he says, in one of his notes on Childe Harold, "nor an admirer of collections." For antiquities, indeed, unassociated with high names and deeds, he had no value whatever; and of works of art he was content to admire the general effect, without professing, or aiming at, any knowledge of the details. It was to nature, in her lonely scenes of grandeur and beauty, or as at Athens, shining, unchanged, among the ruins of glory and of art, that the true fervid homage of his whole soul was paid. In the few notices of his travels, appended to Childe Harold, we find the sites and scenery of the different places he visited far more fondly dwelt upon than their classic or historical associations. To the valley of Zitza he reverts, both in prose and verse, with a much warmer recollection than to Delphi or the Troad; and the plain of Athens itself is chiefly praised by him as "a more glorious prospect than even Cintra or Istambol." Where, indeed, could Nature assert such claims to his worship as in scenes like these, where he beheld her blooming, in indestructible beauty, amid the wreck of all that man deems most worthy of duration? "Human institutions," says Harris, "perish, but Nature is permanent:"—or, as Lord Byron has amplified this thought in one of his most splendid passages:—

"Yet are thy skies as blue, thy crags as wild;

Sweet are thy groves, and verdant are thy fields,

Thine olive ripe as when Minerva smiled,

And still his honeyed wealth Hymettus yields;

There the blithe bee his fragrant fortress builds,

The free-born wanderer of thy mountain-air;

Apollo still thy long, long summer gilds,

Still in his beam Mendeli's marbles glare;

Art, Glory, Freedom fail, but Nature still is fair."

CHILDE HAROLD, Canto II.

At Athens, on this his first visit, he made a stay of between two and three months, not a day of which he let pass without employing some of its hours in visiting the grand monuments of ancient genius around him, and calling up the spirit of other times among their ruins. He made frequently, too, excursions to different parts of Attica; and it was in one of his visits to Cape Colonna, at this time, that he was near being seized by a party of Mainotes, who were lying hid in the caves under the cliff of Minerva Sunias. These pirates, it appears, were only deterred from attacking him (as a Greek, who was then their prisoner, informed him afterwards) by a supposition that the two Albanians, whom they saw attending him, were but part of a complete guard he had at hand.

In addition to all the magic of its names and scenes, the city of Minerva possessed another sort of attraction for the poet, to which, wherever he went, his heart, or rather imagination, was but too sensible. His pretty song, "Maid of Athens, ere we part," is said to have been addressed to the eldest daughter of the Greek lady at whose house he lodged; and that the fair Athenian, when he composed these verses, may have been the tenant, for the time being, of his fancy, is highly possible. Theodora Macri, his hostess, was the widow of the late English vice-consul, and derived a livelihood from letting, chiefly to English travellers, the apartments which Lord Byron and his friend now occupied, and of which the latter gentleman gives us the following description;—"Our lodgings consisted of a sitting-room and two bed-rooms, opening into a court-yard where there were five or six lemon-trees, from which, during our residence in the place, was plucked the fruit that seasoned the pilaf, and other national dishes served up at our frugal table."

The fame of an illustrious poet is not confined to his own person and writings, but imparts a share of its splendour to whatever has been, even remotely, connected with him; and not only ennobles the objects of his friendships, his loves, and even his likings, but on every spot where he has sojourned through life, leaves traces of its light that do not easily pass away. Little did the Maid of Athens, while listening innocently to the compliments of the young Englishman, foresee that a day would come when he should make her name and home so celebrated that travellers, on their return from Greece, would find few things more interesting to their hearers than such details of herself and her family as the following:—

"Our servant, who had gone before to procure accommodation, met us at the gate and conducted us to Theodora Macri, the Consulina's, where we at present live. This lady is the widow of the consul, and has three lovely daughters; the eldest celebrated for her beauty, and said to be the subject of those stanzas by Lord Byron,—

"'Maid of Athens, ere we part, Give, oh, give me back my heart!' &c.

"At Orchomenus, where stood the Temple of the Graces, I was tempted to exclaim, 'Whither have the Graces fled?'—Little did I expect to find them here. Yet here comes one of them with golden cups and coffee, and another with a book. The book is a register of names, some of which are far sounded by the voice of fame. Among them is Lord Byron's, connected with some lines which I shall send you:—

"'Fair Albion, smiling, sees her son depart,

To trace the birth and nursery of art;

Noble his object, glorious is his aim,

He comes to Athens, and he—writes his name.'

"The counterpoise by Lord Byron:—

"'This modest bard, like many a bard unknown,

Rhymes on our names, but wisely hides his own;

But yet whoe'er he be, to say no worse,

His name would bring more credit than his verse.'

"The mention of the three Athenian Graces will, I can foresee, rouse your curiosity, and fire your imagination; and I may despair of your farther attention till I attempt to give you some description of them. Their apartment is immediately opposite to ours, and if you could see them, as we do now, through the gently waving aromatic plants before our window, you would leave your heart in Athens.

"Theresa, the Maid of Athens, Catinco, and Mariana, are of middle stature. On the crown of the head of each is a red Albanian skull-cap, with a blue tassel spread out and fastened down like a star. Near the edge or bottom of the skull-cap is a handkerchief of various colours bound round their temples. The youngest wears her hair loose, falling on her shoulders,—the hair behind descending down the back nearly to the waist, and, as usual, mixed with silk. The two eldest generally have their hair bound, and fastened under the handkerchief. Their upper robe is a pelisse edged with fur, hanging loose down to the ankles; below is a handkerchief of muslin covering the bosom, and terminating at the waist, which is short; under that, a gown of striped silk or muslin, with a gore round the swell of the loins, falling in front in graceful negligence;—white stockings and yellow slippers complete their attire. The two eldest have black, or dark hair and eyes; their visage oval, and complexion somewhat pale, with teeth of dazzling whiteness. Their cheeks are rounded, and noses straight, rather inclined to aquiline. The youngest, Mariana, is very fair, her face not so finely rounded, but has a gayer expression than her sisters', whose countenances, except when the conversation has something of mirth in it, may be said to be rather pensive. Their persons are elegant, and their manners pleasing and lady-like, such as would be fascinating in any country. They possess very considerable powers of conversation, and their minds seem to be more instructed than those of the Greek women in general. With such attractions it would, indeed, be remarkable, if they did not meet with great attentions from the travellers who occasionally are resident in Athens. They sit in the eastern style, a little reclined, with their limbs gathered under them on the divan, and without shoes. Their employments are the needle, tambouring, and reading.

"I have said that I saw these Grecian beauties through the waving aromatic plants before their window. This, perhaps, has raised your imagination somewhat too high, in regard to their condition. You may have supposed their dwelling to have every attribute of eastern luxury. The golden cups, too, may have thrown a little witchery over your excited fancy. Confess, do you not imagine that the doors

"'Self-open'd into halls, where, who can tell

What elegance and grandeur wide expand,

The pride of Turkey and of Persia's land;

Soft quilts on quilts, on carpets carpets spread,

And couches stretch'd around in seemly band,

And endless pillows rise to prop the head,

So that each spacious room was one full swelling bed?'

"You will shortly perceive the propriety of my delaying, till now, to inform you that the aromatic plants which I have mentioned are neither more nor less than a few geraniums and Grecian balms, and that the room in which the ladies sit is quite unfurnished, the walls neither painted nor decorated by 'cunning hand.' Then, what would have become of the Graces had I told you sooner that a single room is all they have, save a little closet and a kitchen? You see how careful I have been to make the first impression good; not that they do not merit every praise, but that it is in man's august and elevated nature to think a little slightingly of merit, and even of beauty, if not supported by some worldly show. Now, I shall communicate to you a secret, but in the lowest whisper.

"These ladies, since the death of the consul, their father, depend on strangers living in their spare room and closet,—which we now occupy. But, though so poor, their virtue shines as conspicuously as their beauty.

"Not all the wealth of the East, or the complimentary lays even of the first of England's poets, could render them so truly worthy of love and admiration."

Ten weeks had flown rapidly away, when the unexpected offer of a passage in an English sloop of war to Smyrna induced the travellers to make immediate preparations for departure, and, on the 5th of March, they reluctantly took leave of Athens. "Passing," says Mr. Hobhouse, "through the gate leading to the Piraeus, we struck into the olive-wood on the road going to Salamis, galloping at a quick pace, in order to rid ourselves, by hurry, of the pain of parting." He adds, "We could not refrain from looking back, as we passed rapidly to the shore, and we continued to direct our eyes towards the spot, where we had caught the last glimpse of the Theséum and the ruins of the Parthenon through the vistas in the woods, for many minutes after the city and the Acropolis had been totally hidden from our view."

At Smyrna Lord Byron took up his residence in the house of the consul-general, and remained there, with the exception of two or three days employed in a visit to the ruins of Ephesus, till the 11th of April. It was during this time, as appears from a memorandum of his own, that the two first Cantos of Childe Harold, which he had begun five months before at Ioannina, were completed. The memorandum alluded to, which I find prefixed to his original manuscript of the poem, is as follows:—

"Byron, Ioannina in Albania.Begun October 31st, 1809;Concluded Canto 2d, Smyrna,March 28th. 1810.

"BYRON".

From Smyrna the only letter, at all interesting, which I am enabled to present to the reader, is the following:—

LETTER 41.

TO MRS. BYRON.

"Smyrna, March 19. 1810.

"Dear Mother,

"I cannot write you a long letter; but as I know you will not be sorry to receive any intelligence of my movements, pray accept what I can give. I have traversed the greatest part of Greece, besides Epirus, &c. &c., resided ten weeks at Athens, and am now on the Asiatic side on my way to Constantinople. I have just returned from viewing the ruins of Ephesus, a day's journey from Smyrna. I presume you have received a long letter I wrote from Albania, with an account of my reception by the Pacha of the province.

"When I arrive at Constantinople, I shall determine whether to proceed into Persia or return, which latter I do not wish, if I can avoid it. But I have no intelligence from Mr. H——, and but one letter from yourself. I shall stand in need of remittances whether I proceed or return. I have written to him repeatedly, that he may not plead ignorance of my situation for neglect. I can give you no account of any thing, for I have not time or opportunity, the frigate sailing immediately. Indeed the further I go the more my laziness increases, and my aversion to letter-writing becomes more confirmed. I have written to no one but to yourself and Mr. H——, and these are communications of business and duty rather than of inclination.

"F—— is very much disgusted with his fatigues, though he has undergone nothing that I have not shared. He is a poor creature; indeed English servants are detestable travellers. I have, besides him, two Albanian soldiers and a Greek interpreter; all excellent in their way. Greece, particularly in the vicinity of Athens, is delightful,—cloudless skies and lovely landscapes. But I must reserve all account of my adventures till we meet. I keep no journal, but my friend H. writes incessantly. Pray take care of Murray and Robert, and tell the boy it is the most fortunate thing for him that he did not accompany me to Turkey. Consider this as merely a notice of my safety, and believe me,

yours, &c. &c.

"Byron."

On the 11th of April he left Smyrna in the Salsette frigate, which had been ordered to Constantinople, for the purpose of conveying the ambassador, Mr. Adair, to England, and, after an exploratory visit to the ruins of Troas, arrived, at the beginning of the following month, in the Dardanelles.—While the frigate was at anchor in these straits, the following letters to his friends Mr. Drury and Mr. Hodgson were written.

Letter 42.

TO MR. HENRY DRURY.

"Salsette frigate, May 3. 1810.

"My dear Drury,

"When I left England, nearly a year ago, you requested me to write to you—I will do so. I have crossed Portugal, traversed the south of Spain, visited Sardinia, Sicily, Malta, and thence passed into Turkey, where I am still wandering. I first landed in Albania, the ancient Epirus, where we penetrated as far as Mount Tomarit—excellently treated by the chief AH Pacha,—and, after journeying through Illyria, Chaonia, &c., crossed the Gulf of Actium, with a guard of fifty Albanians, and passed the Achelous in our route through Acarnania and Ætolia. We stopped a short time in the Morea, crossed the Gulf of Lepanto, and landed at the foot of Parnassus;—saw all that Delphi retains, and so on to Thebes and Athens, at which last we remained ten weeks.

"His Majesty's ship, Pylades, brought us to Smyrna; but not before we had topographised Attica, including, of course, Marathon and the Sunian promontory. From Smyrna to the Troad (which we visited when at anchor, for a fortnight, off the tomb of Antilochus) was our next stage; and now we are in the Dardanelles, waiting for a wind to proceed to Constantinople.

"This morning I *swam* from *Sestos* to *Abydos*. The immediate distance is not above a mile, but the current renders it hazardous;—so much so that I doubt whether Leander's conjugal affection must not have been a little chilled in his passage to Paradise. I attempted it a week ago, and failed,—owing to the north wind, and the wonderful rapidity of the tide,—though I have been from my childhood a strong swimmer. But, this morning being calmer, I succeeded, and crossed the 'broad Hellespont' in an hour and ten minutes.

"Well, my dear sir, I have left my home, and seen part of Africa and Asia, and a tolerable portion of Europe. I have been with generals and admirals, princes and pashas, governors and ungovernables,—but I have not time or paper to expatiate. I wish to let you know that I live with a friendly remembrance of you, and a hope to meet you again; and if I do this as shortly as possible, attribute it to anything but forgetfulness.

"Greece, ancient and modern, you know too well to require description. Albania, indeed, I have seen more of than any Englishman (except a Mr. Leake), for it is a country rarely visited, from the savage character of the natives, though abounding in more natural beauties than the classical regions of Greece,—which, however, are still eminently beautiful, particularly Delphi and Cape Colonna in Attica. Yet these are nothing to parts of Illyria and Epirus, where places without a name, and rivers not laid down in maps, may, one day, when more known, be justly esteemed superior subjects, for the pencil and the pen, to the dry ditch of the Ilissus and the bogs of Bœotia.

"The Troad is a fine field for conjecture and snipe-shooting, and a good sportsman and an ingenious scholar may exercise their feet and faculties to great advantage upon the spot;—or, if they prefer riding, lose their way (as I did) in a cursed quagmire of the Scamander, who wriggles about as if the Dardan virgins still offered their wonted tribute. The only vestige of Troy, or her destroyers, are the barrows supposed to contain the carcasses of Achilles, Antilochus, Ajax, &c.;—but Mount Ida is still in high feather, though the shepherds are now-a-days not much like Ganymede. But why should I say more of these things? are they not written in the *Boke* of *Gell*? and has not H. got a journal? I keep none, as I have renounced scribbling.

"I see not much difference between ourselves and the Turks, save that we have ———, and they have none—that they have long dresses, and we short, and that we talk much, and they little. They are sensible people. Ali Pacha told me he was sure I was a man of rank, because I had *small ears* and *hands*, and *curling hair*. By the by, I speak the Romaic, or modern Greek, tolerably. It does not differ from the ancient dialects so much as you would conceive: but the pronunciation is diametrically opposite. Of verse, except in rhyme, they have no idea.

"I like the Greeks, who are plausible rascals,—with all the Turkish vices, without their courage. However, some are brave, and all are beautiful, very much resembling the busts of Alcibiades:—the women not quite so handsome. I can swear in Turkish; but, except one horrible oath, and 'pimp,' and 'bread,' and 'water,' I have got no great vocabulary in that language. They are extremely polite to strangers of any rank, properly protected; and as I have two servants and two soldiers, we get on with great éclat. We have been occasionally in danger of thieves, and once of shipwreck,—but always escaped.

"Of Spain I sent some account to our Hodgson, but have subsequently written to no one, save notes to relations and lawyers, to keep them out of my premises. I mean to give up all connection, on my return, with many of my best friends—as I supposed them—and to snarl all my life. But I hope to have one good-humoured laugh with you, and to embrace Dwyer, and pledge Hodgson, before I commence cynicism.

"Tell Dr. Butler I am now writing with the gold pen he gave me before I left England, which is the reason my scrawl is more unintelligible than usual. I have been at Athens and seen plenty of these reeds for scribbling, some of which he refused to bestow upon me, because topographic Gell had brought them from Attica. But I will not describe,—no—you must be satisfied with simple detail till my return, and then we will unfold the flood-gates of colloquy. I am in a thirty-six gun frigate, going up to fetch Bob Adair from Constantinople, who will have the honour to carry this letter.

"And so H.'s *boke* is out, with some sentimental sing-song of my own to fill up,—and how does it take, eh? and where the devil is the second edition of my Satire, with additions? and my name on the title page? and more lines tagged to the end, with a new exordium and what not, hot from my anvil before I cleared the Channel? The Mediterranean and the Atlantic roll between me and criticism; and the thunders of the Hyperborean Review are deafened by the roar of the Hellespont.

"Remember me to Claridge, if not translated to college, and present to Hodgson assurances of my high consideration. Now, you will ask, what shall I do next? and I answer, I do not know. I may return in a few months, but I have intents and projects after visiting Constantinople.—Hobhouse, however, will probably be back in September.

"On the 2d of July we have left Albion one year—'oblitus meorum obliviscendus et illis.' I was sick of my own country, and not much prepossessed in favour of any other; but I 'drag on' 'my chain' without 'lengthening it at each remove.' I am like the Jolly Miller, caring for nobody, and not cared for. All countries are much the same in my eyes. I smoke, and stare at mountains, and twirl my mustachios very independently. I miss no comforts, and the musquitoes that rack the morbid frame of H. have, luckily for me, little effect on mine, because I live more temperately.

"I omitted Ephesus in my catalogue, which I visited during my sojourn at Smyrna; but the Temple has almost perished, and St. Paul need not trouble himself to epistolise the present brood of Ephesians, who have converted a large church built entirely of marble into a mosque, and I don't know that the edifice looks the worse for it.

"My paper is full, and my ink ebbing—good afternoon! If you address to me at Malta, the letter will be forwarded wherever I may be. H. greets you; he pines for his poetry,—at least, some tidings of it. I almost forgot to tell you that I am dying for love of three Greek girls at Athens, sisters. I lived in the same house. Teresa, Mariana, and Katinka, are the names of these divinities,—all of them under fifteen.

Your ταπεινοτατος δουλος,

"BYRON."

LETTER 43.

TO MR. HODGSON.

"Salsette frigate, in the Dardanelles, off Abydos, May 5. 1810.

"I am on my way to Constantinople, after a tour through Greece, Epirus, &c., and part of Asia Minor, some particulars of which I have just communicated to our friend and host, H. Drury. With these, then, I shall not trouble you; but as you will perhaps be pleased to hear that I am well, &c., I take the opportunity of our ambassador's return to forward the few lines I have time to despatch. We have undergone some inconveniences, and incurred partial perils, but no events worthy of communication, unless you will deem it one that two days ago I swam from Sestos to Abydos. This, with a few alarms from robbers, and some danger of shipwreck in a Turkish galliot six months ago, a visit to a Pacha, a passion for a married woman at Malta, a challenge to an officer, an attachment to three Greek girls at Athens, with a great deal of buffoonery and fine prospects, form all that has distinguished my progress since my departure from Spain.

"H. rhymes and journalises; I stare and do nothing—unless smoking can be deemed an active amusement. The Turks take too much care of their women to permit them to be scrutinised; but I have lived a good deal with the Greeks, whose modern dialect I can converse in enough for my purposes. With the Turks I have also some male acquaintances—female society is out of the question. I have been very well treated by the Pachas and Governors, and have no complaint to make of any kind. Hobhouse will one day inform you of all our adventures,—were I to attempt the recital, neither *my* paper nor *your* patience would hold out during the operation.

"Nobody, save yourself, has written to me since I left England; but indeed I did not request it. I except my relations, who write quite as often as I wish. Of Hobhouse's volume I know nothing, except that it is out; and of my second edition I do not even know *that*, and certainly do not, at this distance, interest myself in the matter. I hope you and Bland roll down the stream of sale with rapidity.

"Of my return I cannot positively speak, but think it probable Hobhouse will precede me in that respect. We have been very nearly one year abroad. I should wish to gaze away another, at least, in these ever-green climates; but I fear business, law business, the worst of employments, will recall me previous to that period, if not very quickly. If so, you shall have due notice.

"I hope you will find me an altered personage,—do not mean in body, but in manner, for I begin to find out that nothing but virtue will do in this d——d world. I am tolerably sick of vice, which I have tried in its agreeable varieties, and mean, on my return, to cut all my dissolute acquaintance, leave off wine and carnal company, and betake myself to politics and decorum. I am very serious and cynical, and a good deal disposed to moralise; but fortunately for you the coming homily is cut off by default of pen and defection of paper.

"Good morrow! If you write, address to me at Malta, whence your letters will be forwarded. You need not remember me to any body, but believe me yours with all faith,

"BYRON."

From Constantinople, where he arrived on the 14th of May, he addressed four or five letters to Mrs. Byron, in almost every one of which his achievement in swimming across the Hellespont is commemorated. The exceeding pride, indeed, which he took in this classic feat (the particulars of which he has himself abundantly detailed) may be cited among the instances of that boyishness of character, which he carried with him so remarkably into his maturer years, and which, while it puzzled distant observers of his conduct, was not among the least amusing or attaching of his peculiarities to those who knew him intimately. So late as eleven years from this period, when some sceptical traveller ventured to question, after all, the practicability of Leander's exploit, Lord Byron, with that jealousy on the subject of his own personal prowess which he retained from boyhood, entered again, with fresh zeal, into the discussion, and brought forward two or three other instances of his own feats in swimming, to corroborate the statement originally made by him.

In one of these letters to his mother from Constantinople, dated May 24th, after referring, as usual, to his notable exploit, "in humble imitation of Leander, of amorous memory, though," he adds, "I had no Hero to receive me on the other side of the Hellespont," he continues thus:—

"When our ambassador takes his leave I shall accompany him to see the sultan, and afterwards probably return to Greece. I have heard nothing of Mr. Hanson but one remittance, without any letter from that legal gentleman. If you have occasion for any pecuniary supply, pray use my funds as far as they *go* without reserve; and, lest this should not be enough, in my next to Mr. Hanson I will direct him to advance any sum you may want, leaving it to your discretion how much, in the present state of my affairs, you may think proper to require. I have already seen the most interesting parts of Turkey in Europe and Asia Minor, but shall not proceed further till I hear from England: in the mean time I shall expect occasional supplies, according to circumstances; and shall pass my summer amongst my friends, the Greeks of the Morea."

He then adds, with his usual kind solicitude about his favourite servants:—

"Pray take care of my boy Robert, and the old man Murray. It is fortunate they returned; neither the youth of the one, nor the age of the other, would have suited the changes of climate, and fatigue of travelling."

LETTER 44.

TO MR. HENRY DRURY.

"Constantinople, June 17. 1810.

"Though I wrote to you so recently, I break in upon you again to congratulate you on a child being born, as a letter from Hodgson apprizes me of that event, in which I rejoice.

"I am just come from an expedition through the Bosphorus to the Black Sea and the Cyanean Symplegades, up which last I scrambled with as great risk as ever the Argonauts escaped in their hoy. You remember the beginning of the nurse's dole in the Medea, of which I beg you to take the following translation, done on the summit:—

"Oh how I wish that an embargo

Had kept in port the good ship Argo!

Who, still unlaunch'd from Grecian docks,

Had never passed the Azure rocks;

But now I fear her trip will be a

Damn'd business for my Miss Medea, &c. &c.,

as it very nearly was to me;—for, had not this sublime passage been in my head, I should never have dreamed of ascending the said rocks, and bruising my carcass in honour of the ancients.

"I have now sat on the Cyaneans, swam from Sestos to Abydos (as I trumpeted in my last), and, after passing through the Morea again, shall set sail for Santo Maura, and toss myself from the Leucadian promontory;—surviving which operation, I shall probably join you in England. H., who will deliver this, is bound straight for these parts; and, as he is bursting with his travels, I shall not anticipate his narratives, but merely beg you not to believe one word he says, but reserve your ear for me, if you have any desire to be acquainted with the truth.

"I am bound for Athens once more, and thence to the Morea; but my stay depends so much on my caprice, that I can say nothing of its probable duration. I have been out a year already, and may stay another; but I am quicksilver, and say nothing positively. We are all very much occupied doing nothing, at present. We have seen every thing but the mosques, which we are to view with a firman on Tuesday next. But of these and other sundries let H. relate with this proviso, that *I* am to be referred to for authenticity; and I beg leave to contradict all those things whereon he lays particular stress. But, if he soars at any time into wit, I give you leave to applaud, because that is necessarily stolen from his fellow-pilgrim. Tell Davies that H. has made excellent use of his best jokes in many of his Majesty's ships of war; but add, also, that I always took care to restore them to the right owner; in consequence of which he (Davies) is no less famous by water than by land, and reigns unrivalled in the cabin as in the 'Cocoa Tree.'

"And Hodgson has been publishing more poesy—I wish he would send me his 'Sir Edgar,' and 'Bland's Anthology,' to Malta, where they will be forwarded. In my last, which I hope you received, I gave an outline of the ground we have covered. If you have not been overtaken by this despatch, H.'s tongue is at your service. Remember me to Dwyer, who owes me eleven guineas. Tell him to put them in my banker's hands at Gibraltar or Constantinople. I believe he paid them once, but that goes for nothing, as it was an annuity.

"I wish you would write. I have heard from Hodgson frequently. Malta is my post-office. I mean to be with you by next Montem. You remember the last,—I hope for such another; but after having swam across the 'broad Hellespont,' I disdain Datchett. Good afternoon!

I am yours, very sincerely,

"Byron."

About ten days after the date of this letter, we find another addressed to Mrs. Byron, which—with much that is merely a repetition of what he had detailed in former communications—contains also a good deal worthy of being extracted.

Letter 45.

TO MRS. BYRON.

"Dear Mother,

"Mr. Hobhouse, who will forward or deliver this and is on his return to England, can inform you of our different movements, but I am very uncertain as to my own return. He will probably be down in Notts, some time or other; but Fletcher, whom I send back as an incumbrance (English servants are sad travellers), will supply his place in the interim, and describe our travels, which have been tolerably extensive.

"I remember Mahmout Pacha, the grandson of Ali Pacha, at Yanina, (a little fellow of ten years of age, with large black eyes, which our ladies would purchase at any price, and those regular features which distinguish the Turks,) asked me how I came to travel so young, without anybody to take care of me. This question was put by the little man with all the gravity of threescore. I cannot now write copiously; I have only time to tell you that I have passed many a fatiguing, but never a tedious moment; and all that I am afraid of is that I shall contract a gipsylike wandering disposition, which will make home tiresome to me: this, I am told, is very common with men in the habit of peregrination, and, indeed, I feel it so. On the third of May I swam from *Sestos* to *Abydos*. You know the story of Leander, but I had no *Hero* to receive me at landing.

"I have been in all the principal mosques by the virtue of a firman: this is a favour rarely permitted to infidels, but the ambassador's departure obtained it for us. I have been up the Bosphorus into the Black Sea, round the walls of the city, and, indeed, I know more of it by sight than I do of London. I hope to amuse you some winter's evening with the details, but at present you must excuse me;—I am not able to write long letters in June. I return to spend my summer in Greece.

"F. is a poor creature, and requires comforts that I can dispense with. He is very sick of his travels, but you must not believe his account of the country. He sighs for ale, and idleness, and a wife, and the devil knows what besides. I have not been disappointed or disgusted. I have lived with the highest and the lowest. I have been for days in a Pacha's palace, and have passed many a night in a cowhouse, and I find the people inoffensive and kind. I have also passed some time with the principal Greeks in the Morea and Livadia, and, though inferior to the Turks, they are better than the Spaniards, who, in their turn, excel the Portuguese. Of Constantinople you will find many descriptions in different travels; but Lady Wortley errs strangely when she says, 'St. Paul's would cut a strange figure by St. Sophia's.' I have been in both, surveyed them inside and out attentively. St. Sophia's is undoubtedly the most interesting from its immense antiquity, and the circumstance of all the Greek emperors, from Justinian, having been crowned there, and several murdered at the altar, besides the Turkish sultans who attend it regularly. But it is inferior in beauty and size to some of the mosques, particularly 'Soleyman,' &c., and not to be mentioned in the same page with St. Paul's (I speak like a *Cockney*), However, I prefer the Gothic cathedral of Seville to St. Paul's, St. Sophia's, and any religious building I have ever seen.

"The walls of the Seraglio are like the walls of Newstead gardens, only higher, and much in the same order; but the ride by the walls of the city, on the land side, is beautiful. Imagine four miles of immense triple battlements, covered with ivy, surmounted with 218 towers, and, on the other side of the road, Turkish burying-grounds (the loveliest spots on earth), full of enormous cypresses. I have seen the ruins of Athens, of Ephesus, and Delphi. I have traversed great part of Turkey, and many other parts of Europe, and some of Asia; but I never beheld a work of nature or art which yielded an impression like the prospect on each side from the Seven Towers to the end of the Golden Horn.

"Now for England. I am glad to hear of the progress of 'English Bards,' &c.;—of course, you observed I have made great additions to the new edition. Have you received my picture from Sanders, Vigo Lane, London? It was finished and paid for long before I left England: pray, send for it. You seem to be a mighty reader of magazines: where do you pick up all this intelligence, quotations, &c. &c.? Though I was happy to obtain my seat without the assistance of Lord Carlisle, I had no measures to keep with a man who declined interfering as my relation on that occasion, and I have done with him, though I regret distressing Mrs. Leigh, poor thing!—I hope she is happy.

"It is my opinion that Mr. B—— ought to marry Miss R——. Our first duty is not to do evil; but, alas! that is impossible: our next is to repair it, if in our power. The girl is his equal: if she were his inferior, a sum of money and provision for the child would be some, though a poor, compensation: as it is, he should marry her. I will have no gay deceivers on my estate, and I shall not allow my tenants a privilege I do not permit myself—*that* of debauching each other's daughters. God knows, I have been guilty of many excesses; but, as I have laid down a resolution to reform, and lately kept it, I expect this Lothario to follow the example, and begin by restoring this girl to society, or, by the beard of my father! he shall hear of it. Pray take some notice of Robert, who will miss his master: poor boy, he was very unwilling to return. I trust you are well and happy. It will be a pleasure to hear from you.

Believe me yours very sincerely,

"BYRON.

"P.S.—How is Joe Murray?

"P.S.—I open my letter again to tell you that Fletcher having petitioned to accompany me into the Morea, I have taken him with me, contrary to the intention expressed in my letter."

The reader has not, I trust, passed carelessly over the latter part of this letter. There is a healthfulness in the moral feeling so unaffectedly expressed in it, which seems to answer for a heart sound at the core, however passion might have scorched it. Some years after, when he had become more confirmed in that artificial tone of banter, in which it was, unluckily, his habit to speak of his own good feelings, as well as those of others, however capable he might still have been of the same amiable sentiments, I question much whether the perverse fear of being thought desirous to pass for moral would not have prevented him from thus naturally and honestly avowing them.

The following extract from a communication addressed to a distinguished monthly work, by a traveller who, at this period, happened to meet with Lord Byron at Constantinople, bears sufficiently the features of authenticity to be presented, without hesitation, to my readers.

"We were interrupted in our debate by the entrance of a stranger, whom, on the first glance, I guessed to be an Englishman, but lately arrived at Constantinople. He wore a scarlet coat, richly embroidered with gold, in the style of an English aide-de-camp's dress uniform, with two heavy epaulettes. His countenance announced him to be about the age of two-and-twenty. His features were remarkably delicate, and would have given him a feminine appearance, but for the manly expression of his fine blue eyes. On entering the inner shop, he took off his feathered cocked-hat, and showed a head of curly auburn hair, which improved in no small degree the uncommon beauty of his face. The impression which his whole appearance made upon my mind was such, that it has ever since remained deeply engraven on it; and although fifteen years have since gone by, the lapse of time has not in the slightest degree impaired the freshness of the recollection. He was attended by a Janissary attached to the English embassy, and by a person who professionally acted as a Cicerone to strangers. These circumstances, together with a very visible lameness in one of his legs, convinced me at once he was Lord Byron. I had already heard of his Lordship, and of his late arrival in the Salsette frigate, which had come up from the Smyrna station, to fetch away Mr. Adair, our ambassador to the Porte. Lord Byron had been previously travelling in Epirus and Asia Minor, with his friend Mr. Hobhouse, and had become a great amateur of smoking: he was conducted to this shop for the purpose of purchasing a few pipes. The indifferent Italian, in which language he spoke to his Cicerone, and the latter's still more imperfect Turkish, made it difficult for the shopkeeper to understand their wishes, and as this seemed to vex the stranger, I addressed him in English, offering to interpret for him. When his Lordship thus discovered me to be an Englishman, he shook me cordially by the hand, and assured me, with some warmth in his manner, that he always felt great pleasure when he met with a countryman abroad. His purchase and my bargain being completed, we walked out together, and rambled about the streets, in several of which I had the pleasure of directing his attention to some of the most remarkable curiosities in Constantinople. The peculiar circumstances under which our acquaintance took place, established between us, in one day, a certain degree of intimacy, which two or three years' frequenting each other's company in England would most likely not have accomplished. I frequently addressed him by his name, but he did not think of enquiring how I came to learn it, nor of asking mine. His Lordship had not yet laid the foundation of that literary renown which he afterwards acquired; on the contrary, he was only known as the author of his Hours of Idleness; and the severity with which the Edinburgh Reviewers had criticised that production was still fresh in every English reader's recollection. I could not, therefore, be supposed to seek his acquaintance from any of those motives of vanity which have actuated so many others since: but it was natural that, after our accidental rencontre, and all that passed between us on that occasion, I should, on meeting him in the course of the same week at dinner at the English ambassador's, have requested one of the secretaries, who was intimately acquainted with him, to introduce me to him in regular form. His Lordship testified his perfect recollection of me, but in the coldest manner, and immediately after turned his back on me. This unceremonious proceeding, forming a striking contrast with previous occurrences, had something so strange in it, that I was at a loss how to account for it, and felt at the same time much disposed to entertain a less favourable opinion of his Lordship than his apparent frankness had inspired me with at our first meeting. It was not, therefore, without surprise, that, some days after, I saw him in the streets, coming up to me with a smile of good nature in his countenance. He accosted me in a familiar manner, and, offering me his hand, said,—'I am an enemy to English etiquette, especially out of England; and I always make my own acquaintance without waiting for the formality of an introduction. If you have nothing to do, and are disposed for another ramble, I shall be glad of your company.' There was that irresistible attraction in his manner, of which those who have had the good fortune to be admitted into his intimacy can alone have felt the power in his moments of good humour; and I readily accepted his proposal. We visited again more of the most remarkable curiosities of the capital, a description of which would here be but a repetition of what a hundred travellers have already detailed with the utmost minuteness and accuracy; but his Lordship expressed much disappointment at their want of interest. He praised the picturesque beauties of the town itself, and its surrounding scenery; and seemed of opinion that nothing else was worth looking at. He spoke of the Turks in a manner which might have given reason to suppose that he had made a long residence among them, and closed his observations with these words:—'The Greeks will, sooner or later, rise against them; but if they do not make haste, I hope Buonaparte will come, and drive the useless rascals away.'"

During his stay at Constantinople, the English minister, Mr. Adair, being indisposed the greater part of the time, had but few opportunities of seeing him. He, however, pressed him, with much hospitality, to accept a lodging at the English palace, which Lord Byron, preferring the freedom of his homely inn, declined. At the audience granted to the ambassador, on his taking leave, by the Sultan, the noble poet attended in the train of Mr. Adair,—having shown an anxiety as to the place he was to hold in the procession, not a little characteristic of his jealous pride of rank. In vain had the minister assured him that no particular station could be allotted to him;—that the Turks, in their arrangements for the ceremonial, considered only the persons connected with the embassy, and neither attended to, nor acknowledged, the precedence which our forms assign to nobility. Seeing the young peer still unconvinced by these representations, Mr. Adair was, at length, obliged to refer him to an authority, considered infallible on such points of etiquette, the old Austrian Internuncio; —on consulting whom, and finding his opinions agree fully with those of the English minister, Lord Byron declared himself perfectly satisfied.

On the 14th of July his fellow-traveller and himself took their departure from Constantinople on board the Salsette frigate,—Mr. Hobhouse with the intention of accompanying the ambassador to England, and Lord Byron with the resolution of visiting his beloved Greece again. To Mr. Adair he appeared, at this time, (and I find that Mr. Bruce, who met him afterwards at Athens, conceived the same impression of him,) to be labouring under great dejection of spirits. One circumstance related to me, as having occurred in the course of the passage, is not a little striking. Perceiving, as he walked the deck, a small yataghan, or Turkish dagger, on one of the benches, he took it up, unsheathed it, and, having stood for a few moments contemplating the blade, was heard to say, in an under voice, "I should like to know how a person feels after committing a murder!" In this startling speech we may detect, I think, the germ of his future Giaours and Laras. This intense *wish* to explore the dark workings of the passions was what, with the aid of imagination, at length generated the *power*; and that faculty which entitled him afterwards to be so truly styled "the searcher of dark bosoms," may be traced to, perhaps, its earliest stirrings in the sort of feeling that produced these words.

On their approaching the island of Zea, he expressed a wish to be put on shore. Accordingly, having taken leave of his companions, he was landed upon this small island, with two Albanians, a Tartar, and one English servant; and in one of his manuscripts he has himself described the proud, solitary feeling with which he stood to see the ship sail swiftly away—leaving him there, in a land of strangers alone.

A few days after, he addressed the following letters to Mrs. Byron from Athens.

Letter **46.**

TO MRS. BYRON.

"Athens, July 25. 1810.

"Dear Mother,

"I have arrived here in four days from Constantinople, which is considered as singularly quick, particularly for the season of the year. You northern gentry can have no conception of a Greek summer; which, however, is a perfect frost compared with Malta and Gibraltar, where I reposed myself in the shade last year, after a gentle gallop of four hundred miles, without intermission, through Portugal and Spain. You see, by my date, that I am at Athens again, a place which I think I prefer, upon the whole, to any I have seen.

"My next movement is to-morrow into the Morea, where I shall probably remain a month or two, and then return to winter here, if I do not change my plans, which, however, are very variable, as you may suppose; but none of them verge to England.

"The Marquis of Sligo, my old fellow-collegian, is here, and wishes to accompany me into the Morea. We shall go together for that purpose. Lord S. will afterwards pursue his way to the capital; and Lord B., having seen all the wonders in that quarter, will let you know what he does next, of which at present he is not quite certain. Malta is my perpetual post-office, from which my letters are forwarded to all parts of the habitable globe:—by the by, I have now been in Asia, Africa, and the east of Europe, and, indeed, made the most of my time, without hurrying over the most interesting scenes of the ancient world. F——, after having been toasted, and roasted, and baked, and grilled, and eaten by all sorts of creeping things, begins to philosophise, is grown a refined as well as a resigned character, and promises at his return to become an ornament to his own parish, and a very prominent person in the future family pedigree of the F——s, who I take to be Goths by their accomplishments, Greeks by their acuteness, and ancient Saxons by their appetite. He (F——) begs leave to send half-a-dozen sighs to Sally his spouse, and wonders (though I do not) that his ill written and worse spelt letters have never come to hand; as for that matter, there is no great loss in either of our letters, saving and except that I wish you to know we are well, and warm enough at this present writing, God knows. You must not expect long letters at present, for they are written with the sweat of my brow, I assure you. It is rather singular that Mr. H—— has not written a syllable since my departure. Your letters I have mostly received as well as others; from which I conjecture that the man of law is either angry or busy.

"I trust you like Newstead, and agree with your neighbours; but you know *you* are a *vixen*—is not that a dutiful appellation? Pray, take care of my books and several boxes of papers in the hands of Joseph; and pray leave me a few bottles of champagne to drink, for I am very thirsty;—but I do not insist on the last article, without you like it. I suppose you have your house full of silly women, prating scandalous things. Have you ever received my picture in oil from Sanders, London? It has been paid for these sixteen months: why do you not get it? My suite, consisting of two Turks, two Greeks, a Lutheran, and the nondescript, Fletcher, are making so much noise, that I am glad to sign myself

"Yours, &c. &c.

BYRON."

A day or two after the date of this, he left Athens in company with the Marquis of Sligo. Having travelled together as far as Corinth, they from thence branched off in different directions,—Lord Sligo to pay a visit to the capital of the Morea, and Lord Byron to proceed to Patras, where he had some business, as will be seen by the following letter, with the English consul, Mr. Strané:—

LETTER 47.

TO MRS. BYRON.

"Patras, July 30. 1810.

"Dear Madam,

"In four days from Constantinople, with a favourable wind, I arrived in the frigate at the island of Ceos, from whence I took a boat to Athens, where I met my friend the Marquis of Sligo, who expressed a wish to proceed with me as far as Corinth. At Corinth we separated, he for Tripolitza, I for Patras, where I had some business with the consul, Mr. Strané, in whose house I now write. He has rendered me every service in his power since I quitted Malta on my way to Constantinople, whence I have written to you twice or thrice. In a few days I visit the Pacha at Tripolitza, make the tour of the Morea, and return again to Athens, which at present is my head-quarters. The heat is at present intense. In England, if it reaches 98°, you are all on fire: the other day, in travelling between Athens and Megara, the thermometer was at 125°!!! Yet I feel no inconvenience; of course I am much bronzed, but I live temperately, and never enjoyed better health.

"Before I left Constantinople, I saw the Sultan (with Mr. Adair), and the interior of the mosques, things which rarely happen to travellers. Mr. Hobhouse is gone to England: I am in no hurry to return, but have no particular communications for your country, except my surprise at Mr. H——'s silence, and my desire that he will remit regularly. I suppose some arrangement has been made with regard to Wymondham and Rochdale. Malta is my post-office, or to Mr. Strané, consul-general, Patras, Morea. You complain of my silence—I have written twenty or thirty times within the last year: never less than twice a month, and often more. If my letters do not arrive, you must not conclude that we are eaten, or that there is a war, or a pestilence, or famine: neither must you credit silly reports, which I dare say you have in Notts., as usual. I am very well, and neither more nor less happy than I usually am; except that I am very glad to be once more alone, for I was sick of my companion,—not that he was a bad one, but because my nature leads me to solitude, and that every day adds to this disposition. If I chose, here are many men who would wish to join me—one wants me to go to Egypt, another to Asia, of which I have seen enough. The greater part of Greece is already my own, so that I shall only go over my old ground, and look upon my old seas and mountains, the only acquaintances I ever found improve upon me.

"I have a tolerable suite, a Tartar, two Albanians, an interpreter, besides Fletcher; but in this country these are easily maintained. Adair received me wonderfully well, and indeed I have no complaints against any one. Hospitality here is necessary, for inns are not. I have lived in the houses of Greeks, Turks, Italians, and English—to-day in a palace, to-morrow in a cowhouse; this day with a Pacha, the next with a shepherd. I shall continue to write briefly, but frequently, and am glad to hear from you; but you fill your letters with things from the papers, as if English papers were not found all over the world. I have at this moment a dozen before me. Pray take care of my books, and believe me, my dear mother,

yours," &c.

The greater part of the two following months he appears to have occupied in making a tour of the Morea; and the very distinguished reception he met with from Veley Pacha, the son of Ali, is mentioned with much pride, in more than one of his letters.

On his return from this tour to Patras, he was seized with a fit of illness, the particulars of which are mentioned in the following letter to Mr. Hodgson; and they are, in many respects, so similar to those of the last fatal malady, with which, fourteen years afterwards, he was attacked, in nearly the same spot, that, livelily as the account is written, it is difficult to read it without melancholy:—

LETTER **48.**

TO MR. HODGSON.

"Patras, Morea, October 3. 1810.

"As I have just escaped from a physician and a fever, which confined me five days to bed, you won't expect much 'allegrezza' in the ensuing letter. In this place there is an indigenous distemper, which, when the wind blows from the Gulf of Corinth (as it does five months out of six), attacks great and small, and makes woful work with visiters. Here be also two physicians, one of whom trusts to his genius (never having studied)—the other to a campaign of eighteen months against the sick of Otranto, which he made in his youth with great effect.

"When I was seized with my disorder, I protested against both these assassins; —but what can a helpless, feverish, toast-and-watered poor wretch do? In spite of my teeth and tongue, the English consul, my Tartar, Albanians, dragoman, forced a physician upon me, and in three days vomited and glystered me to the last gasp. In this state I made my epitaph—take it:—

"Youth, Nature, and relenting Jove,

To keep my lamp in strongly strove;

But Romanelli was so stout,

He beat all three—and blew it out.

But Nature and Jove, being piqued at my doubts, did, in fact, at last, beat Romanelli, and here I am, well but weakly, at your service.

"Since I left Constantinople, I have made a tour of the Morea, and visited Veley Pacha, who paid me great honours, and gave me a pretty stallion. H. is doubtless in England before even the date of this letter:—he bears a despatch from me to your bardship. He writes to me from Malta, and requests my journal, if I keep one. I have none, or he should have it; but I have replied in a consolatory and exhortatory epistle, praying him to abate three and sixpence in the price of his next boke seeing that half-a-guinea is a price not to be given for any thing save an opera ticket.

"As for England, it is long since I have heard from it. Every one at all connected with my concerns is asleep, and you are my only correspondent, agents excepted. I have really no friends in the world; though all my old school companions are gone forth into that world, and walk about there in monstrous disguises, in the garb of guardsmen, lawyers, parsons, fine gentlemen, and such other masquerade dresses. So, I here shake hands and cut with all these busy people, none of whom write to me. Indeed I ask it not;—and here I am, a poor traveller and heathenish philosopher, who hath perambulated the greatest part of the Levant, and seen a great quantity of very improvable land and sea, and, after all, am no better than when I set out—Lord help me!

"I have been out fifteen months this very day, and I believe my concerns will draw me to England soon; but of this I will apprise you regularly from Malta. On all points Hobhouse will inform you, if you are curious as to our adventures. I have seen some old English papers up to the 15th of May. I see the 'Lady of the Lake' advertised. Of course it is in his old ballad style, and pretty. After all, Scott is the best of them. The end of all scribblement is to amuse, and he certainly succeeds there. I long to read his new romance.

"And how does 'Sir Edgar?' and your friend Bland? I suppose you are involved in some literary squabble. The only way is to despise all brothers of the quill. I suppose you won't allow me to be an author, but I contemn you all, you dogs! —I do.

"You don't know D——s, do you? He had a farce ready for the stage before I left England, and asked me for a prologue, which I promised, but sailed in such a hurry, I never penned a couplet. I am afraid to ask after his drama, for fear it should be damned—Lord forgive me for using such a word! but the pit, Sir, you know the pit—they will do those things in spite of merit. I remember this farce from a curious circumstance. When Drury Lane was burnt to the ground, by which accident Sheridan and his son lost the few remaining shillings they were worth, what doth my friend D—— do? Why, before the fire was out, he writes a note to Tom Sheridan, the manager of this combustible concern, to enquire whether this farce was not converted into fuel, with about two thousand other unactable manuscripts, which of course were in great peril, if not actually consumed. Now was not this characteristic? —the ruling passions of Pope are nothing to it. Whilst the poor distracted manager was bewailing the loss of a building only worth 300,000 *l.*, together with some twenty thousand pounds of rags and tinsel in the tiring rooms, Bluebeard's elephants, and all that—in comes a note from a scorching author, requiring at his hands two acts and odd scenes of a farce!!

"Dear H., remind Drury that I am his well-wisher, and let Scrope Davies be well affected towards me. I look forward to meeting you at Newstead, and renewing our old champagne evenings with all the glee of anticipation. I have written by every opportunity, and expect responses as regular as those of the liturgy, and somewhat longer. As it is impossible for a man in his senses to hope for happy days, let us at least look forward to merry ones, which come nearest to the other in appearance, if not in reality; and in such expectations,

I remain," &c.

He was a good deal weakened and thinned by his illness at Patras, and, on his return to Athens, standing one day before a looking-glass, he said to Lord Sligo—"How pale I look!—I should like, I think, to die of a consumption."—"Why of a consumption?" asked his friend. "Because then (he answered) the women would all say, 'See that poor Byron—how interesting he looks in dying!'" In this anecdote,—which, slight as it is, the relater remembered, as a proof of the poet's consciousness of his own beauty,—may be traced also the habitual reference of his imagination to that sex, which, however he affected to despise it, influenced, more or less, the flow and colour of all his thoughts.

He spoke often of his mother to Lord Sligo, and with a feeling that seemed little short of aversion. "Some time or other," he said, "I will tell you *why* I feel thus towards her."—A few days after, when they were bathing together in the Gulf of Lepanto, he referred to this promise, and, pointing to his naked leg and foot, exclaimed—"Look there!—it is to her false delicacy at my birth I owe that deformity; and yet, as long as I can remember, she has never ceased to taunt and reproach me with it. Even a few days before we parted, for the last time, on my leaving England, she, in one of her fits of passion, uttered an imprecation upon me, praying that I might prove as ill formed in mind as I am in body!" His look and manner, in relating this frightful circumstance, can be conceived only by those who have ever seen him in a similar state of excitement.

The little value he had for those relics of ancient art, in pursuit of which he saw all his classic fellow-travellers so ardent, was, like every thing he ever thought or felt, unreservedly avowed by him. Lord Sligo having it in contemplation to expend some money in digging for antiquities, Lord Byron, in offering to act as his agent, and to see the money, at least, honestly applied, said—"You may safely trust *me*—I am no dilettante. Your connoisseurs are all thieves; but I care too little for these things ever to steal them."

The system of thinning himself, which he had begun before he left England, was continued still more rigidly abroad. While at Athens, he took the hot bath for this purpose, three times a week,—his usual drink being vinegar and water, and his food seldom more than a little rice.

Among the persons, besides Lord Sligo, whom he saw most of at this time, were Lady Hester Stanhope and Mr. Bruce. One of the first objects, indeed, that met the eyes of these two distinguished travellers, on their approaching the coast of Attica, was Lord Byron, disporting in his favourite element under the rocks of Cape Colonna. They were afterwards made acquainted with each other by Lord Sligo; and it was in the course, I believe, of their first interview, at his table, that Lady Hester, with that lively eloquence for which she is so remarkable, took the poet briskly to task for the depreciating opinion, which, as she understood, he entertained of all female intellect. Being but little inclined, were he even able, to sustain such a heresy, against one who was in her own person such an irresistible refutation of it, Lord Byron had no other refuge from the fair orator's arguments than in assent and silence; and this well-bred deference being, in a sensible woman's eyes, equivalent to concession, they became, from thenceforward, most cordial friends. In recalling some recollections of this period in his "Memoranda," after relating the circumstance of his being caught bathing by an English party at Sunium, he added, "This was the beginning of the most delightful acquaintance which I formed in Greece." He then went on to assure Mr. Bruce, if ever those pages should meet his eyes, that the days they had passed together at Athens were remembered by him with pleasure.

During this period of his stay in Greece, we find him forming one of those extraordinary friendships,—if attachment to persons so inferior to himself can be called by that name,—of which I have already mentioned two or three instances in his younger days, and in which the pride of being a protector, and the pleasure of exciting gratitude, seem to have constituted to his mind the chief, pervading charm. The person, whom he now adopted in this manner, and from similar feelings to those which had inspired his early attachments to the cottage-boy near Newstead, and the young chorister at Cambridge, was a Greek youth, named Nicolo Giraud, the son, I believe, of a widow lady, in whose house the artist Lusieri lodged. In this young man he appears to have taken the most lively, and even brotherly, interest;—so much so, as not only to have presented to him, on their parting, at Malta, a considerable sum of money, but to have subsequently designed for him, as the reader will learn, a still more munificent, as well as permanent, provision.

Though he occasionally made excursions through Attica and the Morea, his head-quarters were fixed at Athens, where he had taken lodgings in a Franciscan convent, and, in the intervals of his tours, employed himself in collecting materials for those notices on the state of modern Greece which he has appended to the second Canto of Childe Harold. In this retreat, also, as if in utter defiance of the "genius loci," he wrote his "Hints from Horace,"—a Satire which, impregnated as it is with London life from beginning to end, bears the date, "Athens, Capuchin Convent, March 12. 1811."

From the few remaining letters addressed to his mother, I shall content myself with selecting the two following:—

Letter 49.

TO MRS. BYRON.

"Athens, January 14, 1811.

"My dear Madam,

"I seize an occasion to write as usual, shortly, but frequently, as the arrival of letters, where there exists no regular communication, is, of course, very precarious. I have lately made several small tours of some hundred or two miles about the Morea, Attica, &c., as I have finished my grand giro by the Troad, Constantinople, &c., and am returned down again to Athens. I believe I have mentioned to you more than once that I swam (in imitation of Leander, though without his lady) across the Hellespont, from Sestos to Abydos. Of this, and all other particulars, F., whom I have sent home with papers, &c., will apprise you. I cannot find that he is any loss; being tolerably master of the Italian and modern Greek languages, which last I am also studying with a master, I can order and discourse more than enough for a reasonable man. Besides, the perpetual lamentations after beef and beer, the stupid, bigoted contempt for every thing foreign, and insurmountable incapacity of acquiring even a few words of any language, rendered him, like all other English servants, an incumbrance. I do assure you, the plague of speaking for him, the comforts he required (more than myself by far), the pilaws (a Turkish dish of rice and meat) which he could not eat, the wines which he could not drink, the beds where he could not sleep, and the long list of calamities, such as stumbling horses, want of *tea!!!* &c., which assailed him, would have made a lasting source of laughter to a spectator, and inconvenience to a master. After all, the man is honest enough, and, in Christendom, capable enough; but in Turkey, Lord forgive me! my Albanian soldiers, my Tartars and Janissary, worked for him and us too, as my friend Hobhouse can testify.

"It is probable I may steer homewards in spring; but to enable me to do that, I must have remittances. My own funds would have lasted me very well; but I was obliged to assist a friend, who, I know, will pay me; but, in the mean time, I am out of pocket. At present, I do not care to venture a winter's voyage, even if I were otherwise tired of travelling; but I am so convinced of the advantages of looking at mankind instead of reading about them, and the bitter effects of staying at home with all the narrow prejudices of an islander, that I think there should be a law amongst us, to set our young men abroad, for a term, among the few allies our wars have left us.

"Here I see and have conversed with French, Italians, Germans, Danes, Greeks, Turks, Americans, &c. &c. &c.; and without losing sight of my own, I can judge of the countries and manners of others. Where I see the superiority of England (which, by the by, we are a good deal mistaken about in many things,) I am pleased, and where I find her inferior, I am at least enlightened. Now, I might have stayed, smoked in your towns, or fogged in your country, a century, without being sure of this, and without acquiring any thing more useful or amusing at home. I keep no journal, nor have I any intention of scribbling my travels. I have done with authorship; and if, in my last production, I have convinced the critics or the world I was something more than they took me for, I am satisfied; nor will I hazard *that reputation* by a future effort. It is true I have some others in manuscript, but I leave them for those who come after me; and, if deemed worth publishing, they may serve to prolong my memory when I myself shall cease to remember. I have a famous Bavarian artist taking some views of Athens, &c. &c. for me. This will be better than scribbling, a disease I hope myself cured of. I hope, on my return, to lead a quiet, recluse life, but God knows and does best for us all; at least, so they say, and I have nothing to object, as, on the whole, I have no reason to complain of my lot. I am convinced, however, that men do more harm to themselves than ever the devil could do to them. I trust this will find you well, and as happy as we can be; you will, at least, be pleased to hear I am so, and yours ever."

LETTER 50.

TO MRS. BYRON.

"Athens, February 28. 1811.

"Dear Madam,

"As I have received a firman for Egypt, &c., I shall proceed to that quarter in the spring, and I beg you will state to Mr. H. that it is necessary to further remittances. On the subject of Newstead, I answer as before, *No*. If it is necessary to sell, sell Rochdale. Fletcher will have arrived by this time with my letters to that purport. I will tell you fairly, I have, in the first place, no opinion of funded property; if, by any particular circumstances, I shall be led to adopt such a determination, I will, at all events, pass my life abroad, as my only tie to England is Newstead, and, that once gone, neither interest nor inclination lead me northward. Competence in your country is ample wealth in the East, such is the difference in the value of money and the abundance of the necessaries of life; and I feel myself so much a citizen of the world, that the spot where I can enjoy a delicious climate, and every luxury, at a less expense than a common college life in England, will always be a country to me; and such are in fact the shores of the Archipelago. This then is the alternative—if I preserve Newstead, I return; if I sell it, I stay away. I have had no letters since yours of June, but I have written several times, and shall continue, as usual, on the same plan.

Believe me, yours ever,

BYRON.

"P.S.—I shall most likely see you in the course of the summer, but, of course, at such a distance, I cannot specify any particular month." The voyage to Egypt, which he appears from this letter to have contemplated, was, probably for want of the expected remittances, relinquished; and, on the 3d of June, he set sail from Malta, in the Volage frigate, for England, having, during his short stay at Malta, suffered a severe attack of the tertian fever. The feelings with which he returned home may be collected from the following melancholy letters.

LETTER 51.

TO MR. HODGSON.

"Volage frigate, at sea, June 29. 1811.

"In a week, with a fair wind, we shall be at Portsmouth, and on the 2d of July, I shall have completed (to a day) two years of peregrination, from which I am returning with as little emotion as I set out. I think, upon the whole, I was more grieved at leaving Greece than England, which I am impatient to see, simply because I am tired of a long voyage.

"Indeed, my prospects are not very pleasant. Embarrassed in my private affairs, indifferent to public, solitary without the wish to be social, with a body a little enfeebled by a succession of fevers, but a spirit, I trust, yet unbroken, I am returning *home* without a hope, and almost without a desire. The first thing I shall have to encounter will be a lawyer, the next a creditor, then colliers, farmers, surveyors, and all the agreeable attachments to estates out of repair, and contested coal-pits. In short, I am sick and sorry, and when I have a little repaired my irreparable affairs, away I shall march, either to campaign in Spain, or back again to the East, where I can at least have cloudless skies and a cessation from impertinence.

"I trust to meet, or see you, in town, or at Newstead, whenever you can make it convenient—I suppose you are in love and in poetry as usual. That husband, H. Drury, has never written to me, albeit I have sent him more than one letter;—but I dare say the poor man has a family, and of course all his cares are confined to his circle.

'For children fresh expenses get,And Dicky now for school is fit.'

WARTON.

If you see him, tell him I have a letter for him from Tucker, a regimental chirurgeon and friend of his, who prescribed for me, —— and is a very worthy man, but too fond of hard words. I should be too late for a speech-day, or I should probably go down to Harrow. I regretted very much in Greece having omitted to carry the Anthology with me—I mean Bland and Merivale's.— What has Sir Edgar done? And the Imitations and Translations—where are they? I suppose you don't mean to let the public off so easily, but charge them home with a quarto. For me, I am 'sick of fops, and poesy, and prate,' and shall leave the 'whole Castilian state' to Bufo, or any body else. But you are a sentimental and sensibilitous person, and will rhyme to the end of the chapter. Howbeit, I have written some 4000 lines, of one kind or another, on my travels.

"I need not repeat that I shall be happy to see you. I shall be in town about the 8th, at Dorant's Hotel, in Albemarle Street, and proceed in a few days to Notts., and thence to Rochdale on business.

"I am, here and there, yours," &c.

LETTER 52.

TO MRS. BYRON.

"Volage frigate, at sea, June 25. 1811.

"Dear Mother,

"This letter, which will be forwarded on our arrival at Portsmouth, probably about the 4th of July, is begun about twenty-three days after our departure from Malta. I have just been two years (to a day, on the 2d of July) absent from England, and I return to it with much the same feelings which prevailed on my departure, viz. indifference; but within that apathy I certainly do not comprise yourself, as I will prove by every means in my power. You will be good enough to get my apartments ready at Newstead; but don't disturb yourself, on any account, particularly mine, nor consider me in any other light than as a visiter. I must only inform you that for a long time I have been restricted to an entire vegetable diet, neither fish nor flesh coming within my regimen; so I expect a powerful stock of potatoes, greens, and biscuit: I drink no wine. I have two servants, middle-aged men, and both Greeks. It is my intention to proceed first to town, to see Mr. H——, and thence to Newstead, on my way to Rochdale. I have only to beg you will not forget my diet, which it is very necessary for me to observe. I am well in health, as I have generally been, with the exception of two agues, both of which I quickly got over.

"My plans will so much depend on circumstances, that I shall not venture to lay down an opinion on the subject. My prospects are not very promising, but I suppose we shall wrestle through life like our neighbours; indeed, by H.'s last advices, I have some apprehension of finding Newstead dismantled by Messrs. Brothers, &c., and he seems determined to force me into selling it, but he will be baffled. I don't suppose I shall be much pestered with visiters; but if I am, you must receive them, for I am determined to have nobody breaking in upon my retirement: you know that I never was fond of society, and I am less so than before. I have brought you a shawl, and a quantity of attar of roses, but these I must smuggle, if possible. I trust to find my library in tolerable order.

"Fletcher is no doubt arrived. I shall separate the mill from Mr. B——'s farm, for his son is too gay a deceiver to inherit both, and place Fletcher in it, who has served me faithfully, and whose wife is a good woman; besides, it is necessary to sober young Mr. B——, or he will people the parish with bastards. In a word, if he had seduced a dairy-maid, he might have found something like an apology; but the girl is his equal, and in high life or low life reparation is made in such circumstances. But I shall not interfere further than (like Buonaparte) by dismembering Mr. B.'s *kingdom*, and erecting part of it into a principality for field-marshal Fletcher! I hope you govern my little *empire* and its sad load of national debt with a wary hand. To drop my metaphor, I beg leave to subscribe myself yours, &c.

"P.S.—This letter was written to be sent from Portsmouth, but, on arriving there, the squadron was ordered to the Nore, from whence I shall forward it. This I have not done before, supposing you might be alarmed by the interval mentioned in the letter being longer than expected between our arrival in port and my appearance at Newstead."

LETTER 53.

TO MR. HENRY DRURY.

"Volage frigate, off Ushant, July 17. 1811.

"My dear Drury,

"After two years' absence (on the 2d) and some odd days, I am approaching your country. The day of our arrival you will see by the outside date of my letter. At present, we are becalmed comfortably, close to Brest Harbour;—I have never been so near it since I left Duck Puddle. We left Malta thirty-four days ago, and have had a tedious passage of it. You will either see or hear from or of me, soon after the receipt of this, as I pass through town to repair my irreparable affairs; and thence I want to go to Notts. and raise rents, and to Lanes. and sell collieries, and back to London and pay debts,—for it seems I shall neither have coals nor comfort till I go down to Rochdale in person.

"I have brought home some marbles for Hobhouse;—for myself, four ancient Athenian skulls, dug out of sarcophagi—a phial of Attic hemlock—four live tortoises—a greyhound (died on the passage)—two live Greek servants, one an Athenian, t'other a Yaniote, who can speak nothing but Romaic and Italian —and *myself,* as Moses in the Vicar of Wakefield says, slily, and I may say it too, for I have as little cause to boast of my expedition as he had of his to the fair.

"I wrote to you from the Cyanean Rocks to tell you I had swam from Sestos to Abydos—have you received my letter? Hodgson I suppose is four deep by this time. What would he have given to have seen, like me, the *real Parnassus,* where I robbed the Bishop of Chrissæ of a book of geography!—but this I only call plagiarism, as it was done within an hour's ride of Delphi."

END OF THE FIRST VOLUME.